Party Politics
in New Zealand

Party Politics
in New Zealand

Raymond Miller

OXFORD
UNIVERSITY PRESS

OXFORD
UNIVERSITY PRESS

253 Normanby Road, South Melbourne, Victoria 3205, Australia

Oxford University Press is a department of the University of Oxford.
It furthers the University's objective of excellence in research,
scholarship, and education by publishing worldwide in

Oxford New York

Auckland Cape Town Dar es Salaam Hong Kong Karachi
Kuala Lumpur Madrid Melbourne Mexico City Nairobi
New Delhi Shanghai Taipei Toronto

With offices in

Argentina Austria Brazil Chile Czech Republic France Greece
Guatemala Hungary Italy Japan Poland Portugal Singapore
South Korea Switzerland Thailand Turkey Ukraine Vietnam

OXFORD is a trade mark of Oxford University Press in the UK and in
certain other countries

National Library of New Zealand
Cataloguing-in-Publication data

Miller, Raymond.
Party politics in New Zealand / Raymond Miller.

   Includes bibliographical references and index.
   ISBN 0 19 558413 9

   1. Political parties—New Zealand. 2. Elections—New Zealand.
   I. Title.

324.293—dc22

Typeset by Cannon Typesetting
Printed by Sheck Wah Tong Printing Press Ltd, Hong Kong

Contents

List of Figures

List of Tables

Preface

A book on New Zealand party politics is long overdue. The last specialist text on the country's parties and party system was produced in 1966 by a visiting scholar to New Zealand (Milne 1966). It focused on a two-party system widely regarded as one of the purest in the world, so much so that the only significant minor party of the time was relegated to a cameo appearance in the book's appendix. How different the party landscape is today. The introduction of proportional representation signalled both a consolidation of the multi-party system and the advent of coalition government. Instead of two parties being represented in the nation's parliament, there are now anything up to seven or eight, with an additional twenty or more parties competing unsuccessfully for their share of the 120 seats. These changes and their consequences are one of the two major themes of this book.

With attention having been so firmly focused on the effects of proportional representation, in particular the reconfiguration of the party system, developments within the parties themselves have been largely overlooked. The second major theme of the book is the internal world of party politics in New Zealand. In examining the various types of party organisation, it is important to consider the decline of the mass party and the growing centralisation of power in the parliamentary office of the party leader. This trend raises certain questions: What are the reasons for being a party activist or member? Should party funding be the responsibility of the party or the state? Who should be responsible for choosing the party's parliamentary candidates and leader?

The study then turns to the ways in which parties compete with each other, both during election campaigns and within parliament and government. Given the intense inter-party rivalry for the support of 'middle' New Zealand, it is pertinent to ask whether we are now approaching the end of ideology. Other important questions include the following: Who runs the modern campaign, and in whose interests? To what extent is parliament a more representative body than it was under the former simple plurality voting system? Can any minor party survive the experience of coalition government?

A strand of enquiry running through these discussions concerns the growing problem of civic disengagement. Despite the advent of proportional representation, the proliferation of political parties, and the resulting increase in the opportunities for parliamentary representation, participation in political parties continues to decline. Whereas a number of countries are experimenting with democratic initiatives, the people in charge of New Zealand's political parties generally show little interest in reform. Strategies for increasing participation, discussed in a number of chapters, include having greater grassroots involvement in candidate and leadership selection, making party funding by the state dependent upon the size of a party's membership, and exploiting the interactive capabilities of new technology, especially the Internet.

During the course of writing this book, I gleaned information and advice from a wide range of scholars, politicians, and party officials. I owe an intellectual debt to my present and past colleagues in the Politics Department at the University of Auckland, especially Barry Gustafson, Helena Catt, Peter Aimer, Richard Mulgan, and Jack Vowles. I am particularly grateful to my fellow members of the New Zealand Election Study (NZES), especially the principal investigator, Jack Vowles, for providing access to survey data covering the four general elections between 1993 and 2002. The work of the NZES was funded by the Foundation for Research, Science and Technology.

A number of postgraduate students at the University of Auckland graciously listened to, and frequently challenged, the ideas presented in this book. Some even experimented with draft chapters in their classroom teaching. In particular, I would like to thank Bevan McKenzie, Jane Scott, Darryl Godfrey, Edwin de Ronde, Patrick Hine, Nikki Reid, Doreen Suddens, Marcus Ganley, Hamish McCracken, and Grant Gillon. I also received help from the former head of New Zealand's Electoral Commission, Paul Harris.

Although the primary concern of this book is the political parties of New Zealand, there is much to be gained from comparing New Zealand's political situation to that of other countries. In 1998, and again in 2002, I spent time studying the process of party system change in Canada and the United Kingdom. I was particularly interested in political developments in Scotland, a country with a proportional electoral system very similar to that of New Zealand. From my base at the University of Stirling, I had conversations with a number of scholars, including Stephen Ingle, Peter Lynch, and Eric Shaw (Stirling), Fiona McKay (University of Edinburgh), Lynn Bennie (Aberdeen), and John Curtice (Strathclyde). Among the politicians and party organisers who were prepared to be interviewed were Jim Wallace, Derek Barrie, Alex Rowley, and Mike Russell. At the University of London, I received help from the members of the Constitution Unit. In Canada, I greatly appreciated my discussions with Doreen Barrie, Tom Flanagan, Anthony Sayers, Ted Moreton,

Roger Gibbins (all from the University of Calgary), David Laycock (Simon Fraser), Larry Le Duc (Toronto), Terry Horkoff, and Preston Manning.

Over the years of planning and writing this book I spent an immense amount of time attending party conferences and other meetings, as well as discussing party politics with a range of party leaders, organisers and MPs. I never cease to be amazed at how approachable and available these people are to those of us conducting academic research. While a number have specifically asked not to be named, I would like to thank the following for their time: Peter Dunne, Mike Smith, John Pagani, Rod Donald, Murray McCully, Mike Williams, Matt McCarten, Bob Harvey, and Graham Watson. For some basic information on the functions of the Parliamentary Press Gallery, I am grateful for the help provided by Vernon Small.

Finally, I would like to thank the staff of Oxford University Press for their continuing support. Jill Henry helped get this particular project underway, Heather Fawcett was a wonderful source of encouragement and advice, two anonymous readers made many useful suggestions for improvements to the first draft of the manuscript, Craig MacKenzie lent his expertise to the copy-editing process, and Tim Campbell supervised the overall production.

I owe a particular debt to a former professor of Politics at the University of Auckland, Robert Chapman, who both sparked my interest in New Zealand politics and maintained a close interest in the direction of my work. Bob was unstinting in his support for the project and proved to be a ready source of knowledge and advice, even until shortly before his death in 2004. This book is dedicated to his memory.

Raymond Miller
The University of Auckland

Introduction

Thinking about Participation and the Party System

1

THIS book is concerned with the external and internal worlds of party politics in New Zealand. It is organised around two central themes. The first explores the transition from a two-party system to a multiparty system in which up to seven or eight parties regularly win parliamentary seats and coalitions are the standard form of government. At the core of our investigation are the circumstances that caused New Zealand's two-party system to fracture and fragment. What are the implications of this decline of the two-party system for democracy in New Zealand? Are there common elements in the rise of the new parties? Can the present array of parliamentary parties be sustained? The future of the two major parties may seem assured, but what lies in store for the minor parties, especially those personality-based movements facing the inevitable departure from politics of their founding leaders? As the recent collapse of the Alliance and the formation of the new Maori party illustrate, charting the changing dynamics of multiparty politics in New Zealand is both a highly speculative and endlessly intriguing task.

A central question of this book is whether New Zealand's new multiparty system is a product of proportional representation or of other more complex developments. According to one school of thought, there is a strong causal link between a nation's party system and its social structure. Where the number of divisions in society is low, a two-party system is the likely outcome. On the other hand, countries with complex social structures based on divisions of class, ethnicity, region, and religion will tend to be of the multiparty type. If this theory has any relevance to the present study, then perhaps we should be looking beyond the electoral system to any systemic changes that may have been taking place within New Zealand society.

Whereas the first major theme is concerned with the external relationships of parties one with the other, the second delves inside the parties to consider the problem of public disengagement. Despite the proliferation of parties and increased opportunities for parliamentary representation, participation in New Zealand politics is in decline. We all know that the public's links with voluntary organisations, such as churches, youth groups, social and recreational clubs, and trade unions are becoming progressively weaker. As Robert Putnam (2000) has pointed out, at the core of the problem are changes within Western societies. He and others have identified a number of possible reasons, all of which resonate with the New Zealand experience. They include the growth of more secular and individualistic values, increased access to tertiary education, the privatisation of leisure, and the transformation of work patterns. Also important has been the population drift from the smaller and more integrated provincial communities to the sprawling city suburbs.

Political participation has also been affected by the rising tide of public cynicism and mistrust. There is evidence of declining faith in the legitimacy of government, weakening partisan attachment, the rise of alternative social and political movements, and reduced electoral turnout. In the case of New Zealand, during the 1980s and 1990s public confidence in successive governments was shaken on several fronts. As well as widespread opposition to the pace and pervasiveness of governmental reform, there was growing public concern that the two-party system had become debased and that the first-past-the-post electoral system was undemocratic and unjust. To these can be added the cumulative effect of economic globalisation and privatisation, especially in reducing the nation state's ability to bring about change. As a result, the Labour and National parties were accused of everything from indolence and arrogance to the abuse of power.

The focus of our study will be on how declining participation has manifested itself within the parties themselves. As we will see, individual membership numbers have been dropping, as have many of the voluntary activities traditionally associated with democratic politics. Paralleling this decline has been a shake-up in the relationship between parties and their associated support groups. Whereas parties once represented the interests of clearly identifiable sectional interests, such as unionists, small business proprietors, and farmers, this mediating link has begun to attenuate. As well as discussing these trends, we will explore avenues by which parties can encourage greater participation, especially in policy-making, the selection of candidates and party leaders, and in the provision of party funds. Despite the advent of the professional campaign, with its attendant emphasis on mass marketing, state and corporate funding, as well as centralised planning and control, there may be opportunities for wider public participation through the new technologies, including the use of email and the World Wide Web.

The changing party system

It is tempting to elevate changes to the party system to the level of a 'transformation'. In the heyday of the former two-party system, the combined vote for National and Labour came remarkably close to 100 per cent. As a result, there was never any doubt that one or other of the two parties would have a working majority for the following three years. While the Social Credit Political League offered some third party resistance, its votes were thinly dispersed, with the result that it managed to win only four seats in close to forty years of electoral competition. In recent times, in contrast, the combined two-party vote has averaged a mere 66 per cent. The number and diversity of parties, together with the presence of a genuinely multiparty legislature and government, gives substance to the claim that the party system has undergone fundamental change (see figure 1.1).

This study will argue that the notion of 'transformation' ignores some important common strands between the present multiparty system and earlier stages of development. One source of continuity concerns the adaptive ability of the two major parties. Despite the array of minor parties represented in the New Zealand parliament, the two major parties have continued to attract the lion's share of the vote. An illustration of the resilience of two-party politics can be found in the 'Waitangi Day' poll of 14 February 2004, which gave National a 17-point lift in support in the space of two months (the largest increase on record) and left the five small parliamentary parties with a combined total of only 17 per cent.[1] Even more to the point, over the course of the first three elections under proportional representation (PR), the new parties struggled to lift their electoral support much above the 5 per cent threshold that guarantees representation. Those minor parties that joined a coalition government enjoyed few legislative successes and incurred heavy electoral costs. In short, by demonstrating an ability to adjust to the increase in electoral competition, the two major parties were able to turn a potentially difficult situation, made precarious by the advent of PR, into one of continuing domination.

For most of the last century, the two-party system appeared to be 'frozen' in time. Its survival can be put down to three main factors: the one-dimensional nature of the New Zealand social structure; the broad ideological consensus that existed between the two parties, reflecting the moderate views of most voters; and the highly disproportional electoral benefits resulting from the first-past-the-post electoral system. Despite this record of two-party stability, the first three decades of the twentieth century were characterised by change, as New Zealand moved from a no-party system to a rudimentary single party system, to be followed in quick succession by two-party and three-party phases. The one significant strand running through each transition was that of socio-economic class. With the advent of the mass party, Labour was able to consolidate its support among manual workers and those on low incomes. National, on the other hand, built an impressive record of electoral success by appealing to farmers, white-collar workers, self-employed business proprietors, and professionals.

Figure 1.1   The party system, 2005

Labour
Formed 1916
Leader Helen Clark (1993–)
In government 1935–49; 57–60; 72–75; 84–90; 99–

National
Formed 1936
Leader Don Brash (2003–)
In government 1949–57; 60–72; 75–84; 90–99

New Zealand First
Formed 1993
Leader Winston Peters
In government 1996–98

Green
Formed 1990
Leaders Jeanette Fitzsimons and Rod Donald (1996–)

ACT
Formed 1994
Leader Rodney Hide (2004–)

United Future
Formed 2000
Leader Peter Dunne
Government support party 2002–

Progressive
Formed 2002
Leader Jim Anderton
In government 2002–

Maori
Formed 2004
Leaders Tariana Turia and Pita Sharples (2004–)

Outside parliament

Registered parties include:
Alliance
Aotearoa Legalise Cannabis
Christian Heritage
Democrats (formerly Social Credit)
Destiny New Zealand
Libertarianz
OneNZ
Outdoor Recreation NZ

Support for the Keynesian welfare state formed the cornerstone of New Zealand's postwar consensus. While the two parties frequently claimed to be pursuing divergent ideological goals, their policies in government reflected broad agreement over the rights of citizens and the appropriate functions and powers of the state. Labour's reputation was built on an ideological commitment to economic intervention and welfare reform, whereas National saw itself as the defender of free enterprise, limited government, self-reliance, and individual freedom. Although sincerely held, these doctrines were more the stuff of election campaigns than the guiding principles of government. When in power, Labour generally proved to be a cautious reformer, and National demonstrated considerable ideological flexibility in leaving the postwar mixed economy and universal welfare state largely undisturbed.

It was the breakdown of this consensus that was instrumental in destroying the two-party monopoly and paving the way for the growth of alternative party organisations. The first hint of declining public confidence occurred in the late 1970s, when massive oil price increases, followed by world recession, exposed the weaknesses of New Zealand's dependent economy. Unpopular intervention by the National administration of Robert Muldoon, including high overseas borrowing and a wage and price freeze, followed by the introduction of a radical free market agenda by successive Labour (1984–90) and National (1990–93) governments, had a seriously corrosive effect on electoral support for both parties. As well as provoking deep divisions within party ranks, the reform process resulted in the formation of several splinter parties, beginning with the New Zealand (1983) and NewLabour (1989) parties. The two-party vote, which had averaged 95 per cent in the period of 1945 to 1966, dropped to an average of 87 per cent between 1967 and 1980, and 80 per cent between 1981 and 1993.

New Zealand's experience of two-party decline is far from unique. Beginning in the early 1990s, dramatic shifts in voter support impacted on the party systems of several established democracies, including those of Japan, Italy, Scotland, and Canada. Japan's long-established Liberal Democrat government was replaced in 1993 by a seven-party coalition. In Italy, the collapse of the Christian Democrat vote precipitated a process of transformation, with several old parties either splintering or completely disappearing and new ones, such as the conservative Forza Italia, being formed. At about the same time the Canadian party system underwent dramatic change. Following the governing Progressive Conservative party's heavy defeat at the 1993 election (it lost all but two of its parliamentary seats), the populist Reform (later renamed Alliance) and Bloc Quebecois parties began to compete for the vacant position of main opposition party to the Liberals. At the 2004 election, the Liberals lost their parliamentary majority in a four-way contest with a rejuvenated Conservative party (which had merged with the

Alliance), Bloc Quebecois, and New Democrat party (NDP). Minor parties also enjoyed record levels of support in Scotland following the decline of the Conservative party of Margaret Thatcher and John Major. Historically one of the two main parties in British politics, during the 1990s the Conservatives gradually lost all of their Scottish seats, with the third party beneficiaries being the Scottish Nationalists and Liberal Democrats.

What made New Zealand's experience of change different from that of most other countries, however, was the consolidating role of electoral reform (see figure 1.2). In as much as the unravelling of New Zealand's postwar consensus provided the mood for change, electoral reform was responsible for its reinforcement. A number of scholars have claimed that there is a direct causal link between the electoral and party systems, with Maurice Duverger characterising the connection between first-past-the-post elections and two-partism as 'a true sociological law' (1964, p. 217). PR, on the other hand, is said to have a 'multiplicative tendency' that leads to the formation of new parties, as well as causing long-established parties to fracture and fragment.

Figure 1.2 Chronology of events, 1978–2002

1978	Labour (40.4%) receives more votes than National (39.8%) but 11 fewer seats. Social Credit wins 16% of vote but only 1 seat.
1981	Labour (39.0%) again receives more votes than National (38.8%) but 4 fewer seats. Social Credit gains 20.7% of vote but only 2 seats.
1984	On becoming the government, Labour appoints a Royal Commission to look into the future of the electoral system.
1986	Royal Commission recommends adoption of the German Mixed Member system of proportional representation (MMP).
1987	Labour re-elected with 48.0% of the vote to National's 44.0%. Combined minor party vote 8.0%.
1988	Labour rejects Royal Commission's recommendation.
1990	Incoming National government promises a referendum on the future of the first-past-the-post electoral system.
1992	At the first electoral referendum, 85% of voters opt for change, with MMP being the preferred system of 71%.
1993	At the second electoral referendum, 54% prefer MMP to first-past-the-post. At the general election held the same day, National is re-elected with 35.1% of vote. Combined minor party vote is 30.2%.
1996	First election under MMP. Combined minor party vote is 38%. NZ First (17 seats) opts for majority coalition with National.
1998	Prime Minister Shipley dismisses NZ First leader, Winston Peters, from cabinet. Coalition collapses.
1999	At general election, minority National government is defeated. Labour forms a minority coalition with Jim Anderton's Alliance.
2002	Early election is called by Prime Minister Helen Clark following split within the Alliance. After the election, Labour forms a minority coalition with the breakaway Progressive Coalition.

In contrast to the wasted vote syndrome found in first-past-the-post systems, the votes cast for third, fourth and even fifth-ranked parties under PR have a good chance of producing parliamentary seats, leading Duverger to conclude that he could find no example of a country where PR had either given rise to or sustained a two-party system.

While any assertion of a causal link between New Zealand's electoral and party systems is undermined by the fact that the decline and fracturing of the two-party system occurred long before the advent of PR, it is extremely doubtful whether, without the vote for the Mixed Member Proportional (MMP) system, most of the new parties would have survived much beyond their first or second elections. As the collapse of the Values (1972–78)[2] and New Zealand (1983–85) parties had shown, it is difficult to build electoral support, or even retain a viable electoral organisation, under the highly disproportional rules of first-past-the-post. In this respect, Social Credit proved to be a notable exception, due mainly to the quasi-religious zeal with which successive generations of followers professed their faith in monetary reform. Had the public not supported the move to MMP, Jim Anderton (Alliance) and Winston Peters (New Zealand First) might well have been left as the sole representatives of their parties in parliament. Instead, the 1993 election, which coincided with the electoral referendum,[3] provided an important platform from which the new parties could build their future support (the combined minor party vote rose from 17 per cent in 1990 to 30 per cent in 1993).

As well as helping to consolidate support for the existing minor parties, notably the five-party Alliance and New Zealand First, MMP gave rise to the formation of a number of largely opportunistic parties, mostly through the defection of MPs from the two major parties. Between the electoral referendum and the first MMP election, some thirteen backbench MPs and ministers had broken away to form rival organisations. By the time of the 1996 election, a total of twenty-seven parties had registered with the Electoral Commission. Of the new post-referendum parliamentary parties, only United was returned to parliament. The most successful of the new post-referendum parties formed outside parliament was ACT, which was led by a former Finance minister, Roger Douglas, and included a small group of former MPs and party activists, mainly from Labour.

What is the likely fate of the current multiparty arrangement? According to proponents of the social structural argument, parties represent specific divisions or cleavages within society, hence their appeal to different voting blocs. Just as New Zealand's two-party system was linked to the country's one-dimensional social structure, so the recent growth of a multiparty system might be expected to reflect the emergence of a more complex cleavage structure made up of several new social dimensions. Two American-based scholars, Arend Lijphart (1999) and Jack Nagel (1994), have explored the extent to which New Zealand's cleavage structure remains rooted in the past and ask whether the clutch of new parties are products of greater cultural, ethnic, and religious diversity. The cleavages identified by Lijphart include socio-economic class, the urban-rural split, religion, and ethnicity. Nagel added two possible 'issue' dimensions, namely postmaterialism and economic intervention.

While the residual strength of socio-economic class helps explain the continuing electoral dominance of the two major parties, in what other respects does the social cleavage analysis help us to predict either the number of viable parties or their relative strength? This investigation will look into whether there is some potential for the consolidation of ethnic and religious cleavages, with the likely beneficiaries being the Maori party, which was formed in 2004, and the transformation of United Future into a self-consciously Christian party. As far as issue dimensions are concerned, it is useful to ask whether postmaterialism and neoliberalism have the potential to sustain the Green and ACT parties respectively over the medium to long term. Over the passage of time, the free market versus economic interventionist debate out of which both the ACT and Alliance parties were formed lost much of its resonance with voters. Following ACT's dramatic decline in the opinion polls, in early 2004 its leader, Richard Prebble, canvassed his email subscribers on whether his party should continue as a separate movement or merge with National.[4]

Given the obvious limitations of the social cleavage argument, on what other basis can the persistence of the present array of parties be understood? One possible explanation concerns the growing importance of personal attachment or ties. New Zealand has had more than its share of personality-based parties. While some have appealed to the populist, even anti-party, instincts of voters, others, such as Bob Jones' New Zealand party and Jim Anderton's Alliance, have held to a messianic belief in the need to return the major parties to their founding doctrines. Unlike parties representing society's old cleavage structures, these personality-based movements appear suddenly and, by virtue of being the product of the actions of a particular individual, remained inherently unstable and transient, as illustrated by the collapse of the Alliance and the continuing ebbs and flows of support for New Zealand First.

In his analysis of the party systems of Western Europe, Gordon Smith identifies three stages in the process of change: first, a shake-up of the major parties 'as new parties gain support and electoral volatility rises'; second, 'a period of flux with the core parties in disarray and adopting strategies of adaptation'; and finally, the return of relative stability, with the major parties 'recovering at least a substantial part of their electorate and…reassert[ing] their governing position' (1989, pp. 361–2). As we will see, while Labour was able to reassert its dominant governing position by forging links with several of the new parties, National continued for some time to be in a state of electoral and ideological flux, although its rise in the polls in 2004 suggested that it may be entering Smith's third stage of governing success and electoral stability.

Party participation

The second major theme of this book explores the decline of party membership and activism. Do New Zealand's political parties encourage or discourage participation among rank-and-file members? The case for participation is built on two main claims: first, that it enables individual citizens to assert greater control over the 'public' dimension of their lives; and second, that it helps to energize parties and frustrate the natural inclination of the ruling elite towards an 'elective dictatorship'. Advocates of increased participation believe that direct grassroots control is a prerequisite to responsive government. In theory, if not always in practice, parties maintain a mediating link between the citizenry and the politicians. Those members of the public who wish to become involved in collective action with a view to influencing elite opinion, and perhaps even policy outcomes, can join a political party. As one democratic theorist has observed, parties 'enable citizens to develop ideas about the sort of political future they want and to express their opinions about this in the decision-making process' (Ware 1987, p. 25). Without significant input into decision-making by the party membership, feelings of powerlessness can easily develop, and politicians are apt to get out of step with the views of the wider public. It is this issue of accountability that is at the heart of the debate over the role of party members and activists. Can accountability be achieved simply through the ballot box, or does it require on-going citizen involvement?

The case against grassroots participation, on the other hand, consists of two related but independent strands. The first argument is based on the assumption that voters lack the necessary interest and knowledge to justify any substantive influence over the political process. According to a definition made famous by Joseph Schumpeter, representative democracy is 'that institutional arrangement for arriving at political decisions in which individuals acquire the power to decide by means of a competitive struggle for the people's vote' (1976, p. 269). Having chosen their representatives, voters should be prepared to let them govern, with advice from their bureaucrats and advisors, until the next scheduled election, when they can be either re-elected or replaced. According to this narrow conception of democracy, because political legitimacy resides with the elected representatives, voters are required to accept that 'political action is [the government's business] and not theirs' (1976, p. 295). Participation in the form of 'political back-seat driving' will inevitably lead to weak and unstable government.

The second strand in the anti-participation argument is less concerned with lack of voter interest than with the complexity of modern government.[5] It presupposes that power is the responsibility, not of the non-expert masses, but of professionally trained and equipped bureaucratic and technocratic elites. While participatory democracy could be justified in more 'simple' times, modernisation created a need for specialisation that quickly exposed the intellectual limitations of ordinary voters. As Sartori has observed, 'the more total planning is sought, the more democratic incompetence must unreservedly yield to technocratic competence' (1987, p. 431). Short of a return to the pre-technological age, proponents of this argument believe that the voting public should defer to the superior knowledge and wisdom of experts.

Levels of participation

The steady decline in levels of public engagement has led Whiteley and Seyd (2002) to distinguish between 'low-cost' and 'high-intensity' participation. 'Low-cost' participation takes a variety of forms, including expressing an interest in politics, viewing an election campaign on television, and casting a vote. It may also include accessing party information on the Internet, and perhaps taking out party membership simply as a matter of course. As the name implies, 'high-intensity' participation can be applied to all forms of direct activism. Party activists are normally volunteers who devote part of their leisure time to promoting the party and its message. Their activities may include holding party office, participating in policy formation and in the selection of party leaders and candidates, putting their name forward as a list or electorate candidate, and assisting with the planning and funding of an election campaign.

Low-cost participation

For most of the last century, New Zealand had one of the highest levels of electoral turnout in the non-communist world. The reasons are complex, and may have much to do with the small population base and rich democratic history, New Zealand having been the first country to introduce the universal franchise (in 1893). Other influences on turnout may include high educational standards, low unemployment, and the unitary and unicameral nature of the political system, with only one elected body being chosen at the national level every three years. But the consistently good turnout may also reflect the strength of the link between voters and the two major parties. For much of the postwar period, party identification rates were high, and the two parties had proven methods for mobilising their supporters to cast a vote. As a percentage of the valid vote, turnout reached a postwar peak of 94 per cent in 1984. Since then, and despite the introduction of proportional representation, turnout has dropped by a dramatic 17 points to 77 per cent (or 72.5 per cent of the voting-age population, the average for post-industrial democracies (Norris 2002a, p. 45)).[6] A particular cause for concern are the

37 per cent of eighteen- to twenty-nine-year-olds who failed to vote in 2002.[7] Contributing factors may include the continuing decline of party identification (for example, from 62 to 54 per cent in the space of just one election cycle, that of 1996 to 1999), and lack of contact between the parties and voters during the course of the campaign (Vowles et al. 2002, p. 112).

Figure 1.3   Voter turnout, 1935–2002

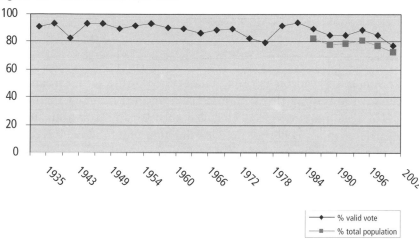

Source of data: *NZ Electoral Compendium*, 3rd edition, 2002, pp. 168–71, 174–5.

High-intensity participation

This brings us to the central issue of whether 'high-intensity' activism is in decline. If it is, what are the reasons? And why have the parties not done more to restore participation among their core activists? The most outstanding feature of party membership in New Zealand, as in most countries, is the unmistakable pattern of decline. Although Labour and National continue to characterise their parties as 'broad churches', both have experienced substantial decreases in the numbers of paid-up members and activists since the heyday of the mass party in the 1940s, 1950s, and 1960s. However, unlike their counterparts in large parts of continental Europe, Britain, and Canada, most of New Zealand's parties have consistently refused to release any membership data, mainly on the grounds that to do so would give the other parties a competitive advantage. While there is truth to Susan Scarrow's assertion that non-disclosure generally indicates a failure on the part of party officials to keep accurate records (2000, p. 85), attitudes in New Zealand are more reflective of the culture of secrecy and mutual suspicion that is endemic to the party system.

Table 1.1 Estimated aggregate party membership, 1954–2002

Year	Raw number (approx.)	% valid vote
1954	290,000	26.4
1960	272,000	23.2
1975	225,000	14.0
1984	170,000	8.8
1993	55,000	2.9
1996	75,000	3.6
1999	65,000	3.1
2002	50,000	2.4[8]

By combining available information obtained by the author from a variety of party sources, together with material from the Electoral Commission, which has a statutory obligation to collect membership data from all registered parties in order to allocate broadcasting time and funding, it is possible to chart the decline in the total estimated numbers of party members in the period since 1954 (see table 1.1). Given the absence of accurate historical data, it is necessary to treat these figures with some caution. As studies on party membership elsewhere have pointed out, there is a temptation for party officials to have overstated any data that has found its way into the public domain (Webb 2000, p. 219).[9] Among the other factors that must be taken into account is Labour's practice of including 'affiliated' union members in its membership totals. In 1960, for example, of an estimated total Labour membership of 180,000, some two-thirds were affiliated members (Chapman et al. 1962, p. 15). At other times the proportion has been as high as four-fifths (Levene 1979, p. 71).

Since the total membership figures provided to the Electoral Commission for 1996 (115,093), 1999 (103,021), and 2002 (83,944) include 'affiliate' members, it is highly likely that aggregate individual membership totals are significantly lower (although the Commission's totals do not include membership figures for ACT (2,900), the Progressive Coalition (2,000), or New Zealand First). Other factors that may contribute to a tendency for aggregate membership numbers to be inflated include: failure to purge membership lists of the names of those whose subscriptions have expired; failure to detect incidences of multiple membership (some are members of more than one party); and significant fluctuations in membership numbers between election and non-election years. With the growing incidence of direct debit bank payments, it is also possible that, unless prompted, a number of members may be unaware of their continuing support.

In accounting for possible reasons for membership decline, Susan Scarrow distinguishes between 'supply-side' and 'demand-side' explanations (2000, p. 83). Supply-side explanations are concerned with changes in the social conditions and outlook of voters, whereas the demand side represents changes occurring within the parties themselves. Perhaps the most widely discussed supply-side explanation is that provided by Robert Putnam. In *Bowling Alone* (2000) and *Democracies in Flux* (2002), he coined the term 'social capital' to describe the social networks that link individuals one with another, thereby instilling a shared sense of friendship, community and belonging. Voluntary organisations that are said to represent some form of social capital include the sports club, church group, professional association, and political party. Activities conducted in the heyday of the mass party typically included organised dances, outings, and retreats. As well as creating social networks, these activities provided a shared sense of belonging, even exclusivity.

Over time, these largely collective benefits of membership began to fall prey to weakening partisan attachments and the more individualistic values and lifestyles of contemporary life, especially among the young. According to Putnam, the rise of television and the new technology were instrumental in the privatisation and individualisation of leisure. Gradually, public interest in joining organisations and devoting spare time to their activities began to weaken. At about the same time the mass party was giving way to a new model of party organisation. The 'catch-all' party expanded its interests beyond the class-based membership of the mass party to a broad range of social groups (Kirchheimer 1966). Among those most severely affected by this repositioning towards the electoral middle ground were the working-class unions, whose association with Labour went back to the party's formation in 1916. In the new era of live television, it was possible for the politicians to reach directly over the heads of these traditional sources of support to a new mass audience. Whereas the mass party had created a sense of belonging and active engagement, under the amorphous catch-all party, 'the role of citizen is coming to be defined more as spectator than as participant' (Putnam 2002, p. 412).

On the demand-side, a change that has impacted on levels of membership and activism has been the emergence of a more professional party organisation. The 'electoral-professional' party is distinguished by its emphasis on strong central control, extensive use of the electronic media, and increasing reliance on professional expertise in preference to amateur activists (Panebianco 1988, pp. 262–7). The process of modernisation has given rise to a more personal, even 'presidential', style of election campaign. To give maximum effect to the opportunities provided by television and the new technology, parties have become increasingly dependent on hired consultants and agencies, such as pollsters, coordinated by a highly centralised and permanent campaign elite. Instead of a busy schedule of public meetings, the party leader's campaign is built around some carefully stage-managed events, most of which are designed to meet the requirements of the 6 o'clock television news.

A further feature of modernisation that has grown in importance since the arrival of MMP has been the use of the tools of mass marketing. Boutique parties competing in a crowded electoral market readily acknowledge the importance of 'branding' and identifying their 'market share'. In the absence of large numbers of rank-and-file members, most also find it necessary to make use of marketing and distribution companies to prepare and distribute their campaign message to a nationwide audience. Because the costs involved in running professional campaigns are clearly beyond the resources of party members and supporters, political leaders are becoming increasingly reliant on corporate donations and funding and other resources, such as staffing, provided by the state.

It would be misleading to suggest, however, that party activism has been superseded by the advent of the professional campaign. Every party with serious parliamentary ambitions continues to regard party membership and activism as important, if for no other reason than to demonstrate that the party is in sound electoral health (Scarrow 2000). In the same way, it is easy to exaggerate the claim that the 'golden age' of parties was characterised by high-intensity participation. Although the ratio of party members to voters was flatteringly high, perhaps giving New Zealand the highest proportion of party members in the Western world, a vast majority did little more than pay their annual membership dues. There were obvious incentives to becoming active, including an opportunity to influence the direction of party policy and the right to be represented in the selection of parliamentary candidates. As a result, party conferences were more robust than they are today, and politicians were more reliant on party workers in organising and attending campaign meetings, canvassing community opinion, and mobilising the vote. By most international standards, however, at no time was the level of democratic involvement high. Of the two major parties, Labour was the more centralised and oligarchic in its decision-making. While local delegates were given some say in the choice of candidate, for example, head office tended to have the upper hand. In neither of the two parties did the members have any formal role in the selection of the party leader, and the most important policy initiatives generally emanated, not from a regional or national party conference, but from the parliamentary caucus and cabinet.

Models of participation

On the assumption that participation is important, to what extent does a party's decision-making structure influence the level of grassroots activism? The present study will propose a modified version of the theoretical framework presented by Whiteley and Seyd (2002) in their analysis of party participation in Britain.[10] We will consider five contrasting models of participation, namely the leadership, elite, delegate, participatory, and plebiscitary models of participation.

Leadership model

Distinguishing features of this model include: a strong, even charismatic, leader; a weak organisational structure; and a loose band of 'supporters' (rather than 'activists'), whose attachment to the party is based almost exclusively on their personal commitment to the leader (Whiteley and Seyd 2002, p. 212). Even though the party's constitution and organisational structure is likely to state otherwise, the leader makes all the important decisions, although on occasions in consultation with an informal group of trusted advisers. Areas over which he or she will exercise final control include the choice of all senior party officials, selection of parliamentary candidates, determining the party's core principles and policy agenda, and being the personification of the movement, especially during an election campaign. The leadership model is most commonly associated with the minor parties, prominent examples of which are Ross Perot's Reform party in the United States, Jean-Marie Pen's National Front in France, and James Goldsmith's Referendum party in Britain.

Elite model

The main feature of this model bears a close resemblance to that of the modern 'catch-all' party, namely a shift in the fulcrum of power away from party members and activists, with their emphasis on participation and the preservation of the party's beliefs, and towards a new class of professionally trained and media-savvy politicians and advisors. According to Whiteley and Seyd, while parties based on the elite model continue to pay lip service to grassroots' involvement through maintaining a party membership and permitting some limited public involvement in areas such as policy formation, candidate selection, and election planning and campaigning, the decisions that count are those of the party hierarchy. Most are no longer made within the wider party organisation, but rather in the offices of the politicians, especially the party leader.

Delegate model

This model is most commonly associated with the former mass-membership party, which had a tiered organisational structure, with cells and branches at the lowest level and with regional and national bodies above. Under this model, members at each level choose one or more of their number to represent the interests of the group at the next level of decision-making within the organisation. Delegates are not chosen to represent their own interests, or to exercise their own individual conscience, but rather those of the group. If this model is applied in the way intended, the party's national conference will be a microcosm of the membership at large. While decisions will need to be made by other bodies of the party between conferences, the powers of the latter are regarded as supreme. For the delegate model to work effectively, close consultation is required between the members and their delegate(s), both before and after any decisions have been reached. Of course, there is always the possibility that delegates will be captured by the views of others, especially the politicians, in which case they will cease to be a conduit for the views of those they represent. While this model has the disadvantage of limiting the opportunities for direct involvement among grassroots members, if properly managed it can produce high levels of responsiveness and accountability.

Participatory model

This is based on the principles of direct democracy, with each member having the opportunity to not only attend party meetings, but also have a voice in all key decisions. Under this model, which works most effectively in minor parties with less than 5,000 members, participants are not delegated to represent the views of others, but rather they represent themselves. On the assumption that only one in five members, and more likely approximately one in ten, will be able to attend a national conference, parties based on the participatory model generally engage in an extensive process of consultation, followed by a majority vote of all those involved. Alternatively, the party may attempt to reach its decisions by consensus.

Plebiscitary model

Those who favour this model over the delegate or participatory approaches are said to be suspicious of the deliberative process, believing that it can readily lead to 'capture...by a closed circle of "special interests" and their benefactors' (Laycock 2002, p. 95). Instead, rank-and-file members are given an opportunity to either endorse or reject the decisions of the party elite. The use of direct primaries to select presidential candidates for the US Republican and Democratic parties is perhaps the most widely known example of this model, although the British Labour and Conservative parties, together with most of the parties of Canada, employ the plebiscitary model, especially in choosing their political leaders. A number of parties, including the British Liberal Democrats and Canadian Alliance party, have also used plebiscites to select their parliamentary candidates. As a number of parties have found, balloting members can have a positive effect on party membership numbers, especially where leadership candidates are permitted to enlist new members during the course of the leadership contest.

The plebiscitary model appeals to those who believe that we are moving towards parties without members, partly because membership is seen to have so little intrinsic value, but also because the costs of participation are becoming too high. Its critics, on the other hand, believe that plebiscitary politics simply creates an illusion of participation, the decisions having already been reached by the party leadership. According to one study, the leaders of the

British Labour and Conservative parties use the device of the plebiscite to reach over the heads of the party activists, who are likely to be critical of their decisions, by going directly to the wider membership to seek endorsement for decisions already made by the party leadership (Whiteley and Seyd 2002, p. 214). No opportunity is presented to effectively scrutinise the proposal, and the plebiscite can be drafted in such a way as to produce a guaranteed outcome.

Plan of the book

The approach of the book is thematic, with the sections and chapters being organised by topic rather than party. While the party-by-party approach has a number of obvious advantages, notably ease of access, with all the relevant information about a particular party being located in the one place, the benefits are outweighed by the potential drawbacks, in particular a cumbersome and repetitive framework which discourages cross-party analysis. The thematic approach, in contrast, makes it possible to be both comprehensive and comparative, with every effort being made to discuss the two major parties and, where relevant, several of the smaller parties within each chapter.

The second section (Part 2—The Party System) focuses on the evolution of the party system. Chapter 2 provides a brief overview of the development of the New Zealand party system, beginning with the one-party phase in the 1890s and concluding with a discussion on the reasons for the decline of the two-party system. Chapter 3 discusses the social and political factors that may have a bearing on the nature and composition of the party system, including class, ethnicity, religion, changing lifestyles and values, and the rise of alternative social and political movements. It asks whether the social structure is sufficiently diverse to sustain the present multiparty arrangement.

In the third section (Part 3—How Parties Organise) we turn to the organisational development of parties. After considering the importance of party organisation, the discussion in chapter 4 turns to the ways in which parties have adjusted to the requirements of democracy and assesses the importance of changing organisational opportunities and developments. It traces the evolution of party organisations through the cadre, mass, and catch-all stages, and, in recent times, into the cartel party phase. Cartel party organisations use the resources of the state to gain an electoral advantage over emerging competitors. This may include manipulating the rules of competition, direct state funding of political parties, the use of state employees to carry out party business, and receiving publicly funded broadcasting time. Although the major parties are best placed to exploit these resources, small parties may be strategically placed to collaborate with a view to receiving their share of available benefits. Anti-competitive moves may include arriving at agreed policies and legislative strategies, shared electoral information, the standing down of candidates, and other forms of electoral accommodation.

Chapter 5 asks whether, in an era of declining civic engagement and the growth of professional parties and campaigns, membership still matters. Why do people join parties, and what are the reasons for the decline in party activism, especially among the young? The chapter also discusses the related issue of party finance, especially given the decline of party membership and the increase in corporate and state funding. Continuing with the theme of linkage in chapter 6, the study explores the mass/elite dichotomy and asks whether party hierarchies genuinely encourage grass-roots participation and influence. How democratic are the candidate selection procedures, for example, and how prepared are the party organisations to engage the public in their decisions? The same theme is carried into a study of leadership selection in New Zealand. Compared with a number of other countries, including Canada and Britain, most of the parties have resisted opening up the leadership selection process to party activists and members. The discussion goes on to describe both the role of leadership and the qualities of a successful leader.

The fourth section of the book (Part 4—How Parties Compete) turns from the theme of party organisation to the ways in which parties compete with one another both within the electorate and inside government. Chapter 8 considers two contrasting accounts of the importance of ideology to party politics. The first is based on the assumption that ideology matters. The families-based approach attempts to cluster parties according to their shared ideological origins and outlook. On the other hand, the vote-maximisation approach pioneered by Anthony Downs adopts the view that parties make policies to win elections rather than win elections to implement policies. The relevance of the latter model to the intriguing two-party battle for the hearts and minds of voters provides a focus for the chapter. The centre-seeking tendencies of the two major parties are illustrated with reference to two recent case studies: Labour's commitment to the politics of the Third Way; and National's orchestration of the race debate in early 2004 to fuel its dramatic rise in the polls.

Chapter 9 considers the approaches and strategies adopted in modern election campaigns, in particular the roles of the media and professional agencies in determining the style, issues, and personalities of the campaign. Returning to the theme of participation, the chapter explores the merits of the view that it is not so much a question of people disengaging from campaigns, but rather of their engaging differently. In weighing up the merits of this perspective, we will draw on survey data on public interest in campaigns and when people make their voting decisions. The chapter will consider fresh opportunities for public participation, especially through the use of interactive television, email, and the World Wide Web.

The advent of the modern election campaign, together with that of MMP, has given rise to speculation about possible changes in the nature and composition of parliamentary representation. In chapter 10 we take the theme of candidate selection one step further by asking who gets into office and why. As well as examining key social indicators, such as levels of female and ethnic representation, the chapter will focus on any operational differences in the roles of list and electorate MPs.

As well as competing for the people's vote, parties vie for legislative and governmental power. Chapter 11 considers the costs, as well as the benefits, of being in power. Because the role of the major parties has been extensively discussed in other studies,[11] this chapter considers the costs that coalitions impose on the minor parties. Drawing on the experiences of minor coalition partners in other countries with a Westminster tradition, notably Ireland and Scotland, and bearing in mind the difficult transition to coalition government by several of New Zealand's minor parties, the chapter asks whether voter rejection is simply a cross the small parties must bear in return for the spoils of office.

Lastly, in chapter 12 we return to one of the central issues of the book, namely the need to reverse the trend towards civic disengagement. Areas of party activity where greater participation can be encouraged include: choosing the party leader; selecting list and electorate candidates; policy initiation and development, party fund-raising; and the interactive use of the Internet.

Notes

1   In the One News/Colmar Brunton poll of 13 February 2004, party support for National rose from 28 per cent in December to 45 per cent in February, largely on the back of the call by the new leader, Don Brash, for an end to 'racial separatism'. Much of the increase was at the expense of New Zealand First (down 5 percentage points to 6 per cent) and ACT (down 5 points to 1 per cent).

2   Although several Values candidates contested the 1981, 1984, and 1987 elections, the party structure was largely disbanded after the 1978 election.

3   There were, in fact, two electoral referendums. The first, which was held in September 1992, was an indicative referendum on the relative merits of five different electoral systems, including first-past-the-post and MMP. Of the 56 per cent of voters who participated, 85 per cent voted for change, and 71 per cent chose MMP. The binding referendum of October 1993 provided a two-way contest between the existing first-past-the-post system and MMP. With 83 per cent of voters participating, the result was a 54 per cent majority in favour of MMP (see figure 1.2).

4   'Letter from Richard Prebble', 16 February 2004, Parliament Buildings, Wellington.

5   For commentaries on Schumpeter, Sartori and other critics of public participation, see, for example, Budge (1993), Parry et al. (1992), and Coe and Wilber (1985).

6   See, for example, Vowles et al. 1995, pp xiii–xiv.

7   *New Zealand Herald*, 1 June 2004, p. A13.

8   The overall pattern of party membership decline in New Zealand mirrors that in many other Western countries. According to data provided by Susan Scarrow (2000, p. 91), however, the rate of decline has been steeper in New Zealand than in any of the other 15 states she looked at. Those countries with greater percentages of party members in the 1990s included Austria (17.1 per cent), Finland (10.5 per cent) and Switzerland (8.7 per cent). Only Australia (1.5 per cent) and the United Kingdom (1.9 per cent) had lower percentages of party members in the population than New Zealand.

9   The figures in table 1.1 were assembled from a variety of scholarly sources, including Chapman et al. (1962), Milne (1966), Levine (1979), Strachan (1985), Gustafson (1986b), Miller (1985), Miller (1987), Gustafson (1997), and Scarrow (2000).

10 The five models discussed in this chapter contain features of the schema of party organisation presented by Whiteley and Seyd (2002). However, the four models of participation offered by these two scholars—extinction, leadership, plebiscitary, and participatory—contain some overlap, especially between the latter two models, and give insufficient attention to participation by delegates. Besides, as they themselves admit, the extinction model is now considered to be an unlikely outcome of party system decline.

11 See, for example, Boston (1997 and 2001), Boston et al. (2000 and 2003).

Further reading

Nagel, J. 1994, 'How Many Parties will New Zealand Have Under MMP?' in *Political Science*, 26/2, pp. 139–60.

Norris, P. 2002a, *Democratic Phoenix: Reinventing Political Activism*, Cambridge University Press, Cambridge.

Putnam, R.D. 2000, *Bowling Alone: The Collapse and Revival of American Community*, Simon and Schuster, New York.

Scarrow, S.E. 2000, 'Parties without Members? Party Organization in a Changing Electoral Environment', in Dalton, R.J. and M.P. Wattenberg (eds), *Parties Without Partisans: Political Change in Advanced Industrial Democracies*, Oxford University Press, Oxford, pp. 79–101.

Whiteley, P. and P. Seyd 2002, *High-Intensity Participation: The Dynamics of Party Activism in Britain*, The University of Michigan Press, Ann Arbor, Michigan.

| part two |

The Party System

Development of the
Party System

2

CHARTING the development of the New Zealand party system reveals a complex pattern of continuity and change. For much of the twentieth century New Zealand enjoyed a reputation for having one of the purest and most stable two-party systems in the world (Epstein 1967, p. 68; Blondel 1968. p. 180; Sartori 1976, p. 185;[1] Lijphart 1999, p. 25). Beginning in the late 1970s, economic crisis and the unravelling of New Zealand's postwar consensus caused major ideological shifts to occur within the two established parties.[2] Their radical economic and social welfare agendas provoked deep divisions within party ranks, brought about the formation of splinter parties, and contributed to a dramatic decline in the two-party vote.

The durability of the two-party system tended to obscure a significant feature in the evolution of the New Zealand party system, namely its capacity for periodic restructuring. Conversely, while the two-party phase has passed, several of its defining characteristics remain in place, notably a narrow cleavage structure and the absence of ideological distance between the two main parties. As one study of party system transition has observed, 'even where changes occurred, older patterns did not disappear' (Wolinetz 1988, p. 4). Thus, while the development of the party system followed clearly discernible stages, each was linked to the other in such a way as to produce a 'collage of successive [party] overlays' (Sundquist 1983, p. 17).

Continuity versus change

Central to the study of political parties is the debate over whether party systems have an inherent tendency towards stability or change. An initial point of reference for any account of the stability thesis is the seminal work of Lipset and Rokkan (1967). Of their four historically important cleavages (centre-periphery; state-church; land-industry; and owner-worker), clearly that between capitalists and workers is the most widely relevant. The early structuring of party competition occurred at a time of growing class conflict, leading Lipset to conclude that elections are 'the expression of the democratic class struggle' (1960, p. 220). The link between class and the franchise can be seen in the rise of a number of left-wing parties, including the Labo(u)r parties of Britain, Australia, and New Zealand. The British Labour party's rise coincided with the 1918 decision to extend the vote to all those over the age of 30. As well as consolidating a sense of political identification among those in the newly enfranchised working class, the party's success resulted in an intensification of anti-socialist sentiment among its opponents (Lipset and Rokkan 1967, p. 22). The electoral bonds formed on both sides of the social divide continued to be a defining feature of the party systems of Britain, New Zealand, and many other Western countries for the next fifty years, leading scholars to conclude that they had become 'frozen'.

Countering the stability argument is the claim that parties have a capacity for significant and often abrupt change (for example, Downs 1957; Carmines 1991). However convincing the 'freezing' hypothesis might have seemed to observers in the 1960s and 1970s, its opponents argue that subsequent events demonstrate that party systems have a marked capacity for change. Possible explanations include changing political values and priorities, rapid expansion of the urban middle class, a blurring of divisions between left and right, declining levels of voter identification and support, and, in the face of mounting economic and social pressures, increasing voter discontent. When confronted with these and other changes, parties and party systems were forced to adapt or be seriously undermined. As we saw in chapter 1, their task was made more difficult by the gradual erosion of any meaningful process by which established parties were linked to the needs and interests of ordinary citizens (Lawson and Merkl 1988; Ignazi 1996). As a result, parties lost much of their effectiveness as channels of public expression and scrutiny. Just as importantly, they also lost the electoral security provided by the old class-based cleavage structure. In a new and more complex world, non-socioeconomic divisions began to destroy much of the social fabric that had made the two-party system such a dominant electoral force.

Rather than proving one and repudiating the other of the stability versus change alternatives, this chapter will argue that the present party system contains strong elements of both.

Four waves of development

An overview of the history of the New Zealand party system reveals a complex pattern of continuity and change, with the socio-economic cleavage being the most visible thread that links the early stages of party system development.

Single party wave (1891–1908)

Before the advent of political parties, the New Zealand parliament was loosely arranged into factions, most of them held together by a combination of personal ties, provincial or community interests, and agreed policy positions (Dalziel 1981). In the absence of even the most skeletal of party systems, candidates tended to run as independents, although by the late 1880s they were under mounting pressure to declare where they stood in relation to the overall plan of action of the government (Richardson 1981, p. 198). By the time the Liberals took office in 1891 it was clear that '"party" was now to be the main determinant of political organization and behaviour in the House' (Hamer 1988, p. 13). In addition to voting together as a bloc, the Liberal members began to develop a collective identity and common core of principles and policies. Cooperation was made easier by the lack of an organised opposition (Hamer 1988, p. 34) and mounting pressure for a government that was both strong and united (Hamer 1988, p. 28).

The Liberals managed to forestall the formation of other parties by drawing support from a broad spectrum of voters—Pakeha and Maori, employers and unionists, skilled and unskilled workers, small traders, urban professionals, and farmers. Although Liberal voters were to be found in the cities and countryside, the party's fortress seats were in the newly prosperous provincial towns, especially the port seats of Gisborne, Napier, New Plymouth, Nelson and Invercargill (Hamer 1988, pp. 150–94. The party's wider coalition was sustained through its endorsement of an inclusive and socially liberal agenda, including graduated taxes, welfare reform, guaranteed recognition of the role of trade unions, and the gradual expansion of the local economy and infrastructure. Although farmers, especially sheep farmers, were less inclined to support the Liberals, with disagreement focusing on the proposed break-up of the large estates, rural opposition was far from universal—support was strong among leasehold farmers, for example, and those in the back-blocks whose standard of living had been improved by the expansion of roads, bridges and railways, as well as the creation of postal and telephone services.

The Liberals' programme of reform laid the foundations for New Zealand's long-time commitment to an active, interventionist state. Under the leadership of William Pember Reeves, landmark industrial legislation was passed to both improve working conditions and create processes for the resolution of industrial disputes (such as the *Industrial Conciliation and Arbitration Act* and the *Factories Act*, both of 1894). In addition, the government introduced a number of welfare reforms, notably old-age pensions for the 'deserving poor' and more humane working conditions for women and young children.

In what may appear to be a rather enlightened initiative for the time, in 1867 the New Zealand parliament had created four separate Maori seats in its seventy-member chamber (a temporary decision which became permanent in 1876). While the decision can be seen as recognition of the political rights of Maori as British subjects and landowners (Sorrenson 1986, A-28), less charitable explanations have been advanced. According to one view, extending the franchise to Maori may have been an attempt to resolve ongoing conflict with the settlers over land. From another perspective, in creating separate seats the government might have been attempting to ring-fence the influence of Maori within the political system. In 1896, the Liberals passed a law preventing Maori of more than half Maori descent from voting in the 'European' seats. By so doing, the government was able to ensure that all non-Maori seats were controlled by and in the interests of Europeans (Mulgan 1989, p. 81).

By the late 1890s the Liberals had gained a firm foothold in the Maori electorates, having captured three of the four available seats (Sorrenson 1986, B-68). Two Maori MPs went on to become cabinet ministers, holding the position of Minister for Native Affairs in successive Liberal governments. When the Liberals decided not to enter federation with Australia in 1901, one of the reasons given was that the terms of federation precluded 'aboriginal natives' from being included in population statistics. They were advised that the exclusion of Maori from any prospect of representation in an Australasian parliament 'would be a great injustice to them'.[3] Despite this expression of support for Maori political rights, a number of electoral anomalies persisted. While the secret ballot was introduced for Europeans in 1890, for example, it was not required in Maori seats for another fifty years.

By the beginning of the new century, the Liberal government's electoral coalition was beginning to unravel. With the burgeoning of the cities and provincial towns (by that time a quarter of the population lived in the four main centres) and the emergence of both an urban middle class and an industrial sector, the image of New Zealand as a 'pioneer-frontier society' was receding (Olssen 1981, p. 253). Thereafter it was the relationship between employer and worker that would determine the structure of the emerging party system. New pressure groups were being formed on the party's right and left flanks in response to growing social and economic divisions within New Zealand society. In the rural heartland, farmers who had been helped onto the land with government assistance now looked for a political party more strongly committed to the protection of their own personal prosperity. In 1898, the Farmers' Union was formed with a view to putting pressure on the government to allow farmers to freehold their leased land. As the debate over the freehold tenure of land became more intense, the government's critics accused it of standing for 'revolutionary socialism' (Bassett 1995, p. 31). In the cities, a new pressure group, the New Zealand Employers' Federation, came to represent the views of an increasingly disaffected business community. With the help of the Farmers' Union and its freehold land supporters, it formed a new right-wing political movement, the Reform party. Under the leadership of a Mangere farmer, W.F. Massey, it took power in 1912.

Figure 2.1   Party development, 1890–1978

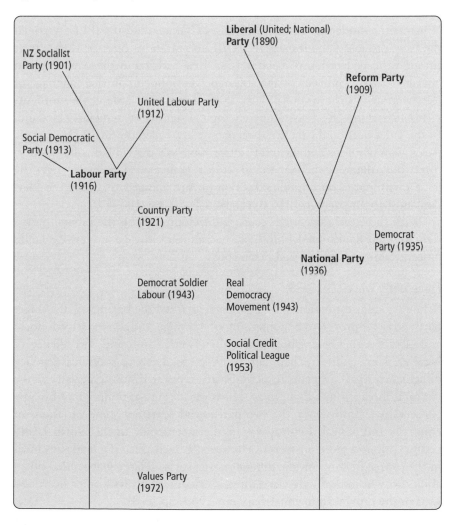

On the left of the political spectrum, a number of moderate and militant trade unions had been formed with a view to advancing workers' rights. Their growing opposition to what they came to regard as the pro-capitalist, anti-worker policies of the Liberals, especially in response to the demands of the well-to-do farming and city business interests (Gustafson 1980, p. 14), resulted in the formation of breakaway socialist and workers' parties. Following the electoral success of the Australian Labor party—in 1901 it held the balance of power in the federal parliament (Brown 1962, p. 4)—the Independent Political Labour League (IPLL) was formed with a view to nominating its own slate of parliamentary candidates. Although its eleven candidates suffered humiliating defeat at the 1905 election, three years later the IPLL won its first seat, that of Wellington East (Gustafson 1980, p. 19). However, a more militant political movement had begun to emerge in the wake of a series of bitter industrial disputes on the South Island's West Coast. Whereas the moderates backed the Trades Councils and the IPLL (renamed the New Zealand Labour party in 1910), the militants directed their efforts through the Federation of Labour (the 'Red Feds') and the New Zealand Socialist party, a movement that framed its arguments in the 'language of class warfare' (Richardson 1981, p. 208). Prominent among the militants were Michael Joseph Savage, Robert Semple, Peter Fraser, and Harry Holland. At the 1914 election the more radical party (now called the Social Democratic party) won two seats and the moderate group (now the United Labour party) three. In parliament they tended to work together until, primarily over the issue of military conscription, the two groups merged to create the New Zealand Labour party in 1916 (Gustafson 1980, pp. 105–19).

With these early twentieth century developments on the Liberal party's right and left flanks the defining socio-economic cleavage of New Zealand's nascent two-party system had taken root.

Three-party wave (1916–36)

While Labour's formation as a single party marked the beginning of a three-party phase, it proved to be something of a mirage, the conservative Reform and Liberal parties having been cast as the 'Tweedledum' and 'Tweedledee' of New Zealand politics (Chapman 1969, p. 5). Lack of substantive policy disagreement gave impetus to periodic attempts at fusion, especially as the electoral threat from Labour grew. However, despite appealing to a broadly conservative constituency, the two parties did represent some variations of emphasis and appeal. Reform was in the ascendancy in the North Island countryside and more prosperous city seats, as well as having made advances in the towns. In contrast, the Liberal party's survival largely depended on an ability to win increasingly close three-way contests in its former heartland seats in the provincial towns (Chapman 1969, pp. 7–8).

Despite Reform's avowed conservatism on taxes, overseas borrowing and freehold land, its two most prominent leaders, Massey (prime minister 1912–25) and Gordon Coates (1925–28), developed a reputation for moderation and pragmatism. As Bassett has pointed out, much of Coates' wide appeal in the mid-1920s lay in his having 'no clear line of thought, no consistent adherence to any set of principles' (1995, p. 92). Sheer pragmatism drove a low-tax, small-government administration to undertake a capital development programme involving extension of the roads, main truck railway, and electricity and telephone systems.

In contrast, a deeply ideological Labour party was still not regarded as a party for whom 'the "respectable" could easily vote' (Chapman 1969, p. 55). The party fell victim to a number of extravagant claims, including the charge that the contest with Reform was 'one between order and revolution' (Bassett 1995, p. 59). Its opponents focused on Labour's call for a steeply progressive tax regime, the nationalisation of land, and a more general commitment to ownership by the state of the means of production, distribution, and exchange. Given Labour's narrow sectional appeal among low-income workers and the unemployed in the country's largest cities, its only chance of electoral success lay in its ability to replace this radical agenda with the more blandly expressed goals of humanitarianism, economic recovery, and improved welfare (Chapman 1981, p. 335). Initial steps towards building a winning alliance included reaching an accommodation with the farmer-based Country party and the powerful Maori politico-religious organisation, the Ratana Church. The accommodation with Maori proved to be especially productive, giving Labour the lion's share of the Maori vote for the next six decades. As well as attracting non-core voters, these alliances with Maori and the Country party helped to choke off potential third party competition.

At the 1928 election, and on the eve of the Great Depression, Reform faced the most formidable challenge of its sixteen years in government. Confronted with the promise of huge state spending on the part of Sir Joseph Ward's Liberal party (now called United), together with the more moderate stance adopted by Labour, Reform suffered a massive loss of support, especially in the cities (Chapman 1969, p. 55). With twenty-nine and twenty-eight seats respectively, Reform and United were well short of a forty-one-seat majority. Having combined with Labour to defeat Reform on a Confidence motion, Ward was given his chance to form a government. However, the veteran statesman had neither the flair nor the imagination to be able to deal with the growing economic crisis. By September 1931 it was clear that the only way to avoid a Labour government was for the two conservative parties to coalesce. At that year's election the two parties reached an accommodation whereby neither put up candidates in the other's winnable seats. The United party's farmer leader, George Forbes, remained prime minister, with Reform's Downie Stewart (1931–33), followed by Gordon Coates (1933–35), taking responsibility for finance. With large-scale unemployment, low export prices, declining purchasing power, and rising cost of credit, the scene was set for a sharp shift in the balance of popular opinion away from an increasingly hapless Coalition and towards Labour.

Two-party wave (1936–78)

Following the fusion of the United and Reform parties to create National in 1936 (an election vehicle, the National Political Federation, was formed the previous year), the party system underwent its longest period of electoral and political stability, with one-party majority outcomes at every election between 1935 and 1993. Although a number of small parties emerged, most survived for only one or two elections, the significant exception being Social Credit, which contested every campaign following its creation in 1953. The last elected Independent to leave parliament was Harry Atmore (Nelson) in 1943. This two-party dominance can be put down to three main factors: the one-dimensional nature of the cleavage structure; the absence of ideological distance between the two parties, reflecting the centripetal inclinations of most voters; and the highly disproportional electoral benefits enjoyed by National and Labour under the first-past-the-post electoral system.

1. Narrow focus of appeal

To secure victory in 1935 and at every subsequent election, Labour had to broaden its appeal beyond its low-income, manual-worker base in the inner cities. This involved drawing support from the more socio-economically mixed city suburbs and provincial towns, together with some predominantly rural seats with clusters of railway, agricultural, and other unionised workers, such as Nelson and the South Island's West Coast. The party's 1935 victory turned into a rout (Labour fifty-three seats, National nineteen) following endorsement from some unusual sources, notably the monetary reform Social Credit Association, which commanded strong support in a number of traditionally conservative seats. Social Credit's unorthodox monetary ideas, which were based on the writings of a Scottish engineer, Major C.H. Douglas, held obvious and simple appeal to many people left helpless by the Depression; not only did it provide an alternative solution to that of the tired Coalition government, but it offered remedies that were immediate, substantial, and tax-free. Conservative voters, particularly dairy farmers and businesspeople of small means, concluded that its proposed reforms directly threatened neither their capitalist values and assets, nor the established social arrangement of their community (Graham 1963, p. 193). For those disillusioned with the Coalition but afraid of socialism, with its more rigorous economic analysis and cure, Social Credit was a convenient 'corridor', as John

A. Lee described it, along which they could travel to deliver electoral support to Labour (Sinclair 1976, p. 116). Michael Joseph Savage had predicted at the outset that reform of the money supply would be the most important issue of the election campaign, a view endorsed with varying degrees of enthusiasm by virtually every Labour candidate.[4]

When the electoral tide eventually turned against Labour in the 1940s (see Appendix), it was in the conservative countryside and city suburbs where the losses were greatest (Chapman 1981, p. 353). Years of wartime restrictions had taken their toll, and the National party was quick to cash in on the growing demand for greater individual freedom and opportunity. Beginning in 1949, it built a more solid reputation than Labour for expanding and retaining its electoral support (between then and 1984 it was out of office for a total of only six years). Whereas in the 1930s it had been reduced to little more than a country party, a condition which gave temporary hope to an urban-based libertarian alternative, the Democrat party (a precursor to the New Zealand party of the 1980s), in the postwar years National was able to consolidate its appeal among the 'buffer-zone' voters, a group described as being 'little if at all better off than the workers, but whose status aspirations are to the groups above them rather than to those below' (Robinson 1967, p. 96). These predominantly white-collar workers tended to live in the sprawling city suburbs and the more prosperous provincial towns. That National was able to win them over without jeopardising its heartland rural support illustrates its strength as an electoral organisation. Indeed, so broad was National's appeal that none of the small alternative conservative parties that emerged during the postwar period (such as a new Liberal party, which contested the 1963 election, and the durable Social Credit Political League) proved capable of making serious inroads into the National vote.

Prior to the 1930s, Maori political representation had been in the hands of highly educated and politically conservative leaders. With the formation of a Maori party by a religious prophet, Tahupotiki Wiremu Ratana, the main thrust of Maori politics turned towards ways of improving the socio-economic well-being of an increasingly poor and landless people (Sorrenson 1986, B-40). In 1936, the Ratana movement forged a highly successful alliance with Labour. As Alan Robinson has stated, 'tribal ties and the strong influence of the minority Ratana sect with its commitment…to support the Labour party have combined to make Labour dominance of the four Maori seats unchallenged since 1943' (1967, p. 96). Ethnic differences became less important and that of socio-economic class grew following the urban migration of Maori and the replacement of labouring jobs in the countryside with those in the industrial sector. From then until 1993, when a third party took the seat of Northern Maori, Labour managed to retain all Maori seats at every election.

Although successive Labour governments had focused on improving the social and economic status of Maori, the party's attitude to Maori representation was characterised by complacency and paternalism. Despite being a beneficiary of the loyalty of a vast majority of Maori voters, Labour was indifferent to the idea of selecting Maori candidates in 'general' (formerly 'European') seats. As a result, the postwar growth in the Maori population brought with it a corresponding decline in levels of representation. Labour's policy of enforced segregation even extended to the executive. Despite ensuring Maori representation in cabinet, Labour consistently relegated that minister to the portfolio of Maori Affairs. The legislation allowing Maori to stand in general seats was not passed until 1975. At that time 'Maori' was redefined to allow anyone of Maori ancestry to vote in Maori electorates. Since the number of seats remained the same as in 1867, creating a more liberal definition of Maori potentially exacerbated existing levels of under-representation.

Maori representation proved to be an even bigger problem for National than for Labour. Having conceded that its chances of winning a Maori seat were slim, National turned its attention to both selecting Maori candidates in general seats and arguing in favour of the abolition of separate Maori representation (mainly on the grounds that it was separatist). By selecting Maori in general seats, National was able to draw attention to Labour's complacency. Compounding Labour's problems were growing allegations by Maori leaders of neglect—in 1980, for example, Matiu Rata, a former Labour Minister of Maori Affairs, formed a breakaway Maori party, which he named Mana Motuhake.[5]

2. Small ideological distance

As in many other Western democracies in the postwar period, the two-party system was characterised by broad agreement over the importance of preserving and enhancing the welfare state within the framework of a mixed economy. Although the two mass membership parties drew from different constituencies and claimed to be pursuing divergent ideological goals, when in government they upheld broadly similar values and concurred on such matters as the rights of citizens, foreign and defence policy, and the appropriate functions and powers of the state. Labour was known as the party of economic intervention and comprehensive welfare, whereas the National party enjoyed a reputation as the defender of '"unfettered" free enterprise, limited government, and the values of self-reliance and the freedom of the individual' (Miller and Catt 1993, p. 12). However, such doctrinal positions became more the stuff of election campaigns than the guiding principles of government. On the few occasions when Labour held power it proved to be a cautious reformer. National, meanwhile, was content to administer

Labour's 'from the cradle to the grave' universal welfare state, with occasional embellishments of its own (such as Robert Muldoon's generous and vastly expensive retirement scheme for all those of sixty years and above). It also pursued an economic agenda based on a steeply progressive tax regime and requiring significant levels of state intervention and control. In this way Labour and National were able to nurture New Zealand's growing reputation for two-party dominance.

3. First-past-the-post elections

The only challenge to the two-party juggernaut in the period from 1936 to the 1980s was the Social Credit Political League, a movement launched with the sole purpose of increasing the money supply with a view to creating cheap credit.[6] Although it continued to exist in various guises for close to five decades, it was largely unable to extend its support beyond the small entrepreneurial class living in a few North Island country districts (notably some orchardists and dairy farmers) and neighbouring small towns (retailers, small manufacturers, and self-employed manual workers). Social Credit's electoral support waxed and waned, with consequent distortions to its sectional character in times of political unrest, such as in the early 1980s, when it won significant victories in the hitherto safe National metropolitan seats of East Coast Bays and Pakuranga.

However, even in its heyday Social Credit's success was severely constrained by the effects of plurality voting. Despite receiving an average of 11 per cent of the vote in the ten elections between 1954 and 1981, it managed to hold a total of only three parliamentary seats. Its electoral woes are best illustrated with reference to the results of the 1978 and 1981 elections. In 1978 Social Credit won 16.1 per cent of the vote and only 1.1 per cent of the seats. Three years later it received a record 20.7 per cent of the vote but only 2.2 per cent of the seats (in contrast, National's 38.8 per cent gave it 51.1 per cent of the seats).[7]

Wave of electoral multipartism (1978–1993)

Whereas the two-party phase had its roots in the social structure, the advent of multipartism reflected the public's growing disillusionment with the pace and magnitude of social and economic change. The first hint of declining public confidence in the two-party system occurred in the late 1970s, when massive oil price increases, followed by a world recession, exposed the weaknesses of New Zealand's dependent economy. Between 1972 and 1975 the Labour government was confronted simultaneously with record levels of inflation, shrinking markets and prices for New Zealand's primary produce, and rising import costs. Maintaining the high levels of state spending, especially on welfare, required massive borrowing. There was hardly time to absorb the effects of successive oil price increases and deepening recession when the country was dealt a further blow with the release of the terms under which Britain had entered the Common Market. The New Zealand–Britain trade link had been so close that up to 90 per cent of the former colony's agricultural produce had ended up on the British market. That dependence was now at an end. In 1975 the opposition National party used the size of the overseas debt as a potent election weapon. National's memorable campaign promise of 'New Zealand the way you want it' more than hinted at a dramatic change for the better under a conservative administration. But instead of improving, the key economic indicators continued to worsen. By 1978, for instance, the level of unemployment was higher than at any time since the 1930s. The decisive change of government in 1975 had produced high expectations but few economic solutions. Both major parties having been found wanting, a growing number of voters turned their attention towards Social Credit (see Appendix).

Whereas Social Credit's brand of political nostalgia was inconsonant with the needs of a nation in crisis, the economic and political volatility of the late 1970s made the party a safe haven in which to shelter briefly from the passing storm. That the party survived as long as it had can only be explained in terms of the quasi-religious commitment of members to the socio-economic truth and relevance of their doctrine. Their conviction had made them highly disputatious and sectarian, as religious faith is prone to do, with damaging consequences for the internal stability and electoral credibility of the party. Yet without the sustaining presence of these doctrinally motivated members the party almost certainly would not have survived to take advantage of the emerging unpopularity of National and Labour.

Social Credit had always strenuously denied the existence of a significant protest component to its electoral support. However, beginning in 1978 the protest vote was openly courted. Voters were encouraged to 'register a massive protest vote against the two tired old parties that between them have led us into the present mess'.[8] Encouraged by an immediate and dramatic rise in its popular support, the party began to modernise and moderate its message by talking less about monetary reform and more about the themes of discontent and distrust. Social Crediters referred nostalgically to a more simple, homogeneous and egalitarian New Zealand, and when pressed to locate it they referred to the financial and social welfare reforms of the first Labour government in the mid-1930s. In those days, they claimed, the government actively cared, the banking, financial, and 'ivory-tower-intellectual' fraternities were kept in check, and social institutions, particularly the family, were treated with respect.

Such sentiments had been expressed by Social Crediters countless times before, but now there was a conscious effort to turn them into a radical and coherent political outlook. The recurring image was that of a small entrepreneurial class struggling for material independence and prosperity against the forces of big business, big foreign investors, big unions, and a big bureaucracy. Social Credit, on the other hand, claimed to stand for self-reliance, small enterprise, and the public observance of 'Christian' standards of morality. Over the next few years the movement would successfully tap the fears and frustrations of many New Zealanders and offer solutions appealing to their social conservatism, nationalism, and belief in a lean but benevolent state.

But because Social Credit's core constituency remained small, electoral success always threatened to be brief. In early 1981 the level of support peaked at 30 per cent, making the party as popular as Labour.[9] Membership more than doubled in the space of six weeks, only to drop just as quickly a few months later when the party's two MPs were persuaded by the government to bolster its slender parliamentary majority by supporting legislation to override any successful judicial appeal against the government's decision to build a high dam on the Clyde River. Their decision was greeted with widespread disapproval and contempt, with the Law Society describing it as 'an act of emasculation to the judicial system'[10] and environmentalists asking 'Can Social Credit be believed any more?'[11] As the impact of the decision began to be assimilated into the public consciousness; the party's support plummeted. For many lapsed Labour and National voters who had made the calculated choice in 1981 of supporting Social Credit with a view to removing the sitting member or giving the government a scare, the Clyde Dam decision was an act of betrayal.

Figure 2.2   Combined two-party vote, 1946–2002

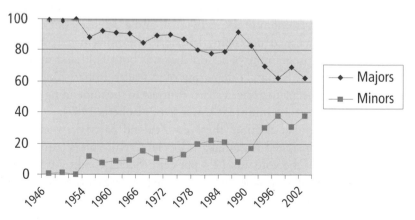

If Social Credit's sudden rise was sparked by crisis, that of the New Zealand party in 1983 was in response to a demand for ideological change. Under the leadership of Muldoon, the National government fought recession with increased levels of borrowing and spending. Muldoon regulated to control wages and prices and attempted to solve the unemployment and fuel dependency problems by initiating a publicly funded industrial development programme ('Think Big'), including large aluminium and steel mills, as well as synthetic energy and oil refining plants. The funds for these projects were mostly borrowed from overseas and at demanding rates of interest and repayment. Even before the new industries came on stream the demand and international prices for aluminium, steel, and oil began to drop. As they were being completed, some plants were either mothballed or sold off at below-construction costs. Only a small proportion of the promised jobs ever materialised. The government also borrowed to prop up prices in the agricultural and manufacturing sectors and to maintain New Zealand's generously funded welfare provisions. Muldoon's enthusiasm for economic intervention and, in stark contrast, National's stated commitment to free enterprise and individual freedom became the subject of increasing intra-party debate, with one of the 'dry' ministers being forced to resign for questioning the direction of government economic policy.

Thus the New Zealand party was 'born and nurtured in protest' against National and its leader (Aimer 1987, p. 189). The founders of the new party, most of whom had been National party activists, accused the government of 'socialism', which became the byword for everything that was undesirable in Muldoon's economic policies and management, and abandonment of princi-ple. However, the so-called 'restoration' of National party principle promised by the new party was more backward looking and radical than that contem-plated by National's founders in the mid-1930s. In fact the ideal society of the New Zealand party had its roots in nineteenth century laissez-faireism. Policies included drastic reductions in state spending and control, a largely deregulated economy, increased freedom of the individual, and a defence policy based on the principle of unarmed neutrality. In short, the movement's third-party status permitted a programme of action that was both bold and uncompro-mising. Moreover, the flair and ostentation of its leader, Robert (Bob) Jones, a wealthy property speculator, was in sharp contrast to the unbending and often grim control of the prime minister (Aimer 1987; Roberts 1987).

At the 1984 general election, the New Zealand party drew most of its support from disillusioned National and Social Credit voters (Aimer 1987, p. 198). Its share of the vote was 12.3 per cent (Social Credit 7.6 per cent), a highly respectable performance given that the party was less than a year old. Although it failed to win a seat, the party had achieved its primary objective, the defeat of the Muldoon-led National government. Jones, who was credited with bankrolling the party during the election campaign, kept it going until the middle of 1985. However, following a poor by-election result in one of the party's strongest seats, Jones decided to close it down. The announce-ment was greeted with outrage and derision by many of its activists and officeholders, although Jones reasoned in his defence that, since Labour was now implementing most of the New Zealand party's policies it deserved his support. He advised the rest of the party to do likewise. At the 1987 election the combined minor party vote was at its lowest (8.0 per cent) in thirty years (see figure 2.3).

Figure 2.3   Share of the vote, 1987

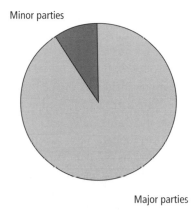

The seeds of electoral multipartism, having been planted in the late 1970s and early 1980s, began to germinate with the formation of Jim Anderton's NewLabour party in 1989. Together with the Liberal and New Zealand First parties, NewLabour was born in crisis and nurtured in opposition to the gov-ernment's radical agenda. Labour's free market reforms continued to be implemented after the October 1987 stock market crash, with telling effect on the internal cohesion of the government and party. Despite having been through a period of unparalleled economic, social, and foreign policy reform at the 1987 election, the Labour government was returned with an increased parliamentary majority. During the campaign the prime minister, David Lange, had indicated that, unlike its first term, Labour's second term in office would be devoted to the reform and further expansion of the welfare state. Instead, the government reduced taxes, closed down unprofitable commu-nity services, including neighbourhood post offices, and continued to corporatise, then privatise, many of the most prominent state-owned assets. Some social policy reforms were introduced, although more on the grounds of a need for greater efficiency, often to be achieved through greater target-ing and user-pays, than increased provision.

Jim Anderton, a backbench MP and former president of the Labour party, became the catalyst for growing opposition to the free market reforms within Labour's non-parliamentary organisation. Anderton vigorously opposed Roger Douglas's flat tax proposal, and in 1988 he was expelled from caucus for refusing to endorse the government's privatisation legislation. Although none of Anderton's parliamentary colleagues followed him out of the party, he was joined by a number of former Labour party activists. All those who made up the new party's inaugural governing body, for example, were former officeholders of the Labour party, and almost two-thirds of the delegates attending NewLabour's 1990 conference were former members of the parent party (Miller 1991, p. 6). The consensus of opinion within the new party was that, with Labour having lurched irrevocably to the ideological right, NewLabour was now the true Labour party. The party's policies reflected this view, with a strong commitment to a universal and free welfare state, a high level of state intervention in the economy, including a steeply progressive tax regime, and a controversial pledge to re-nationalise several newly privatised state assets, including Telecom.

Despite its organisational strengths, NewLabour failed to capitalise on the strength of the anti-Labour vote. Its 5.2 per cent share of the nationwide vote at the 1990 election was significantly less than that of the recently formed Greens, who averaged 9 per cent in the seats they contested. Of particular chagrin to NewLabour's leadership was the fact that the Greens went into the campaign without a leader, an organisation, or even much of a manifesto. Conscious of the damage they and other small parties might do to NewLabour if they continued to compete for the anti-Labour vote, in December 1991 Anderton convinced them to form a minor party alliance with a view to nominating a single candidate in each electorate at the 1993 election. Other founding members of the Alliance were Social Credit (renamed the Democratic party in 1985) and Mana Motuhake, a Maori party formed in 1980. In 1992 they were joined by a fifth party, the Liberal party, which was formed out of National and in protest at the new government's welfare reforms. Although they retained some organisational autonomy, the five constituent parties spent the next two years harmonising their resources and policies and promoting the Alliance as an example of what politics could be like under the more consultative and cooperative spirit of proportional representation.

The final significant participant during this wave of electoral multipartism was New Zealand First, a splinter party formed from National shortly before the 1993 election. New Zealand First was the personal political instrument of Winston Peters, a Maori politician and former Minister of Maori Affairs. Even as a cabinet minister and MP, Peters had engaged in repeated attacks on the government over a range of issues, including broken manifesto promises, the free market, and National's radical social policy reforms, especially its imposition of a pension surtax. A poll conducted at the height of his attacks found that 81 per cent of respondents believed that there was corruption in New Zealand politics.[12] Peters then turned his anti-corruption campaign towards big business, especially members of the Business Roundtable. He alleged that he and other politicians had been offered bribes in exchange for their support for policies favourable to big business, and there were repeated claims of exploitative acts against ordinary New Zealanders by wealthy bankers, property speculators and industrialists. The new party, which was formed in July 1993, offered a mixed bag of promises including less government, greater assistance to small business, an end to the 'internationalisation' of New Zealand, and the establishment of an anti-corruption commission. As a demonstration of good faith with his supporters, Peters promised to take a 40 per cent pay cut in the event of his becoming prime minister.[13] There was every expectation that New Zealand First would make an immediate impact on the electorate, with one poll showing that some 32 per cent of voters intended voting for it.[14] Three months later its support had fallen to 11 per cent and, at the election two months after that, the party attracted a disappointing 8.4 per cent of the vote. New Zealand First's result notwithstanding, the total minor party share of the vote was the highest in almost a century of party competition (see figure 2.4).

Figure 2.4   Share of the vote, 1993

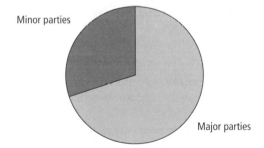

Conclusion

New Zealand continued to be seen as a bastion of two-partism long after the combined two-party vote commenced its steep decline. It is easy to see why a number of political commentaries overlooked the transition to multipartism until shortly before the advent of MMP. New Zealand's small population and geographical remoteness give it little international exposure, hence a tendency simply to repeat information gathered at some earlier time. Moreover, by including only those parties deemed to be 'relevant', as measured by a party's ability to win parliamentary seats (see, for example, Ware 1996, pp. 162–3), the nature and magnitude of change were easily missed. As a result, even as recently as the early 1990s, New Zealand continued to be ranked alongside the USA as a model of two-partism. Indeed, it was only when attention turned to the causes and consequences of electoral reform that the full extent of the restructuring of the party system began to be widely recognised.

A second misconception, also linked to New Zealand's two-party tradition, concerns the debate over whether the dominant tendency is one of stability or change. That the party system appeared remarkably stable for much of the postwar period should not detract from the fact that, in the space of only twenty years, New Zealand had moved from a no-party system to a rudimentary single-party system, to be followed in quick succession by two-party and three-party phases. Throughout each transition the dominant force in determining the nature of the party system was that of socio-economic class. In contrast, beginning in the late 1970s, the gradual fragmentation of the party system had little to do with changing social structures. Rather, it was primarily a consequence of public disquiet over the actions of successive governments, something that a number of the minor parties were fortuitously placed to exploit. Each sought to represent public discontent by devising an anti-government agenda which romanticised the past (in the case of the New Zealand party the nineteenth century, whereas the others looked nostalgically in the direction of the creation of the welfare state in the 1930s), judged the political process to be too remote and oligarchic, and appealed to the nationalistic tendencies of New Zealand voters.

Notes

1   Sartori considers New Zealand to have been one of only three countries (along with the USA and the United Kingdom) to fulfil all the requirements of a pure two-party system.
2   For a discussion on the link between crises and party change see, for example, S. Wolinetz, "The Transformation of Western European Party Systems Revisited," *West European Politics* 2 (1979), pp. 4–28.
3   'Report of the Royal Commission on Federation', *AJHR*, vol. 1, A-4, 1901.
4   *New Zealand Herald*, 1 November 1935, p. 13.
5   Rata's resignation from the Labour party forced a by-election in the Northern Maori seat in 1980. His share of the vote dropped from 71.5 per cent as the Labour candidate at the 1978 general election to 37.9 per cent as the Mana Motuhake candidate in 1980. At the 1981 general election Rata's share of the vote dropped even further, to 23 per cent.
6   Apart from Social Credit, the only small party to make inroads into the two-party vote between 1936 and 1978 was the Values party, which was formed in

1972 by a university student, Tony Brunt, and a public relations officer, Norman Smith. Arguably the first environmental party in the world, Values appealed to young, middle-income voters with a liberal position on issues such as abortion, drug laws, and the role of women. At the 1972 election it received 2 per cent of the vote, and in 1975 it reached over 5 per cent. Following internal conflict between the party's pragmatists and ideological purists over the merits of direct political action, during the 1980s Values adopted the role of a pressure group. In 1989 the party was formally disbanded, and the following year a number of its activists formed the Green party of Aotearoa/New Zealand.

7   The source of these figures is J. Wallace (chair), *Report of the Royal Commission on the Electoral System*, Wellington, 1986, p. 15.

8   *Auckland Star*, 24 January 1978, p. 1.

9   Heylen Research Centre, Auckland, January 1981.

10   Radio NZ, *Checkpoint*, 24 August 1982.

11   *NZ Herald*, 27 August 1982, p. 3.

12   *The Dominion*, 20 June 1992, p. 1.

13   *The Dominion*, 19 July 1993, p. 1.

14   Heylen Research Centre, 'One Network News/Heylen Political Poll', 29 May 1993. Percentages for the other parties were: National 22; Labour 30; and the Alliance 14.

Further reading

Bassett, M. 1982, *Three Party Politics in New Zealand, 1911–1931*, Historical Publications, Auckland.

Chapman, R. 1969, *The Political Scene 1919–1931*, Heinemann, Auckland.

Chapman, R. 1981, 'From Labour to National', in W.H. Oliver (ed.), *The Oxford History of New Zealand*, Oxford University Press, Wellington, pp. 333–68.

Gustafson, B. 1980, *Labour's Path to Political Independence: The Origins and Establishment of the New Zealand Labour Party, 1900–19*, Auckland University Press, Auckland.

Gustafson, B. 1986, *The First Fifty Years: A History of the New Zealand National Party*, Reed Methuen, Auckland.

Richardson, L. 1981, 'Parties and Political Change', in W.H. Oliver (ed.), *The Oxford History of New Zealand*, Oxford University Press, Wellington, pp. 197–225.

The Party System under Proportional Representation

THE advent of the Mixed Member Proportional (MMP) electoral system caused some to speculate about the potential size and shape of the emerging multiparty system. One observer noted 'strong pressure towards fragmentation', and there were predictions of up to ten parliamentary parties once the new electoral system had settled down (Mair 1997, p. 204). As well as the two major parties and their offshoots, notably the Alliance and New Zealand First, a number of new parties were formed by incumbent MPs with a view to exploiting the opportunities for representation and influence provided by MMP.[1] With the exception of the United party's Peter Dunne, none managed to retain their seats following the first MMP election. In addition, a number of more ideologically motivated parties were formed outside parliament, with ACT (formerly the Association of Consumers and Taxpayers) proving to be the most conspicuous. At the 1996 election some twenty-seven parties registered with the Electoral Commission, with six going on to win seats in the first MMP parliament.

This chapter will ask whether *institutional* change, especially the move to MMP, offers the most convincing explanation for the expansion of the party system both inside and outside of parliament. *Social structural* explanations, on the other hand, look beyond institutional factors to the basic composition of society. Where the incidence of social cleavages is low, with only one or two significant divisions, a stable two-party system is the likely outcome (Lipset and Rokkan 1967). On the other hand, in countries with diverse and complex cleavage structures, with class, ethnicity, region, and religion being obvious points of division, the resulting multiparty system is likely to be fragmented. This second explanation is posited on the assumption that there is a direct causal link between the social structure and the party system. If this proves to be the case, then the durability of New Zealand's multiparty system is dependent upon the presence of a broadly equivalent number of cleavages within society at large.

Yet another explanation for the emergence of a multiparty system rejects the sociologist's argument that parties simply mirror the divisions within society. Rather, it regards parties as being in charge of their own destiny, capable of interacting in ways that will promote inter-party competition and maximise their vote (Sartori 1976; Downs 1957). Consistent with this dynamic, as opposed to a largely static, model has been the growth of personality-based parties, whose predominantly populist message has been found to resonate with the fears and needs of many voters. Although jarring with more traditional explanations, this *socio-psychological* approach focuses on the growing importance of personal attachments or ties. This chapter will consider the relative merits of the institutional, social structural, and socio-psychological arguments on the nature of the present party system. It will conclude that, despite the consolidating influence of MMP, today's multiparty system remains a highly unstable and artificial construct.

Which parties count?

Given the number of parties regularly contesting New Zealand elections, with a total of twenty-five registered[2] and a further thirteen unregistered parties contesting the 1999 election (including the exotically named 'Wall of Surf' and 'Blokes Liberation Front', as well as the values-based 'Christians Against Abortion' and 'Communist League'), it is useful to distinguish one level of inter-party competition from another.

Of the various approaches to the classification of party systems, three stand out:
1 numbers-based
2 size-based
3 'relevance'-based.

Numbers-based approach

The numbers-based approach, the most straightforward of the three options, proved to be of greatest value when the only distinction considered important was that between two-party and multiparty systems. Although little attention was given to outcomes, studies adopting this approach were able to offer a clear and simple comparison of the effects each party system had on the structure of government, with two-party systems producing single party majorities and multiparty systems normally resulting in coalitions (see, for example, Duverger 1964). Apart from the most straightforward examples, such as the USA and New Zealand on the one hand and the multiparty Scandinavian countries on the other, it became clear that there were analytical difficulties in simply counting the number of parties. By this time scholars were beginning to recognise that even 'pure' two-party systems were experiencing increasing minor party competition. They could also see that multiparty systems were becoming more varied and complex. As Sartori has pointed out, counting all parties as if they were of equal size and value was almost as unhelpful as not counting them at all (1986, p. 44).

An early typology developed by Blondel (1968), while still clustering countries by numbers of parties, began to offer a more variegated approach based on the intensity of the two-party vote, with the USA scoring an average of 99 per cent and Finland a mere 49 per cent. His four tiers consisted of: two-party; three-party; multiparty; and 'genuine' multiparty systems. In exploring the relative strength of the various parties in each type, with the three-party systems of Australia and Germany being further refined to 'two-and-a-half' party systems, Blondel helped draw an important distinction between moderate (three to five parties) and fragmented multiparty systems, as well as signalling the emergence of a more complex size-based approach.

Size-based approach

In an attempt to distinguish large from small parties, the somewhat derogatory 'half party' category was introduced, although it has been largely superseded by the terms 'minor' or 'third' (once reserved for the party coming third in an election contest, but now used with reference to all small parties). In addition to the two-party system, Ware (1996, p. 162) identified four size-based categories:

- two-and-a-half party systems
- one major and several minor parties
- two major and several minor parties
- 'even' multiparty systems.

In combining the number and size of parties to achieve the above classifications, Ware drew attention to the relationship that exists among parties, including any inter-party rivalry. Examples of a two-and-a-half party system

Figure 3.1 Party development, 1978–2004

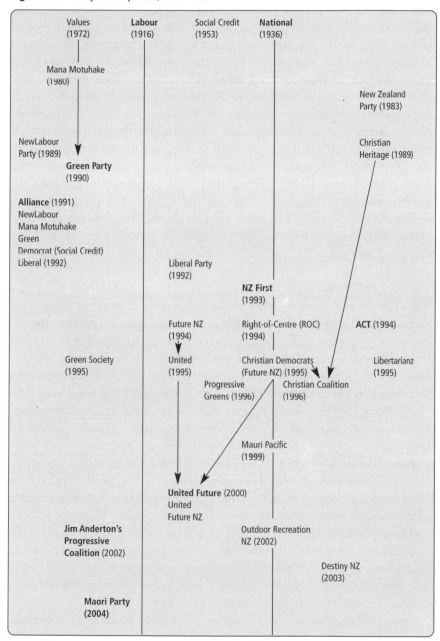

included Australia in the days when National was the sole minor party, and Germany during the heyday of the Free Democrats. In an even contest between the two major parties, the 'half party' is likely to exercise the balance of power, perhaps resulting in a role in government.

An example of Ware's one-large-several-small parties category was Canada during the period of 1993 to 2004. Following the collapse of the ruling Conservatives, the Liberal party was able to command a legislative majority, with the third-party vote being spread among the minor parties, notably the Western Canada Reform/Alliance party, the Bloc Quebecois, and, to a lesser extent, the New Democrats and Conservatives. However, this was not quite the sort of outcome that Ware had predicted under a one-major-and-several-minor parties arrangement. Based on the Scandinavian model, he expected minority governments to be the norm. Similarly, his two-major-and-several-minor category included the arbitrary ruling that the two major parties would win two-thirds and none of the minor parties more than one-seventh of the available seats (Ware 1996, p. 166). New Zealand under MMP fits into this category, along with Scotland and Ireland. On the other hand, Switzerland and Belgium, with their complex cleavage structures, highly fragmented party systems, and multiparty coalitions, are exemplars of the 'even' multiparty category.

Relevance-based approach

While size is an obvious measure of the importance of political parties, the relevance-based approach is potentially more revealing and accurate. One test of relevance is proximity to power, which can be measured either in terms of whether or not a party has seats in parliament or, more precisely, whether those seats give it an ability to influence legislative or governmental outcomes. For example, while the United Future and Green parties had fewer seats than New Zealand First between 2002 and 2005, their formal undertaking to support the broad thrust of the government's legislative agenda guaranteed them greater access to ministers and public servants, together with a more generous allocation of select committee seats and parliamentary resources.

Relevance can be achieved through negative as well as positive behaviour. It has been said that parties have relevance only if they can demonstrate either 'coalition potential' or 'blackmail potential' (Sartori 1976, pp. 122–3). Coalition potential can be measured by a party's utility to a potential governing party or party bloc. Alternatively, in the absence of coalition potential a party may be able to blackmail the government, with common strategies including the threat to block a piece of legislation or the supply of funds, or to defeat the government on a confidence motion.

Sartori's classification has a number of obvious weaknesses, especially when applied to two-party systems. Almost by definition, in such systems the criteria for 'relevance' are too rigorous to allow minor parties to qualify. Throughout its long history as New Zealand's most prominent third party, for example, Social Credit failed the test on both counts; not only was it never required to form a coalition, nor even exercise the balance of power, but its influence on the nature and direction of two-party competition was, at best, slight. The one possible exception involved the party's 1982 stance over the government's Clyde (High) Dam Empowering legislation. In exchange for supporting Sir Robert Muldoon's attempt to override any successful judicial appeal against the high dam option, Social Credit's two MPs attempted to extract certain guarantees for the surrounding communities. However, the government later claimed that the Social Credit MPs had been outfoxed, arguing that it had agreed to their demands even before they had been put.

When applied to New Zealand's present multiparty system, Sartori's test of relevance is more promising, if less clear-cut. While all the minor parties have coalition potential, the potency of their claim depends on the distribution of seats after an election. Following the 2002 election, for example, the New Zealand First and Green parties effectively excluded themselves from consideration by virtue of their uncompromising stands on immigration and the commercial release of genetically modified (GM) organisms. The same two parties also found blackmail to be an unlikely option, United Future having guaranteed the government confidence and supply for the following three years.

This debate over which parties to include in the party system has a number of practical implications, not least in determining the amount of media attention given to each party during the course of an election campaign. In the first multiparty election, New Zealand's electronic media adopted the 'stop-watch' approach to news coverage, studio interviews, and debates, with the two large parties attracting the lion's share of broadcasting time. In subsequent campaigns, however, the notion of an 'even' multiparty system began to take hold, although media organisations were apt to defend their decisions on commercial or news worthiness grounds. As a result, media coverage during the 2002 campaign bore little resemblance to each party's importance or size (see chapter 9). In the event that eight party leaders were accorded roughly equal time to debate the issues on television, for example, the opposition point of view was bound to receive five or six times that of the government.

Explaining today's multiparty system

Institutional explanation

Advocates of the institutional explanation posit a causal link between the electoral system and the party system (Riker 1986). Duverger, who believed that the two-party system was a product of plurality or first-past-the-post voting, identified two barriers, one mechanical and the other psychological, to the success of small parties in plurality systems. Under plurality voting, the 'vanquished' are confronted with the inevitable fate of either non- or under-representation (1964, p. 224). But there is also a psychological barrier, which prompts voters to question whether they should 'waste' their votes on parties that are unlikely to win seats. As a result, many voters opt for the 'sophisticated' alternative of casting their vote for one of the major parties, despite it being their second or third choice (Riker 1986, p. 33). The wasted vote syndrome had a punishing effect on the electoral prospects of New Zealand's minor parties dating as far back as the fledgling Labour party in the 1920s. This long history of minor party under-representation notwithstanding, it was only when the Royal Commission on the Electoral System (Wallace 1986, p. 14) described the voting system as neither representative nor fair that the magnitude of the gap between plurality voting and representation became a focus for public debate.

The Westminster democratic model adopted by New Zealand had a number of interlocking features that served to reinforce plurality voting's disproportional effects. The absence of either a bicameral legislature (the upper house was abolished in 1951) or federal system of government deprived minor parties of any countervailing loci of political power to that of the House of Representatives. Under its highly centralised 'majoritarian' system of government (the last time either of the major parties won a majority of the votes was in 1951), there was little or no scope for 'local' parties to become established.[3] This 'pure' form of Westminster democracy can be contrasted with the democratic systems of Canada, Australia, and even the United Kingdom. In Canada, for example, the Social Credit and New Democrat parties, as well as the separatist Quebec party, have been elected to govern at provincial level despite poor federal performances. Similarly, the Australian Democrats have used the Senate as an alternative source of influence to that of the lower house. Even the British Liberal Democrats, although faced with the same hostile electoral environment as New Zealand prior to 1996, have had a long association with local body or council politics, especially in Scotland's border districts and northern isles.

In addition to arguing the case for a causal link between plurality voting and two-party systems, Duverger repeated the claim with respect to the relationship between proportional representation and multiparty systems. In his view, proportional representation 'always coincides with a multiparty system: in no country in the world has proportional representation given rise to a two-party system or kept one in existence' (1964, p. 245). Largely drawing on anecdotal evidence, Duverger argued that there was little incentive for parties to merge, as they are inclined to do in plurality systems. Rather, proportional representation's 'multiplicative tendency' resulted in the formation of new parties, as well as causing long-established parties to fracture and fragment. In contrast to the wasted vote syndrome found in plurality systems, the votes cast for third-, fourth-, and even fifth-ranked parties under proportional representation stood a strong chance of resulting in parliamentary seats.

Superficially at least, New Zealand's early experience of MMP appears to confirm this multiplicative tendency, with a rapid growth in the number of parties both inside and outside parliament in the period between the electoral referendum and the first MMP election. Some thirteen MPs from the two major parties took stock of the opportunities provided for minor parties under the new electoral system. Having been made aware that the total number of electorate seats would be reduced from ninety-nine to sixty-five, and that the leadership of the two main parties was keen to recruit new talent for the party lists, they either created their own party or joined an existing alternative. The new political vehicles created within parliament were the Right of Centre (later renamed Conservative) party, the Christian Democrats, Future New Zealand, and United (which replaced Future New Zealand). But the MMP decision also led to an increase in the number of parties formed outside parliament. The most successful of this group was the ACT party, although it was forced to share the limelight with a more radical free market group, the Libertarianz. As well as exploiting the more congenial electoral environment of MMP, these non-parliamentary alternatives offered voters greater ideological choice than at any previous election.

Far from disappearing with the arrival of MMP, the wasted vote syndrome manifested itself in a new guise, that of the 5 per cent threshold. Under MMP, there are two thresholds. The first is the requirement that a party win a minimum of 5 per cent of all the party votes. Alternatively, it is entitled to its proportion of the available 120 seats if it wins at least one electorate seat, the contest for which is decided by the old rules of first-past-the-post or plurality voting. While the original purpose of the party vote threshold was to discourage postwar Germans from supporting an extreme party, such as the Communists or Fascists, its adoption in New Zealand has posed a potential problem for all minor parties. Because the threshold has been set so high (the Royal Commission recommended a threshold of 4 per cent), small parties have continued to suffer from the perception that a vote for a small party is a wasted vote. For example, in 1996 the Christian Coalition's prospects were dealt a mortal blow by campaign speculation that it was unlikely to cross the threshold (it ended up getting 4.3 per cent).

On the other hand, as the Green party of Aotearoa-New Zealand has found, the threshold may act as an incentive for undecided voters. Encouraged by opinion polls and media conjecture showing that support for the Greens was close to 5 per cent and rising, during the 1999 campaign the party exploited its underdog status in a last-minute appeal to voters (Miller 2002). As well as narrowly winning the Coromandel seat, it was able to lift its party vote to 5.2 per cent. A similar phenomenon occurred in 2002, when

ACT's immediate future was as precarious as the Greens had been three years earlier. Although there was no chance of a centre-right government, the prospect that ACT could lose all its parliamentary seats presented centre-right voters with a strategic motivation for lifting the party vote above the 5 per cent threshold.

Imposing a 'hard' threshold (that is, with no provision for any additional entitlement as a result of having won an electorate seat) would act as a deterrent to any further fragmentation of the party system. Of the seven parties elected to parliament in 1999, two (New Zealand First and United) failed to cross the threshold (see table 3.1). In 2002, the new Progressive party was guaranteed a role in the next parliament and government by virtue of Jim Anderton's firm hold on the Christchurch seat of Wigram. While its party vote was only marginally better than that of the Christian Heritage and Outdoor Recreation New Zealand parties, its 1.7 per cent entitled it to a second 'list' seat. Although submissions to the parliamentary select committee chosen to review MMP called for a 'hard' threshold of either 4 or 5 per cent, a view supported by the former chairman of the Royal Commission on the Electoral System, Justice Wallace, it was decided by a majority decision that the 'soft' threshold would be retained.

In summary, despite the consolidation of the multiparty system under MMP, the evidence for a direct causal link between the new electoral system and the advent of multiparty politics is at best problematic. As we saw in chapter 2, multiparty voting was a recurring feature of general elections long before the decision to adopt MMP, with the combined minor party vote averaging 20 per cent at the six elections between 1978 and 1993.[4] However, there is no disputing the fact that MMP has been instrumental in enabling small parties to play a role at the institutional level, both within the legislature and as a partner in government.

Social structural explanation

The social structural argument posits a direct link between the nature of the party system and the incidence of divisions that exist within a regional or national community (Rae and Taylor 1970, p. 23). While the most visible divisions are socially or culturally based, with obvious examples being class, ethnicity, language, and religion, the concept of cleavage has been extended to include political actions and attitudes (1970, pp. 1–2). Attitudinal cleavages or 'issue dimensions' may come in many different guises, including those divisions that exist between economic interventionists and market liberals, materialists and postmaterialists, and moral liberals and conservatives. Cleavages based on political action are more difficult to pin down and may include the contrasting beliefs of voters and non-voters, militants and non-militants, or trade unionists and employers.

Table 3.1 Results of the 1996, 1999, and 2002 general elections

Party	1996				1999				2002			
	Vote %	Elect seats	List seats	Total seats	Vote %	Elect seats	List seats	Total seats	Vote %	Elect seats	List seats	Total seats
Labour	28	26	11	37	39	41	8	49	41	45	7	52
National	34	30	14	44	31	22	17	39	21	21	6	27
NZ First	13	6	11	17	4	1	4	5	10	1	12	13
Greens*					5	1	6	7	7	0	9	9
ACT	6	1	7	8	7	0	9	9	7	0	9	9
United Future**	1	1	0	1	1	1	0	1	7	1	7	8
Progressives									2	1	1	2
Alliance	10	1	12	13	8	1	9	10	1	0	0	0
Other	7	0	0	0	5	0	0	0	4	0	0	0

*Greens part of Alliance in 1996.
**United renamed United Future in 2000 following merger of United and Future NZ.

Political parties tend to represent particular cleavages within society, hence their appeal to different voting blocs (Maor 1997, p. 22). Belgium, Italy and Israel, with their traditional religious, linguistic, regional, and socio-economic cleavages, provide extreme examples of the effects of social structural divisions on party fragmentation (Winter and Dumont 1999, p. 203). On the other hand, mildly pluralistic societies, such as the United Kingdom, Germany, and the USA, tend to produce party systems that are dominated by two major parties.

New Zealand's former two-party system has been described as a product of a one-dimensional social structure, although the Maori/non-Maori ethnic cleavage was long regarded as having the potential to offer an additional strand to that of socio-economic class. By extending this line of reasoning, it is possible to extrapolate that New Zealand's current multiparty system reflects the development of a more complex cleavage structure made up of a number of new social and issue dimensions. Two American-based scholars, Arend Lijphart (1999) and Jack Nagel (1994), have explored the extent to which New Zealand's cleavage structure remains rooted in the past and ask whether the clutch of new parties are products of greater cultural, ethnic, and religious diversity.

Shortly after the second electoral referendum and before the first MMP election, Nagel (1994) compiled a checklist of issue dimensions upon which numerical judgments could be made about the party system under MMP.[5] According to his analysis, the relevance of any given issue dimension is based on two criteria: first, each side in the dispute must have the support of at least 5 per cent of all electors; and second, the issue concerned must be of sufficient importance to the affected group to justify the creation of a sustainable political party.[6] At the core of his list are six dimensions developed by Lijphart (1984, pp. 127–41), including socio-economic class, the urban-rural split, religion, and ethnicity. To these Nagel added regionalism and gender. But he also added two possible 'issue' dimensions, namely postmaterialism and economic intervention.

Socio-economic class

As we saw in the previous chapter, class has long been the dominant cleavage in New Zealand politics. In the mid-1960s it was noted that 'there is a high political distinctiveness of the professionals, businessmen, and farmers who vote mainly for the National Party; and of "blue-collar" workers, both skilled and unskilled, who vote mainly for the Labour Party' (Robinson 1967, p. 96). While socio-economic divisions continued to be the most reliable guide to voting behaviour into the 1980s and 1990s, there were signs that they were becoming 'less and less powerful predictors' (Vowles 2003, p. 192). For example, social scientists noted the decline in the incidence of manual workers, a group that had long been associated with support for Labour.

This declining influence of class voting should not be overstated, however. While the number of those in manual occupations has been dropping, they continued to make up a larger slice of the Labour vote (51 per cent in 1999) than non-manual workers (41 per cent) (Vowles et al. 2002, p. 93). Moreover, National continued to draw significantly more support from farmers (50 per cent) and those in managerial positions (40 per cent) than did Labour (15 and 30 per cent respectively). The persistence of the socio-economic cleavage was also reflected in the incomes of the two sets of voters, with one in four National voters earning over $50,000, compared with only one in ten of those supporting Labour.

While the class cleavage has continued to offer a guide to the division of votes between the two major parties, it has proved less helpful in comparing the social bases of support for the major parties with those of the minor parties. NewLabour (the core party of the Alliance) attempted to lay claim to low-income workers and beneficiaries. While it enjoyed modest support among these groups (see Vowles et al. 1995, pp. 25–6), most remained loyal to Labour, despite that party's foray into right-wing economics. New Zealand First enjoyed strong support among low-income Maori voters in 1996, but the association was brief, with most Maori returning to Labour at the following election. While the right-wing ACT party appeared to carve a reliable niche among high-income and predominantly male voters, this vote was successfully cannibalised by National following Don Brash's Orewa speech on race relations in early 2004.

Urban/rural

Much of the pioneering research of Robert Chapman focused on the sectional division between urban and rural New Zealand, a cleavage that had 'revealed itself in our politics for as long as there have been parties' (Chapman et al. 1962, p. 235). As with socio-economic class, the urban/rural cleavage continued to be largely the preserve of the two main parties, with Labour's electoral heartland being in the main urban centres, specifically Dunedin, Christchurch, Wellington, and Auckland, while National's tended to be in the countryside and North Island provincial towns. However, as Chapman himself pointed out, the urban and rural variations were best understood as differences of socio-economic class. Voting patterns long mirrored the basic class divisions, with the richer city and provincial town seats being won by National and the poorer city and town seats by Labour. As a result, elections tended to be decided in the highly marginal mixed-income electorates, such as the Auckland seats of Eden, Roskill and Birkenhead.

Competition with National for the vote of farmers once came from the Country party, a movement that won seats in the dairying communities of Northland and Auckland before finally disappearing in the 1930s (Graham 1963). With the advent of MMP, there was speculation that a farmers' party might enjoy niche support, although National continued to command broad support across most of the rural seats. However, in recent years formidable obstacles have stood in the way of regional parties, mostly on the grounds that narrow regional or sectional interests are not reflected in the attitudes of a vast majority of voters. A registered South Island party received a total of only 2,912 party votes and 2,408 electorate votes at the 1999 election.

Ethnicity

While the most significant line of division remained that of socio-economic class, demographic trends within the Maori population, together with a changing political climate, gave rise to growing speculation about the possible impact of ethnicity on the character of the new multiparty system. Writing many years earlier, Lijphart had argued that the Maori population was too small and the rest of the population too homogeneous to support an ethnic cleavage (1984, pp. 17–18). What he had overlooked, however, was the existence of a politico-religious Maori organisation, the Ratana movement, in the 1920s and early 1930s. At the peak of its popularity it held two of the four Maori seats. Long after it had merged with Labour, Chapman observed that Maori voters engaged 'only sporadically and partially in the parallelism of the other New Zealand electors' (1963, p. 250). His study of voting patterns between 1928[7] and 1960 identified both a distinctive culture and social stress as the primary causes of their divergent paths.

The size of the Maori population (approximately 15 per cent of the population claim Maori ancestry)[8] revived interest in the potential viability of an indigenous party under MMP. However, doubts remained over whether a separate Maori party could be sustained above the 5 per cent threshold. One of the notable features of the 1996 election was the decisive movement of Maori voters in the direction of New Zealand First, with that party winning all five Maori electorate seats. Success gave rise to speculation that the party's Maori leader (Winston Peters) and deputy-leader (Tau Henare) had the warrior-like qualities required to achieve a permanent realignment of the Maori vote. However, New Zealand First's other major constituency was elderly European voters, most of whom had supported Peters on the understanding that he would put a stop to the preferential treatment of Maori on such issues as social welfare and land claims (Miller 1998, p. 207). The return of Maori voters to Labour in 1999 proved to be as decisive as their departure, with the party winning all six Maori seats and 55 per cent of the party vote (Vowles et al. 2002, p. 67).

However, Labour's success in recapturing the Maori seats failed to quell speculation about the possible formation of a separate Maori party capable of winning seats. Following Derek Fox's narrow 1999 defeat to the Labour candidate, Parekura Horomia, in the North Island east coast seat of Ikaroa-Rawhiti, there was some hope that the charismatic Maori broadcaster might lead a new party with the support of several Maori MPs. There was also interest in the plans of the Mana Motuhake party, which, under the leadership of a former MP, Willie Jackson, had broken away from the Alliance in 2002 with a view to contesting the next election as a separate organisation. Driving these and other moves was a conviction among some Maori leaders that Labour was both paternalistic and indifferent to the needs of its mainly low-income Maori constituency.

The driving force behind the new pan-tribal 'Maori party' was indeed a warrior-like leader, although hardly in the mould of a Winston Peters or a Derek Fox. Tariana Turia had used her high profile as a Labour minister to oppose the government's foreshore and seabed legislation, taking her fight to Maori tribal meetings ('hui') in many parts of the country, and culminating in a march ('hikoi') on parliament buildings in Wellington. Having resigned her seat, thereby forcing a by-election in the electorate of Te Tai Hauauru, a contest she easily won,[9] Turia and her co-leader Pita Sharples launched the new party in July 2004. While its underlying philosophy remained unclear, with radical elements supporting a separatist agenda and conservatives calling for a policy platform that even moderate non-Maori could endorse, the party's founders were united in their opposition to the government's plans to abolish their customary rights over the country's foreshore and seabed (for a further discussion on this issue, see chapter 8). A poll taken shortly before the launch of the new party showed that some 62 per cent of Maori voters would support a new Maori party.[10]

Religion

Even more problematic than the ethnic cleavage is that of religion. Although a Christian Coalition enjoyed unexpected success at the 1996 election, attracting some 4.3 per cent of the party vote, its two constituent parties disagreed on a range of social issues, with the less conservative Christian Democrats expressing concern over the hard-line position being adopted by the Christian Heritage party on such matters as abortion and gay rights. Of the two, only the Christian Heritage party remained (the Christian Democrats, renamed Future New Zealand, later merged with the United party to form United Future).[11] Christian Heritage's electoral support averaged less than 2 per cent in the four elections it contested on its own between 1990 and 2002. In 2003, the Destiny Church of New Zealand formed its own party. Under the spiritual guidance of its pastor, Brian Tamaki, the party attacked the 'secular humanism' of consecutive governments, which it blamed for the breakdown of families, lowering of the drinking age to eighteen years, and sanctioning of de facto and same-sex relationships. Among the party's proposals was the provision of financial incentives for being married.

Religious groups in New Zealand have not been politicised in the way they have in the USA, with the result that there is no group consciousness, let alone an agreed conservative agenda. This helps to explain why tensions within the Christian Coalition proved insoluble in 1996. While noting that the importance of the religious dimension has been slight, Nagel observed that a potentially significant religious constituency could be built around core conservative social values, especially on abortion, homosexual law reform, and the rights of the nuclear family. United Future has assumed something of a 'Christian' character, as exemplified by its conservative stand on family values and the significant number of evangelical Christians occupying the top few positions on its party list. Despite being a support party to Labour between 2002 and 2005, the party strongly opposed several government-sponsored initiatives, including the Prostitution Reform Bill (2003) and Civil Unions Bill (2004). The latter bill, which would give legal recognition to a range of civil unions, including those between de facto heterosexual and same-sex couples, was described by United Future as 'more "Pink Think" from a government that imposes its prejudices on New Zealanders'.[12] Despite the party's conservative social agenda, its leader, Peter Dunne, stoutly opposed any suggestion that it had morphed into a 'Christian' party. Instead, he preferred to characterise it as a multi-ethnic, secular political party.

Gender

Prior to the introduction of MMP there was media speculation that a women's party was about to be formed. Beginning in the 1970s, the women's movement had made a significant impact on the political culture of New Zealand. As the electoral reform gathered momentum, women's groups lent their support to the pro-MMP campaign, partly on the grounds that MMP was seen to be a fairer electoral system and more likely to increase the level of representation among women, but also in the hope that it would result in a less adversarial and more cooperative style of politics. With most of the parties responding favourably to the need for more women candidates, especially on the party lists, any prospect that women were likely to channel their energies through a separate women's party proved to be short-lived (for a discussion on the representation of women in parliament and cabinet, see chapter 10).

Economic interventionism

Given the extent to which it resonates with those on either side of the left–right divide, the economic interventionist 'issue' dimension is arguably an extrapolation of that of social class. Because it was the product of a dramatic series of events endogenous to the major parties, the economic interventionist dimension always threatened to be caught in a 1990s time warp. While the libertarian ACT party continued to attract the support of a modest number of ideological refugees from National, the motivation of its voters had less to do with shared beliefs than ACT's potential as a coalition partner for National (Vowles et al. 2002, p. 30). Despite maintaining a make-or-break average well below 5 per cent for much of the 1999–2002 period, the party's 7.1 per cent election result meant that its future prospects could not be written off, although its failure to withstand National's resurgence in the polls in 2004 caused its strategists grave concern and led to the resignation of Richard Prebble as party leader. On the left, in early 2002 the Alliance imploded following a rift between its left and centrist wings over the extent to which, as a junior coalition partner to Labour, the party should endorse government decisions on a range of policies, including fiscal spending, free trade, and military support for the American occupation of Afghanistan. Although the party's president and three of its MPs continued to promote an interventionist agenda, by the time of the 2002 election the Alliance's left-wing constituency had all but disappeared.

Postmaterialism

With between 12 and 15 per cent of all voters identifying the environment as the most important issue for them personally (Miller 1995), the electoral prospects of a distinctly postmaterialist party had been speculated upon since the heyday of the Values party, the precursor to the Green party, in the mid-1970s. At the time of the first MMP election three environmental parties existed: the deep-green Green Society; a blue-green Progressive Green party; and the established red-green movement, the Green party of Aotearoa. Of the three, the Green party of Aotearoa proved the most successful at tapping into public concern over a range of quality-of-life issues. While its 2002 pledge to bring down a Labour government if it did not extend the moratorium on the commercial release of genetically modified organisms attracted significant media attention and pushed the party's level of popular support above 9 per cent, this could not be sustained. As the results of the 1999 and 2002 elections show, the party's electoral base remained small, being concentrated heavily among young urban voters (Vowles et al. 2004).

There is merit in Nagel's conclusion that there were only two 'active' dimensions or cleavages in New Zealand politics, with socio-economic class being the more important. His second 'active' dimension was economic interventionism, although, of the two issue dimensions identified in his analysis, the long-term prospects of postmaterialism appeared somewhat brighter. Three further dimensions, including ethnicity and religion, were seen as having some potential to support minor party representation. By also factoring in the 'institutional carrying capacity' of MMP (Nagel 1994, p. 153), Nagel ended up with a potential upper limit of six parliamentary parties, but with the further possibility that one or two more might emerge if additional social cleavages were to manifest themselves over the medium to long term.

To summarise, while the residual strength of socio-economic class helps explain the continuing electoral dominance of the two major parties, especially Labour, in most other respects the social cleavage analysis fails to accurately measure or predict party strength. As Vowles has pointed out, rather than clarifying and strengthening the relationship between the social structure and the party system, the advent of MMP appears to have had the opposite effect (Vowles et al. 2002, p. 94). Whether the formation of the Maori party adds a substantial ethnic dimension to the social structural argument time alone will tell.

Socio-psychological explanation

Whereas the social structural explanation has suffered from 'sociological reductionism' to the point where parties are sometimes viewed as mere receptacles for discrete social groups (Broughton and Donovan 1999, p. 259), the socio-psychological explanation views parties as dynamic organisations capable of adapting to shifting political conditions, as well as to the changing interests and needs of voters. As Katz and Mair (1994) have pointed out, voters in many Western countries have become less constrained by their social and ideological backgrounds, resulting in an increasingly ambivalent attitude towards political parties. Although the level of penetration of New Zealand society by political parties has never run deep, as we have seen, declining partisanship has been a feature of the modern party system. This has led to the emergence of new parties, often built around strong personalities and appealing to the populist, even decidedly anti-party, instincts of voters (Katz and Mair 1994, p. 19; Schedler 1996, pp. 292–3). Unlike parties representing society's old cleavage structures, these personality-based movements appear suddenly and, by virtue of being the product of the actions of a particular individual, remain inherently unstable and transient (Blondel 2001).

New Zealand's recent political history is replete with examples of personality-based parties. As we saw in chapter 2, Social Credit's transformation in the late 1970s from an old-fashioned, conspiratorial party to a modern, populist movement owed much to the personal appeal of its leader, Bruce Beetham. From the time he assumed the leadership in 1972, the young Teachers' College lecturer personified 'new' Social Credit, a party that had come to replace its 'funny-money' and vaguely anti-Semitic image with one reflecting the increasingly nationalistic concerns of voters, especially in relation to defence, foreign ownership, and investment. When Beetham first won the seat of Rangitikei, at a by-election in 1978, his campaign stressed personality over policy, with slogans such as 'Give Beetham a Go' and 'It's Beetham Versus the Rest'. In openly courting aggrieved major party supporters, he was able to rejuvenate the party, increasing the membership to over 30,000 by 1981. Following the Clyde Dam incident (see chapter 2) and the party's poor electoral performance at the 1984 election, Beetham's leadership began to be questioned by key party officials. In the late 1980s he formed his own breakaway movement, which outpolled the largely discredited Social Credit party (renamed the Democrats) at the 1990 election.

So closely was Robert (Bob) Jones linked with the formation and development of the New Zealand party that members of the media and the public preferred to refer to it as the 'Jones' party. As well as largely bankrolling the party during the 1984 election campaign with the injection of an estimated one million dollars, the high-profile property developer, boxing commentator, and media personality adopted a hands-on approach to the party, personally recruiting the slate of parliamentary candidates, conceiving and drafting party policy, and, in 1987, abruptly closing the party down. Much of the New Zealand party's support came from young well-to-do businesspeople and professionals who, but for having been inspired by Jones' free market agenda and sense of derring-do, would have continued to support National.

As a former Auckland mayoral candidate, Labour party president, and one of *Time* magazine's political leaders of the future, Jim Anderton enjoyed a high public profile well before his election as the Labour MP for Sydenham in 1981. His expulsion from the Labour caucus in 1989 following his decision to oppose the government's privatisation legislation was the catalyst for a split with the party. While none of his parliamentary colleagues, including several ideological allies, could be persuaded to accompany him into the NewLabour party, Anderton enjoyed the strong personal loyalty and support of a large number of mainly young Labour party activists and grassroots members, including Matt McCarten, Laila Harre, and Matt Robson. When the five-party Alliance was forged some two years later, Anderton became its personification and driving force, so much so that when he temporarily resigned from the leadership in 1994, the Alliance suffered a dramatic loss of popular support.

The link between populism and a psychological dependency on the 'great leader' has been noted in a number of studies of radical right-wing movements (for example, Blondel 1987; Schedler 1996; Betz and Immerfall 1998). As Betz has observed, 'Often led by charismatic figures who are at least as comfortable in press conferences and TV talk shows as they are among their supporters, the new parties of the right are among the most prominent representatives of a new political entrepreneurialism' (Betz and Immerfall 1998, p. 2). More than any other New Zealand politician of recent times, the New Zealand First leader, Winston Peters, has been able to mobilise public resentment against a range of targeted groups, notably immigrants, refugees, foreign investors, and 'corrupt' politicians and bureaucrats. Despite his 'well-publicised late night revelry and the use of parliamentary privilege to launch bitter personal attacks' (Miller 1997, p. 172), Peters was widely regarded by his followers as being 'the only honest politician' in the country. His ability to command the unswerving loyalty of his core constituency and to adapt his message to the changing fears and concerns of voters were the main reasons for his party's continuing success.

The potential influence of the socio-psychological factor is well illustrated by the events surrounding the implosion of the Alliance in 2002. Jim Anderton's feud with his party's activists, its director Matt McCarten, and three Alliance MPs over their criticism of his excessively 'compliant' role within the Labour-Alliance government resulted in the formation by Anderton of his own personal political vehicle, the 'Jim Anderton Progressive Coalition'. His departure was instrumental in leading to the Alliance's sub-sequent electoral defeat. What this schism helps to illustrate is that, not only are personal ties important, but personality-based parties are only as durable as their leader. Inasmuch as it is hard to imagine the Progressive party surviving the eventual retirement from politics of Jim Anderton, so the futures of both the New Zealand First and the United Future parties have been inextricably linked to the political careers of Winston Peters and Peter Dunne.

Conclusion

While neither the institutional, nor the social structural, nor even the socio-psychological argument is sufficient to fully account for today's multiparty system, each provides a partial explanation. The New Zealand experience certainly refutes any suggestion of a causal link between the advent of pro-portional representation and the rise of multiparty voting (although the consolidation of a multiparty presence in parliament is directly attributable to MMP). Nevertheless, it is clear that the new rules of MMP, particularly with respect to the party vote threshold, act as both an incentive and a barrier to political representation on the part of the small parties. The pre-dicted growth in the incidence and influence of social cleavages has not materialised, although socio-economic class (Labour and National), postmaterialism (Greens), and economic interventionism (ACT) can be said to have had some bearing on levels of party support. Certainly there is some potential for the consolidation of ethnic and religious cleavages, with the likely beneficiaries being the Maori party and the transformation of United Future into a self-consciously Christian party. Overall, however, there is much to be said for the view that the social structural explanation has less credibility than in the heyday of the two-party system. If the social structural and personality explanations are placed on a continuum, as suggested by Blondel (2001), then a strong argument can be made for the view that, bolstered by the growing 'personalisation' of politics and campaigns, especially with respect to the role of the electronic media, New Zealand's political parties are moving away from the more traditional social cleavage explanation and in the direction of personal attachments or ties.

Notes

1   New parties formed in the wake of the MMP referendum included the Christian Democrat and Right-of-Centre (renamed Conservative) parties.

2   In order to put up a party list, a party must be registered with the Electoral Commission. Unregistered parties are entitled to stand candidates, but only in electorate or constituency seats.

3   Anti-partisan sentiments in New Zealand local body politics run deep. Those political parties that put up candidates in local body elections tend to mask their identity by running as Independents or in ostensibly non-partisan organisations. Examples of such bodies in Auckland include Citizens and Ratepayers, City Vision, and Auckland Now. Bush found that, in 1998, a mere 16 per cent of elected local body politicians were affiliated to a political organisation or group (2003, p. 167).

4   Canada and Australia (alternative vote) are even more glaring examples of countries with a non-PR electoral formula and a history of multiparty voting.

5   Nagel was influenced by the propositions of Taagepera and Grofman (1985, pp. 341–52): first, that one issue dimension will result in two and only two political parties; and second, that each new dimension will produce one and only one additional party (that is, a formula of N = I (Issue) plus 1).

6   Had Nagel followed the Sartori definition of 'relevance' (that is, having either coalition or blackmail potential), then the figure of six might seem more realistic (two of the current crop of six parliamentary parties gained representation with less than 5 per cent of the vote by winning an electorate seat, and both potentially have either blackmail or coalition potential).

7   New Zealand's two-party system can be dated from 1928, when the conservative Reform and United (previously Liberal) parties combined to form a coalition government. The two parties merged as the National party in 1936.

8   Some 194,114 voters were registered on the Maori roll in 2002. An additional 125,000 chose to be registered on the general roll.
9   Neither Labour nor National, nor any of the parliamentary minor parties, contested the by-election. Tariana Turia received over 92 per cent of the votes cast.
10 TVNZ/Marae-DigiPoll, 23 May 2004.
11 A subsequent merger occurred in April 2004 between the United Future and Outdoor Recreation NZ parties. The latter party received 1.3 per cent of the party vote in 2002.
12 P. Dunne, 'Why is the Civil Unions Bill Being Promoted?', *New Zealand Women's Weekly*, 17 May 2004, p. 47 (political advertisement).

Further reading

Blondel, J. 1968, 'Party Systems and Patterns of Government in Western Democracies', *Canadian Journal of Political Science*, 1/2, pp. 180–203.
Chapman, R., 1963, 'The Response to Labour and the Question of Parallelism of Opinion, 1928–1960', in R. Chapman and K. Sinclair (eds), *Studies of a Small Democracy*, Pauls Books, Auckland, pp. 221–54.
Lijphart, A. 1984, *Democracies: Patterns of Majoritarian and Consensus Government in Twenty-One Countries*, Yale University Press, New Haven.
Nagel, J. 1994, 'How Many Parties will New Zealand Have Under MMP?' in *Political Science*, 26/2, pp. 139–60.
Vowles, J. 2003, 'Voting Behaviour', in R. Miller (ed.), *New Zealand Government and Politics*, Oxford University Press, Melbourne, 3rd edition, pp. 188–200.
Ware, A. 1996, *Political Parties and Party Systems*, Oxford University Press, Oxford.

How Parties Organise

Organisation

4

PARTY organisations play a significant role in helping to transform public opinion into government policy. Classical studies of political parties refer to a two-way link between voters and politicians, with party members and activists providing the vital point of contact between the two groups (e.g. Duverger 1964; Key 1961). One scholar has likened this process to a relay race, with voters at one end of the track or pool and the politicians at the other (Kirchheimer 1966, p. 189). The mass party, with its large membership, ability to mobilise public support, and realistic expectation of being in government, has long been regarded as the standard-bearer for the democratic goals of participation and accountability. Accordingly, any departure from the mass party model represents a slide into party decline. 'Linkage failure' is said to have been manifesting itself in a number of important ways, including: the concentration of power in the hands of political elites; declining party membership; increased public disengagement from politics; voter volatility; the emergence of new parties; and the rise of alternative organisations, such as environmental and communitarian movements (Lawson and Merkl 1988, pp. 13–38; Coleman 1996, pp. 5–10).

While agreeing with aspects of the 'linkage failure' thesis, critics reject the prediction of terminal party decline, believing it to be based on the mistaken assumption that the mass party is 'the standard against which everything should be judged' (Katz and Mair 1997, p. 93). The revisionist position is based on the assumption that parties are dynamic organisations capable of responding to societal and political change. In the same way that the mass party reflected the emergence of a clearly defined working class, so the blurring of social divisions and advent of a number of associated trends, including the increased availability of tertiary education, diversification of the labour market, changing attitudes to leisure, and gradual public disengagement from social and political groups, are said to have resulted in the decline of the mass party and the emergence of more appropriate forms of party organisation.

This chapter will focus on different types of party organisation, assessing the continuing relevance for New Zealand of the mass party and considering the claims of alternative models. While Labour and National retain features of the mass party, they, along with the minor parties, have developed a number of the characteristics of what have become known as the 'catch-all' and 'cartel' models of party organisation. The chapter will conclude that these developments have resulted in a weakening, not a strengthening, of internal party democracy.

Types of party organisation

Studies of comparative parties offer at least four models of party organisation, each representing a different stage in the development of the modern political party: the cadre party (nineteenth and early twentieth centuries); mass party (1920s–1960s); 'catch-all' party (1945–); and the 'cartel' party (1970–) (Katz and Mair 1997, pp 110–11). This is not to suggest that there is no overlap between one stage and the next; indeed, today's parties commonly display characteristics of more than one model (Katz and Mair 1997, p. 109).

Cadre party

Cadre or elite parties constitute the earliest form of party organisation. They can be defined as weakly organised collections of socially homogeneous notables or 'parliamentary clubs' (Kirchheimer 1966, p. 180). Rather than being motivated by an overriding commitment to the public interest, such parties have tended to be shaped around and reflect the electoral ambitions and personal priorities of their leaders and key candidates. While they may have significant numbers of supporters and voters, cadre parties are distinguished by their skeletal extra-parliamentary (meaning 'outside' parliament) structure and limited ability to mobilise grassroots support. Fund-raising and the planning of election campaigns are activities, not for the members and wider party organisation, but for the parliamentary elite, together with its wealthy individual and corporate backers and associated experts (Duverger 1964, p. 64).

A number of the earliest political parties (those formed in the nineteenth and early twentieth centuries), especially conservative parties, were of the cadre or elite type. These included the British Conservative party and the American Republican party. Although New Zealand's first political party, the Liberal party, which was formed after the Liberals became the government in 1890, developed an extensive network of branches and grassroots supporters, it was essentially the brainchild and political vehicle of a small group of parliamentary notables comprising the prime minister, Richard Seddon (1893–1906), and his senior government ministers (Richardson 1981). As such, it exemplified more of the structural characteristics of a cadre party than of a modern mass party. (For a fuller account of the embryonic stage of the Liberal party's organisational development, see chapter 2).

Mass party

The mass party model is the starting-point for any discussion on the link (sometimes referred to as the transmission or conveyor belt) between decision-makers and the voting public. As predominantly left-wing movements, the early mass parties attempted to integrate the newly enfranchised working class into the political system. Lacking the support of wealthy individuals, they were forced to rely on the income provided by fee-paying members and like-minded associations, notably trade unions. To this end, and to equip their membership with the means to influence decision-making, mass parties developed a complex structure outside of parliament, or in the community at large. In time, the success of the mass party would result in a 'contagion [effect] from the Left', with parties on the ideological right seeking to adopt the same organisational characteristics as their left-wing opponents (Duverger 1964, p. xvii).

According to the mass party model, party organisations have three main functions: nurturing and expanding party membership and resources; developing policies that can be implemented by elected officials; and preparing the party for election campaigns (Ware 1996, p. 111). By maximising its membership, the mass party is able to garner sufficient resources and support to contest and win elections. In return, members are presented with opportunities for political representation and accountability. Through a system of vertical links, with the lowest common denominator being the local branch or cell, the mass party is able to assist with the recruitment and political education of the rank-and-file, some of whom go on to become parliamentary candidates. In this way, the mass party is able to preserve its 'unity and homo-geneity', even in the face of the inevitable pressure towards centralised control (Duverger 1964, p. 49).

Key's seminal work on parties and public opinion elaborates on the role played by mass parties in 'the translation of mass preferences into public policy' (1961, p. 432). The process entails direct involvement by grassroots members in the development of an agreed policy platform, often by way of remits proceeding from the cells or branches to party conferences, where they are debated and either rejected, amended or endorsed. Having formulated policies that win the approval of the voters in an election campaign, the elected mass party is given a mandate to govern 'in accord with the majority will' (Key 1961, p. 432). But as well as aggregating the views of its members and voters, the party also provides the leadership with a means to make and shape public opinion. As Key has observed, 'by their evangelism party advocates create opinion' (1961, p. 454). In more recent times the main instrument of persuasion has shifted from the party and its more 'evangeli-cal' members to the mass media (see chapter 9).

Catch-all party

The 'catch-all' party is said to have had its roots in the changes that began to occur in Western societies in the postwar period. The class divisions between workers and capitalists that largely defined the party systems of Britain and other parts of Europe became less clear-cut in the wake of a number of important social and economic developments, including growing economic prosperity and a diversification of the job market at the expense of traditional blue-collar occupations. As a result, the numerical strength and influence of the working class gradually declined, to be replaced by the demands of a large and growing middle class. For example, whereas the resources of the welfare state had once been heavily targeted towards the poor, they were now in danger of being 'captured' by middle-income groups, especially in the high-cost areas of health and education.

These societal changes coincided with another major development, namely the growing accessibility of the mass media, especially television, to ordinary voters. Instead of working through traditional channels, such as door-knocking and public meetings, politicians were able to reach directly over the heads of party organisers to a mass television audience. In a series of developments we have come to associate with the 'Americanisation' or 'presidentialisation' of politics, parties were forced to adapt in ways that led to a transition from the mass party, with its strong linkage with discrete social groups, to an amorphous, or 'catch-all', movement that sought to maximise its electoral appeal among all sectors of society. To this end, it projected a media image that emphasised leadership, inclusiveness, and a moderate policy agenda.

Masking this paradigm shift were some residual features of the mass party, including members and activists, local branches, and regional and national conferences. Slowly but surely, however, the fulcrum of power was moving away from the extra-parliamentary organisation, with its emphasis on participation and the preservation of the party's founding beliefs, and towards the party's more electorally ambitious and pragmatic parliamentary elite (Katz and Mair 1997, p. 101).

Thus, the catch-all party has a number of characteristics that distinguish it from the mass party:

- *Membership*—A reduced role for party members in traditional areas of party activity, such as policy-making, the selection of leaders and candidates, fund-raising, and campaigning.
- *Organisation*—Greater recognition of the importance of professionals (such as public relations and advertising agencies) and interest groups. The role of the catch-all party is not to be captive to any one group, but rather to consult widely.
- *Ideology*—Diluting the party's ideology and policies, thereby creating a character that has been described as 'non-utopian, non-oppressive and ever so flexible' (Kirchheimer 1966, p. 199).
- *Party positioning*—While recognising the importance of brand differentiation, maintaining a close proximity to the party's main rival in the moderate centre of the political spectrum, thereby nurturing and sustaining a nationwide constituency.
- *Focus on personnel*—In the absence of divergent political ideologies or policies, emphasising differences of personnel, hence the importance assigned to the nomination and election of parliamentary candidates.
- *Leadership*—With the help of the mass media, placing particular emphasis on the personal style and image of the leader, who is frequently presented as the personification of the party.
- *Media role*—Rather than using conventional means of communicating with the wider community, such as rank-and-file members, appealing directly to voters through the mass media.

The catch-all party's ability to attract broad electoral support from its position in the moderate centre has the dual effect of both forcing the other dominant party into the ideological centre ground and pushing smaller parties to the extremes, thereby thwarting any plans to expand their base of electoral support. Thus, in predominantly two-party systems, such as that of the USA and Great Britain, the effect of the catch-all tendency has been to reinforce the existing party system.

Cartel party

Whereas the mass party was founded on a large grassroots membership, reinforced by a network of branches and electorate committees, and the catch-all party pays lip-service to party membership while removing most of its functions, the cartel party finds no substantive purpose in party membership, preferring to pin its future success on its access to the vastly superior resources and powers of the state. Membership numbers may continue to be used to promote its overall image, but the cartel party resembles the cadre party of old in focusing almost exclusively on the interests of the parliamentary leadership.

The cartel model as formulated by Katz and Mair (1997) is based on the symbiotic relationship that has come to exist between parties and the state. As with a corporate cartel, this new model recognises the capacity of legislative and governing parties to access the resources of the state in order to gain an electoral advantage over emerging competitors. These resources may include the manipulation of the rules of competition, direct state funding of political parties, the use of state employees to carry out party business, and access to publicly funded broadcasting time. Although the main beneficiaries are likely to be the major parties, small parties may be strategically placed to collaborate with a view to receiving their share of available benefits. Anti-competitive moves may include: arriving at agreed policies and legislative strategies; sharing electoral information; and reaching electoral accommodation, including standing down a candidate in preference to one from another party.

Because the cartel party operates largely within the confines of parliament, any non-parliamentary organisation is skeletal at best (perhaps a more appropriate metaphor would be 'dismembered head'). In the case of some of the small cartel parties, party 'headquarters' and the MPs' parliamentary offices are virtually one and the same. Party leaders assume responsibility for matters once considered to be part of the sphere of influence of party members and activists, including policy development, political recruitment, and election tactics and strategies.

The distinguishing features of the cartel model can be summarised thus:

- *Membership*—While individual 'members' are still valued for providing evidence of grassroots endorsement, they are treated as little different from 'supporters'; indeed, the two categories are frequently merged in a party's contact list (Katz and Mair 1997, p. 113). The political elite's reliance on state resources has made the role and functions of members less valued and important.
- *Organisation*—The extra-parliamentary organisation is largely submerged within the governing or legislative organisation of the state. While an

organisational structure of sorts may continue to operate outside the state apparatus, its functions will be tightly constrained, being limited to communication with members, maintaining membership lists, and some fund-raising.

- *Ideology*—Policy differences are ironed out in the interests of inter-party cooperation and consensus. As a result, policy positions tend to be fluid and pragmatic and are heavily influenced by the perspectives and priorities of the state bureaucracy. In contrast, relatively little attention is paid to the views of the general public.
- *Party positioning*—The anti-competitive impetus behind the cartel model reduces the importance of party space or distance.
- *Focus on personnel*—Given the emphasis on politics as a skilled profession, it is hardly surprising that management skills and incumbency are highly valued. Under the cartel model, election campaigns are viewed as 'almost exclusively capital-intensive, professional, and centralized...' (Katz and Mair 1997, p. 113)
- *Leadership*—Consistent with the growing trend under the catch-all model, substantial powers are given to the party leader, especially in forging alliances with other parliamentary parties.
- *Media role*—Increased state funding has made the use of the media, especially the electronic media, more accessible and important.

National and Labour as mass parties

Adopting the trade union movement's organisational template, during the 1920s and early 1930s the Labour party began to adopt the essential features of a mass party, including a tiered organisation and mass membership. It represented a significant departure from the dominant cadre party model of the late nineteenth and early twentieth centuries. The latter was characterised by a loose organisational structure, the informal selection of parliamentary candidates, many of whom were the friends or associates of the party leader (often a local provincial mayor, lawyer or businessman), and tight central control of party finance by the leader and his inner parliamentary group. At the National party's formation in 1936, there was general agreement that it should also be organised along mass party lines. As well as an electorate structure, National created five divisions, which fed into the central bodies of the party. Although policy discussions were much more highly moderated than in Labour, with conference delegates generally deferring to their MPs, local activists were delegated the important power of being able to select their own parliamentary candidates.

At its peak in the 1940s and 1950s, National reportedly had a membership of close to 300,000, making it on a per capita basis the most successful mass party in the Western world. Not far behind was Labour, with a combined affiliated and active branch membership approaching 200,000 (Gustafson 1989, p. 208). This gave the two parties a total membership approaching one in three voters. Although a sizeable proportion of Labour's members were recruited directly, a vast majority were filtered through the party's trade union affiliates (as many as eight out of every ten members), giving it the overall character of Duverger's 'indirect' party type (1964, p. 17). In contrast, National's membership has always been indisputably 'direct', its organisational strength being founded on an ability to conscript an army of individual supporters. To this end, membership fees have been kept at an attractively low level (for example, a modest twenty-five cents in the mid 1960s and an unspecified donation in 2004).

Extra-parliamentary party organisation

Early in their history both major parties established distinct parliamentary and extra-parliamentary or organisational wings, although there has always been considerable overlap between the two (for example, it has not been uncommon for a Labour MP to serve simultaneously as party president).[1]

Figure 4.1 Mass party organisation

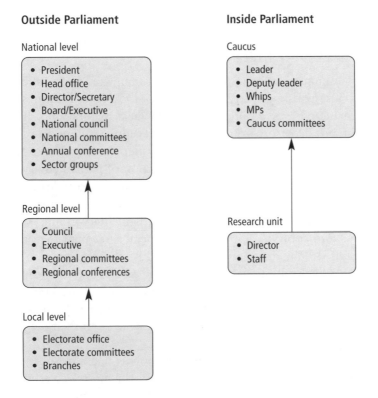

Electorate-level

At the base of the extra-parliamentary organisation is the local branch, of which there have been as many as 200 nationwide, and the local electorate committee (one per electorate). Trade unions can affiliate separately with the Labour party, with their membership being allocated to individual electorates (New Zealand Labour Constitution July 2001: Rule 44b). The primary tasks of the branch and local electorate committee members (constituencies that lack branches are deemed by National to be 'unitary' electorates) are to raise money for the local organisation and party head office, disseminate party propaganda, and prepare the local electorate for the next election. Each party also has a number of ancillary organisations, such as special youth, women's, university, industrial, Maori, and Pacific Island branches. One of the most prominent of Labour's special branches is the University of Auckland's Princes Street branch, which was formed in the early 1960s and has been responsible for the early political socialisation of a number of prominent Labour politicians, including Jonathan Hunt, Helen Clark, Richard Prebble, and Judith Tizard (Godfrey 2003). The Young Nationals have a similarly influential history, having been something of a nursery for future politicians and officials since the creation of a separate youth division in 1938 (Gustafson 1986b, pp. 255–66).

Regional level

Above the electorate organisation are regional or divisional bodies. The decision to introduce this intermediate level within the party structure was initiated by National at the time of its formation. National's regional councils, which meet every three months, are primarily made up of the chairs of each of the electorates within that region. Labour's regional structure is less elaborate and more recent, having been formed in 1971. The regional councils are responsible for the promotion of party activities across several electorates, including the coordination of fund-raising and candidate list selection, as well as communication between the local organisation and head office. They also convene regional conferences and seminars. Following an internal power-struggle between some regions and the national body, the powers of Labour's regional bodies were greatly reduced. However, when a similar attempt was made within National in the 1980s, it was successfully rebuffed. Each of National's five regions (three in the North Island and two in the South Island) maintains a committee structure, which may include policy, women's and youth committees (National Party Constitution April 1999: Rule 64). As we will see, the powers of National's regional offices were finally reduced as part of a review of the party's disastrous election campaign of 2002.

National level

At the apex of the extra-parliamentary organisation of each party are a national head office, an elected council (the governing body when conference is not in session), and a smaller working executive. Labour's Council has a membership of eighteen, made up of a combination of nationally and regionally elected officials. It meets in Wellington at least six times a year. The nine-member executive meets at least once a month. National's Board of Directors also has nine members, including the leader, a second member of the parliamentary caucus, and the party president. Of the Board's seven elected members, at least one must be from each of the three large geographic regions of the North Island (Northern, Central, and Southern), together with the South Island. The executive body of each party is empowered to interpret the party's rules, control the finances, and direct the day-to-day business of the organisation. At the national level, there are also a number of standing committees on matters such as finance, policy, and publicity. Until recently the party president, vice-presidents, and other senior officers were elected by the annual conference, though the positions were sometimes uncontested. However, in 2003 National transferred the power to elect the president from the annual conference to the Board of Directors. The Board also employs the party's general manager.

Constitutionally, though not in practice, the chief decision-making body of the mass party is the annual conference. Party delegates (and, in Labour's case, union affiliates) are given the opportunity to introduce and debate constitutional and policy remits with a view to shaping the direction of the party in opposition and in government. Reports are presented, officers elected, and informal networking takes place both within the conference precincts and at the social events that are part of any party conference. In recent times the annual conference has also been used to discuss election plans, enthuse party members, and present the party in a positive light to a wider public. Conferences typically last for two to four days and attract 400 to 600 voting delegates, together with their non-voting social partners (a common feature of National gatherings), interested observers, and members of the media and foreign diplomatic corps.

Parliamentary party organisation

In contrast to the elaborate extra-parliamentary party organisation, until recently the parliamentary wing was notable for its simplicity. In the interests of party cohesion and discipline, early in the development of the two-party system both groups of MPs began to meet or 'caucus' on a regular basis. Internal relations are generally less fractious among opposition MPs, but the party caucus presents government backbench members with a private forum in which to question their ministers. Over time each caucus began to develop a network of standing and ad hoc caucus committees. The main aims of these committees are to improve the party's performance and support its legislative agenda. The president and general secretary have long been able to attend caucus, thereby providing MPs with an extra-parliamentary perspective, although such officials are not permitted to vote. The smooth running of the parliamentary party has been further facilitated by the addition of several key support services, including larger parliamentary staffs and party research units.

The decision-making processes employed by Labour and National have long reflected a predominance of centralist over decentralist tendencies, to the extent that the use of the term 'democratic centralist', once a driving principle of the Communist Party of the Soviet Union, while somewhat ironic, is not entirely misplaced (Duverger 1964, p. 57). In describing the relationship between the political elite and the party organisation, R. S. Milne once stated that 'caucus treats the wishes of the [party] organization with about as much respect as the management in paternalistic business firms accords to workers' suggestions; ideas for minor improvements are in order, but advice on how to run the business would be regarded as an impertinence' (1966, p. 165). Or, as a former Labour president found when attending her regular meetings with the party's senior parliamentarians, 'party representatives were viewed as the poor relations from the wrong side of the tracks who were invited to the family gathering only out of duty' (Wilson 1989, p. 44).

Labour has decidedly more centralist tendencies than National, with the party leadership exercising firm control over a wide range of activities, including policy formation, especially when the party is in government, candidate and leadership selection, and the discipline of elected representatives. However, this was not always the case. In the early years of the party, for example, attempts by Michael Joseph Savage to give the executive the power to veto nominated parliamentary candidates was defeated by the party's annual conference, which took the view that the final choice of candidate was the sovereign right of all party members in a given electorate (Brown 1962, p. 34). During those early years, conference was also given an instrumental role in the formulation and approval of party policy, with some heated debates occurring over such issues as foreign and defence policy, immigration, land policy, and monetary reform (Brown 1962).

As the Labour party began to grow and enjoy electoral success many of the powers hitherto enjoyed by grassroots activists began to be transferred to the organisation's national office, as well as to the parliamentary wing. But the leadership's oligarchic tendencies did not stop there. As with the Australian Labor party, on the occasions when Labour has been in government there is a marked tendency for cabinet to overrule not only the party organisation, but also the caucus, especially on policy matters. Attempts by backbench MPs to hold the cabinet to account, or even to convene a special meeting of caucus to discuss a topic of mutual interest, such as the proposed Springbok Tour of 1973 (Bassett 1976, p. 39), have tended to be treated with impatience bordering on contempt by their senior colleagues. Individual MPs are also bound by the party's constitution to support the decisions made by caucus. Any MP found to be breaching this rule faces the prospect of expulsion from the caucus, a fate experienced by Jim Anderton in December 1988 over his decision to oppose the privatisation of Postbank. This intolerance of dissent has a number of possible explanations, including the influence of the trade union movement, with its well-known emphasis on group solidarity and opposition to 'scabbing' (Milne 1966, p. 137; Gustafson 1992, p. 284), as well as concern within the leadership over how to control the informal factions that tend to develop within caucus. One notable factional dispute occurred around the time of the stock-market crash in late 1987 and led to caucus 'being in continual uproar—relations between Left and Right were poisonous' (quoted in Debnam 1994, p. 58).

From the time of its landslide victory in 1984 the Labour cabinet had raised the spectre of democratic centralism to unprecedented heights. As Debnam (1994), Easton (1989), Gustafson (1992) and others have pointed out, the prime minister, David Lange, and his senior ministers were prepared to systematically dishonour policy pledges made to voters during the election campaign (Debnam 1994, p. 56). In response, the extra-parliamentary party began to explore ways of restraining government ministers who were 'seriously considering policy in conflict with the manifesto, or outside of subsequent agreed conference decisions' (Debnam 1994). While ten policy committees were set up to review and monitor government action, the oligarchic nature of the New Zealand cabinet system of government under the former first-past-the-post electoral system seriously undermined any chance of success.

National's local party organisation has greater involvement and influence over candidate selection at the electorate level than that of Labour (to be discussed in chapter 6). Local party members also exercise a much stronger claim to ownership of their MPs, regarding them primarily as constituency representatives rather than as party delegates. In most other respects, however, the party's parliamentary wing exercises considerable influence. As Wood has pointed out (2001, p. 249), the parliamentary leadership dominates the policy-making process, especially when in government, as well as all significant decisions over election strategy. Moreover, while backbench MPs are given some freedom to vote against the party if they regard its position to be in conflict with the prevailing mood within the local constituency, in practice the pressure to conform is almost as strong as it is within Labour.

Appearance in New Zealand of the catch-all party

Although the two parties' extra-parliamentary organisations continued to be based on the mass party model, by the 1970s there were signs that the mass party phenomenon was beginning to wane. Among the explanations which had pertinence to New Zealand were: rising living standards and advances in the availability of education, particularly tertiary education, resulting in an obscuring of differences between classes; the gradual decline of socio-economic voting (Vowles et al. 1995, p. 39); the growing pervasiveness of the mass media, especially television; and, despite its small population base, clear evidence of atomisation, with fewer people wanting to join or be associated with large and increasingly amorphous political organisations (see chapter 5). The political party was once described as a 'community', and one of the benefits of active membership was the opportunity to meet and socialise with politicians and like-minded grassroots members. Apart from the impact of these social changes on the integrative role of the mass party, during the 1980s the emergence of a more professional political elite began to threaten the role traditionally carried out by rank-and-file party members.

Despite having divergent ideological traditions, during the 1960s and 1970s the National and Labour parties began to converge on a number of political values and policy goals. Areas of concurrence included the rights of citizenship and the appropriate functions and powers of the state. Labour had established its reputation as the party of economic intervention and comprehensive welfare. Nationalists, on the other hand, were the defenders of 'unfettered' free enterprise, limited government and the values of self-reliance and individual freedom. In practice, however, Labour had shown itself to be a cautious reformer, and National had been content to administer some significant Labour reforms, with occasional embellishments of its own. By pursuing policies that were moderate and pragmatic, both major parties were trying to appeal to the centripetal tendencies of the New Zealand electorate. This goal was nicely encapsulated in National's 1975 campaign slogan, which blandly offered voters 'New Zealand the Way You Want It'.

Following National's landslide victory in 1975, attempts were made to modernise the defeated Labour party's image with the voting public. As well as streamlining the extra-parliamentary organisation and channels of public communication (Strachan 1985), unsuccessful efforts were made to replace the decidedly uncharismatic leader, Bill Rowling, with a young Auckland lawyer, David Lange, and to broaden the party's appeal among middle class voters by dropping 'Labour' from the title in favour of 'Social Democratic'. However, by the late 1970s a new generation of Labour leaders had begun to emerge. Lange, Geoffrey Palmer, David Caygill, and Anne Hercus were university educated and professionally trained politicians (all were lawyers), with little or no background in the traditional roots of the Labour movement, specifically the working class and affiliated trade unions. Being part of a new postwar generation of politicians, they were more media-savvy than their predecessors and quickly recognised that the party's future lay in broadening its appeal among New Zealand's burgeoning middle class, especially on the issue of economic policy. By the time Lange assumed the leadership in 1983, the party was becoming well positioned for an electoral assault on the increasingly authoritarian and ideologically rigid Muldoon government.

Any hope that Labour would be able to consolidate support among middle class voters proved to be short-lived, as the party's disastrous performance in the 1990 election clearly illustrates (from 48 per cent and fifty-four seats in 1987 to 35 per cent and twenty-eight seats in 1990). While the radical nature of the reforms introduced by successive Labour (1984–90) and National (1990–93) governments are at odds with the bland ideological and policy prescription laid down in the catch-all party model, the same cannot be said for organisational and election campaign developments. In the face of bitter opposition to their policies from grassroots party members, the key political leaders of both major parties appealed over their heads to the wider electorate. As we are about to see, this required extensive use of professional agencies and parliamentary staff, a development that was bound to further depress the parties' already shrinking membership numbers. (For a fuller discussion on the application of the catch-all model to New Zealand, see chapters 5, 8, and 9.)

Advent of the cartel party

As we have seen, the cartel party is able to access the resources of the state in order to gain an electoral advantage over emerging competitors (Katz and Mair 1995; Katz and Mair 2002; Katz 2002). Although the focus of Katz and Mair's work is on major parties, the advent of MMP has resulted in multi-layered cartels, with available state resources being distributed among a number of quite small parliamentary parties. But the notion of a cartel also carries with it connotations of cooperation, even collusion, between blocs of parties and their opponents.

Of the numerous social, economic and political developments that help account for the emergence of the cartel model in New Zealand, three stand out: the rise of neo-liberalism; the reconfiguration of New Zealand's predominantly two-party system into a multiparty one; and the advent of MMP. By the late 1970s and early 1980s the unsettling effects of economic recession, electoral pressure from the third parties, and the unravelling of the social consensus upon which the old two-party system had been built was followed by a repositioning of the major parties on the right of the political spectrum. The introduction of MMP in 1996 resulted in a further consolidation of this trend.

New Zealand's dramatic shift towards the free market was driven by the political leadership of the two major parties, together with their advisers and the members of key government departments, especially Treasury. According to its chief architect, Roger Douglas, the country's economic problems had their roots in the 'extravagant promises' that had been made by the political parties over the previous two or more decades (Oliver 1989, p. 26). Consistent with the public choice model that had been adopted by the Finance minister and some of his cabinet colleagues, party members and activists came to be regarded with the same suspicion, even hostility, as other 'vested interests'. Although the incoming Labour government convened an Economic Summit at which various future options were discussed, there was little input from its extra-parliamentary party. Besides, by this time the government's economic agenda had already been put in place by its political leadership (Oliver 1989, p. 38).

Over the next few years, the political leaders largely circumvented party channels of communication, preferring to use the media to influence public values and opinions. Party membership was in dramatic decline, party activists had become disillusioned over the extent to which their role had been usurped by the political leaders and their professional advisers, and the funding of both major parties was becoming more and more dependent on large corporate donors and the state institutions (Miller and Catt 1993). By the late 1980s and early 1990s, successive Labour and National governments were in open conflict with their party members and activists.

Beginning in the late 1980s, within the Office of the Prime Minister an overtly political wing was created. The sharp increase in the availability of administrative expertise and political advice can be dated from 1989, when Geoffrey Palmer's Labour government restructured the Prime Minister's Department by creating separate bureaucratic and political wings. The Prime Minister's Office was given the task of providing a 'political advice function, liaising with political parties as well as carrying out administrative and ceremonial functions' (Palmer and Palmer 1997, p. 58). Staffing was immediately increased from eight to twenty, and a communications unit was added in the early 1990s. In order to gain the National opposition party's support for these reforms, additional staffing was made available to the leader of the opposition (Palmer and Palmer 1997, p. 59). This development weakened the role of the extra-parliamentary wing of each party, as evidenced by the gradual reduction in the number of head office staff. To head his new political wing, Palmer turned to Margaret Wilson, a former Labour party president.

One of the most visible features of the chasm that had opened between the political leaders and their party members was the formation of breakaway movements. The creation of NewLabour in 1989 removed an entire tier of activists from the parent organisation, helping to set the scene for Labour's landslide defeat at the following year's election. In recognition of the threat these new parties posed to the two-party system, at the 1992 Tamaki by-election Labour colluded with National by sharing canvassing data. It helped to ensure the defeat of the front-running Alliance candidate by National's Clem Simich (Miller and Catt 1993, p. 71). When the public was offered a referendum on a new electoral system later the same year, a decision that was strongly opposed by the parliamentary elites of both major parties, together with prominent representatives of the business community, the scene was set for the final stage in the development of the cartel model, that of parliamentary and governmental power-sharing with the minor parties.

Because the new parliamentary parties had relatively few members, they were particularly susceptible to the attraction of the 'spoils' of office. (Katz and Mair 1997, p. 107). As part of its bid to persuade New Zealand First to enter into a coalition arrangement with it rather than Labour in 1996, for example, Bolger's National government granted the small party's negotiating team a significant slice of the total funding of $563,000 that had been set aside for legal, administrative, and other forms of assistance (National decided not to draw on the fund). Among those paid from it was Winston Peters' brother, a Whangarei lawyer, who had been hired by the party as a legal advisor. This was in addition to the $1.3 million that had already been set aside to pay for the party's research and other expenses.

Subsequent efforts to foster inter-party cooperation and enhance the electoral fortunes of the small parliamentary parties included providing generous office space in the executive Beehive building for the Independent MP, Alamein Kopu (at the time the government enjoyed a one-seat majority), payment by the Parliamentary Services Commission of a $28,000 legal bill incurred following her defection from the Alliance,[2] and, following the formation of her Mana Wahine party, awarding the sum of $77,000 to help pay for research and office expenses, as well as to employ a 'spin doctor'.[3] In addition to her parliamentary salary of $83,000, Kopu, a list MP, also received an annual amount of $34,200 towards operating an electorate office. Despite this level of assistance, at the 1999 general election Kopu's party received a total of only 296 votes.

MPs also enjoy a range of tax-free perquisites, including free domestic air travel for MPs and their partners, heavily discounted international air travel, accommodation expenses, and generous superannuation provisions. During the 2001–02 financial year, for example, the total cost of MPs' domestic air travel was $5.2 million.[4] One analysis has indicated that these additional benefits effectively push an MP's base salary up to a gross income of between $130,000 and $140,000.[5]

Consistent with the cartel model, parliamentary parties receive a significant boost to their taxpayer-funded resources simply by virtue of their presence in parliament. The division between legitimate parliamentary activity and party organisational activity is frequently blurred, with extra-parliamentary business being conducted in the parliamentary offices of the party leader and MPs, and parliamentary employees being deployed to assist with the party's election campaigns and other related activities. Although the New Zealand First party headquarters were listed as being in Hamilton, until recently the actual address was the private residence of the president, Doug Woolerton. In practice, most of the significant organisational functions of the party were carried out in the parliamentary offices in Bowen House (opposite the Beehive) of Woolerton and his fellow New Zealand First MPs. Similarly, from its inception in 2001, United Future was organised out of the parliamentary office of its leader, Peter Dunne. As for the major parties, while Labour's national headquarters are quite separate from the offices of the party's MPs and ministers, being located in Fraser House, Wellington, the role of its seven-member staff, including the general secretary, is limited to a small number of largely non-political functions, specifically administering the party's membership lists (at the time of writing, the party had not attempted any significant recruitment campaign since the early 1980s), maintaining contact with branch members and party officials, and some fund-raising.

Between 1999 and 2002, the Alliance operated its Electoral Liaison Unit inside parliament. The party president, Matt McCarten, and general secretary maintained a parliamentary office as employees of Parliamentary Services. Unbeknown to the party leadership, party membership information and mailing lists were stored on parliament's computers. For most of its time as a parliamentary party, the Alliance stipulated that its MPs and ministers tithe 10 per cent of their taxpayer-funded salary to the party.[6] In addition to this total gross income of $125,225, each MP pooled approximately $20,000 of her or his Parliamentary Services allowance to help fund: two parliamentary research staff; approximately six full-time staff employed by the Electoral Liaison Unit and based in parliament; as well as out-of-parliament secretaries in a number of centres (including Auckland, Hamilton, Rotorua, and Dunedin). Most of these staff came under the direct supervision of the party president, through the general secretary. While some of their activities could be directly linked to the needs of MPs and constituents, others had to do with the internal politics, organisation, electoral strategies, and policies of the party. When the Alliance became irreconcilably divided in 2001 and early 2002, a number of MPs alleged that McCarten was using the resources made available by them through a combination of tithes and Parliamentary

Services' entitlements to undermine the parliamentary leadership of the party and promote the ideological and leadership aspirations of the party's left-wing. Several MPs discontinued the practice of tithing and allocating their share of the parliamentary budget to the Election Liaison Unit, action that effectively resulted in their dismissal from the party.

In 2003 it was alleged that the ACT leader, Richard Prebble, had charged his party rent for use of his company-owned Wellington townhouse as its electorate office. For several years the party had paid up to seven electorate agents to work part-time in parliament as researchers and press officers. According to reports, 'most of the agents were not given keys to the... townhouse and some had never known the address'.[7] There was also the suggestion, made by Winston Peters, that Prebble had used public money to fund a 'mobile electorate office' during his three years as MP for Wellington Central.[8] The ACT party also received $34,200 annually (plus an expenses allowance of $8,477) to run an electorate office for each of its list MPs, although only two were reported to have set up such offices.[9] The scheme was said to have boosted ACT's budget by up to $150,000 per year.[10]

Finally, parties receive direct assistance with their election campaigns, including state-funded broadcasting allocations, eligibility for which includes the number of MPs a party has at the time of the allocation. In 2002, for example, there was a total allocation of $2,081,000, of which only $167,784 (or 8 per cent) went to the non-parliamentary parties (Electoral Commission 2002, p. 35). Moreover, at the 2002 election the electronic media, which in the past had been scrupulous in apportioning time, began to broaden participation in key debates and studio interviews to include all eight parliamentary parties, regardless of their level of representation and electoral support. The exclusion of parties such as Christian Heritage, which had a better voting record than either United Future or the Progressive Coalition, put non-parliamentary parties at an electoral disadvantage.

Despite the relevance of the cartel model with respect to the allocation of state resources, inter-party cooperation in the electoral arena has been surprisingly rare. One such occasion occurred in 1996, when National decided not to contest the Wellington electorate of Ohariu-Belmont, thereby enabling United's Peter Dunne to carry the seat with an 8,513-vote majority. Other examples of electoral accommodation between potential coalition partners have included the belated effort of both major parties to encourage their supporters to vote for an electorate candidate whose party was at risk of falling below the 5 per cent party-vote threshold. In 1996, National strategists made it clear that they would not be unhappy if National voters in Wellington Central gave their vote to the ACT party candidate, Richard Prebble, rather than the National candidate, advice that helped Prebble to a narrow victory. Three years later, Helen Clark sent a similar message to those

Labour supporters in the Coromandel who were considering giving their vote to Jeanette Fitzsimons of the Greens. Such arrangements tend to be the exception rather than the rule. In 1999, the electorate of Tauranga was vigorously contested by both major parties, a decision that almost cost New Zealand First all its parliamentary seats—having fallen below the 5 per cent threshold, the party was saved by Winston Peters' 63-vote majority over the Labour candidate, Margaret Wilson.

Conclusion

Although most parties either retain or aspire to the main organisational features of the mass party, together with the electoral characteristics of the catch-all party, it has been the contention of this chapter that the dominant contemporary model is that of Katz and Mair's cartel party. Whereas the mass party is distinguished by a large grassroots membership, reinforced by a network of branches and electorate committees, the new cartel party tends to look more like the cadre party of old, being formed by and in the interests of its parliamentary leadership.

The cartel model has quite serious implications for the future of electoral democracy, as illustrated by the results of National's Strategic Review, which was conducted in the aftermath of that party's landslide defeat at the 2002 election. Despite a stated commitment to a large and active membership and pressure from within the party for greater grassroots involvement in the selection of candidates and in the election of the party leader, the Review led to a further concentration of power in the hands of a smaller national executive, renamed the Board of Directors, including the right to choose the president, a decision previously made by delegates attending the party's annual conference. No effort was made to open up candidate selection or to remove the power of caucus to choose the party leader. The Review also resulted in a reduction in the role of the party's regions and the disestablishment of several elected committees, with a number of their powers being transferred to the Board of Directors.

But the anti-democratic nature of the cartel model also has implications for the level of inter-party competition. As we have seen, because the parliamentary parties are able to monopolise the material benefits offered by the state, small and emerging parties such as the Maori party, not to mention the array of non-parliamentary parties, struggle to compete.

Notes

1 These included Norman Douglas (MP for Auckland Central) and Arthur Faulkner (MP for Roskill), both of whom served terms as president during the 1970s.
2 *Sunday Star Times*, 14 November 1999.
3 *New Zealand Herald*, 28 May 1999.
4 *New Zealand Herald*, 20 January 2003.
5 J. Shewan, 'Outrageous Vote Highlights Travel Perk Bonanza', *New Zealand Herald*, 27 December 2002, Section C, p. 2.
6 In 1999 $8,300 for each of the four backbench MPs; $16,100 for Jim Anderton as deputy prime minister; $14,540 for each of the other three cabinet ministers; $12,925 for the one minister outside of cabinet; $10,450 for the parliamentary under-secretary; and $8,930 for the party whip.
7 *New Zealand Herald*, 6 March 2003.
8 *New Zealand Herald*, 7 March 2003.
9 *New Zealand Herald*, 4 March 2003.
10 *New Zealand Herald*, 5 March 2003.

Further reading

Duverger, M. 1954, *Political Parties: Their Organisation and Activity in the Modern State*, Methuen, London.
Gustafson, B. 1989, 'The Labour Party', in H. Gold (ed.), *New Zealand Politics in Perspective*, Longman Paul, Auckland, 2nd edition, pp 199–222.
Katz, R.S. and P. Mair 1997, 'Party Organisation, Party Democracy, and the Emergence of the Cartel Party', in P. Mair, *Party System Change: Approaches and Interpretations*, Oxford University Press, New York, pp. 93–119.
Kirchheimer, O. 1966, 'The Transformation of the Western European Party Systems', in J. LaPalombara and M. Weiner (eds), *Political Parties and Political Development*, Princeton University Press, Princeton, pp. 177–200.
Panebianco, A. 1988, *Political Parties: Organization and Power*, Cambridge University Press, Cambridge.
Wood, A. 2003, 'National', in R. Miller (ed.), *New Zealand Government and Politics*, Oxford University Press, Melbourne, 3rd edition, pp. 251–60.

Members, Activists, and Funding

5

THERE is much to debate on the subject of party finance. Opinion is divided on a number of issues, including the growth of funding by corporations and wealthy individuals, the increasing incidence of anonymous donations, and whether or not parties should be funded by the state. Those endorsing spending limits point to the USA, which spends approximately $NZ8 billion on its presidential and other election campaigns, with close to $NZ500 million being spent on the presidential pre-nomination process alone (Eldersveld and Walton 2000, p. 255). Others are more concerned about a lack of transparency and accountability and call for the full disclosure of sources, especially in relation to large donations. While Britain's 'cash-for-access' and 'cash-for-questions' affairs[1] may have no direct counterpart in New Zealand, there is an irresistible logic to the claim that money is given in the expectation of personal access and material gain. Still others express concern that present funding laws prevent fair and open competition, with a few parties receiving the lion's share of available corporate and state funding, while others receive little or none. They ask what chance a new political party will have when it is starved of the resources it needs to compete against more established, though conceivably less popular, political movements.

Party finance has long been closely linked with that of party membership and activism. Members not only provide political parties with a sense of legitimacy and a core of committed activists, but also substantial financial assistance and support. Important functions include making annual sub-scriptions and periodic donations, as well as helping with fund-raising activities and the recruitment of new fee-paying members. However, with advances in technology and the advent of the modern election campaign, a number of the functions once carried out by members and activists have been contracted out to paid political advisors and professional consultants (see chapter 9). The resulting rise in the cost of running a party, especially at elec-tion time, has shifted much of the fund-raising emphasis away from individual members and towards large institutional and private donors and, even more importantly, the resources provided by the state. While the era of membership-based parties is by no means over, it is gradually being replaced by one in which small elite parties function as 'agents of the state' (Katz and Mair 1995).

Does party membership still matter? In an article provocatively entitled 'Forget the Party Activists. They Make No Difference',[2] one leading British newspaper has argued that the sort of things members have always done, especially canvassing and raising money, are now largely peripheral to a party's success. This chapter will argue that members are the life-blood of a party. As well as being an essential feature of party democracy, an active membership provides a necessary check on the powers of the politicians. We will consider the extent of membership decline in New Zealand, together with any possible explanations, before turning our attention to the likely implications of this decline for the future of party funding.

Party members and activists

There are a number of reasons why someone may wish to join and become active in a political party:

1. Sense of belonging

As with other social groups, political parties provide their members with the opportunity to be part of a community of like-minded individuals. There was a time when parties engaged in a wide range of social and recreational activities, including organised dances, outings, and weekend retreats. Although this social function has fallen victim to the more individualistic values of contemporary society, most parties still maintain a network of social groups, such as Labour's youth, Maori, women's, rainbow, Pacific Island, and regional bodies. The social activities organised by National are even more renowned. The Young Nationals' organisation, which for many years held an annual weekend retreat at Mt Ruapehu's Chateau hotel, provided an opportunity to forge friendships, debate issues, and become socialised into National party politics. Many of the party's senior officials and cabinet ministers, including Murray McCully, Michelle Boag, and Ruth Richardson, are former members of this youth division.

2. Shared beliefs

Parties perform the further important function of giving shape and purpose to the incomplete, and often incoherent, values and beliefs of their members and supporters. For some, discovering that others hold the same views may assume the importance of a religious conversion or awakening. At a reunion of the University of Auckland's Princes Street branch of the Labour party in 2000, for example, several former branch members, including Helen Clark and her cabinet colleague, Judith Tizard, described their involvement in the anti-Vietnam movement as a defining moment in their initiation into party politics. Similar accounts of a shared belief-system or ethos are frequently heard within other, notably cause, parties, including Social Credit (renamed the Democrats), ACT, and the Greens. In such parties, organised meetings provide an opportunity to converse with and draw sustenance from fellow believers.

3. Political ambition

Since New Zealand lacks any recent experience of elected Independent MPs (the sole exception since 1943 was the election of Winston Peters in the Tauranga by-election of 1993), becoming a party member is an essential prerequisite to a career in parliament. Most parties require that a candidate must have been a party member for at least a year, although this requirement can be waived at the party's discretion (see chapter 6). Nurseries for aspiring National and Labour MPs have included the aforementioned Young Nationals (Gustafson 1986b) and Labour's Princes Street branch (Godfrey 2003). While a member's political ambitions may be frustrated by the preference normally shown for incumbent MPs, office-holding experience and commitment within the party continues to be an important criterion for selection, especially within the two major parties (Miller and Karp 2004).

4. Material and psychological benefits

During the nineteenth and early twentieth centuries, it was not uncommon for parties to be able to offer material incentives to potential members. In the USA, for example, the Democratic party machine operating in Cook County, Illinois, was able to offer jobs, housing and other material benefits to those new immigrants who chose to join and become active in the party. In contrast, New Zealand's governing parties have scrupulously avoided offering direct financial incentives to their members. Indirectly, however, party members have long been beneficiaries of patronage politics. This may take the form of positions on the numerous statutory bodies to which the government is empowered to make appointments, and for which appointees may receive a stipend and expenses. Senior party officials may also receive appointment to diplomatic posts overseas (during the 1990s, for example, a former president of the National party, John Collinge, was appointed to a term as New Zealand High Commissioner to London). Another perennial source of political patronage has been the British Imperial Honours system, which has allowed parties to award titles and other distinctions (Member of the British Empire, Order of the British Empire, etc) for community and public service. Although this Imperial system was recently replaced by a New Zealand award system, the latter is no less susceptible to patronage politics. For a vast majority of party members, however, the chances of receiving some material benefit will be slight. For such people, simply rubbing shoulders with cabinet ministers and other prominent MPs at a party conference may be reason enough to be involved in politics.

A vast majority of party members are inactive, their participation being limited to the payment of an annual subscription fee and receipt of party information and other printed material. In the larger branches, members may be asked to provide assistance with fund-raising and election campaign activities, although the use of professional fund-raisers and mail-out companies makes much of that work redundant, especially in the better resourced party organisations. Partly because the most pressing demands on members are money and time, party membership is skewed towards middle-aged and elderly supporters—whereas only 1.5 per cent of those in the eighteen- to twenty-four-year age group are party members, some 5.7 per cent of those in the fifty- to fifty-nine-year age group are members, and among the sixty-plus group it is 10.8 per cent (see figure 5.1). The age profile of members is similar to that in other Western democracies and parallels the gradual decline in partisanship among the young (Dalton 2000, p. 30–1).

Why non-participation among the young?

There are at least two possible explanations for the low association of the young with politics (see figure 5.2). According to the *life cycle* argument, younger age groups have always been less inclined to join parties. Reasons may include lack of time and money, as well as low partisanship and a general indifference to voluntary work of this sort (Norris 2002a, p. 89). While the young may choose to join a sports club or students' union, or perhaps even an environmental movement, there is much less personal incentive to become associated with partisan politics. As they move into their middle and older years, however, changing personal circumstances will increase the likelihood of some form of direct political involvement (see figure 5.3). The *generational* argument, on the other hand, is based on the assumption of a gradual decline in levels of participation among successive postwar generations. In his analysis of the reasons for declining civic engagement, Robert Putnam presents data showing that the 'cohort born between 1973 and 1982 show a remarkable decline in their pattern of associability' (Putnam 2002, p. 216). He explains this decline in relation to a number of developments in the post-Vietnam War period of the 1980s and 1990s, including the decline of the peace and anti-nuclear movements, the rise of individualism and consumerism, and the impact of neo-liberalism.

Figure 5.1 Interest in politics, party membership, and activism, 2002 voters

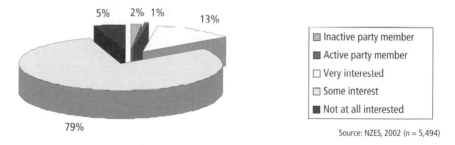

Source: NZES, 2002 (n = 5,494)

Figure 5.2 Very interested in politics by age, 2002 voters

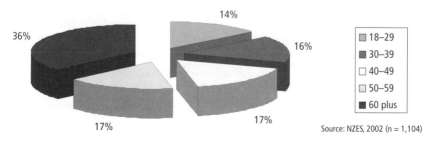

Source: NZES, 2002 (n = 1,104)

Anecdotal evidence certainly bears out the relevance of the *generational* argument in explaining the changing age profiles of most of today's political parties. During the 1960s and 1970s, the young were highly visible and vocal participants in the organisations of both major parties. At the risk of slight exaggeration, today they look more like a 'retired person's club' (Whiteley and Seyd 2002, p. 100). With the notable exception of the Greens, the minor parties have been no more successful at recruiting young members than the two established parties. It is a source of some embarrassment and concern to party officials, as illustrated by the recent efforts of a party conference organiser to get two student observers to sit at the front of the conference hall 'near the television cameras'.

Figure 5.3   Party membership by age, 2002

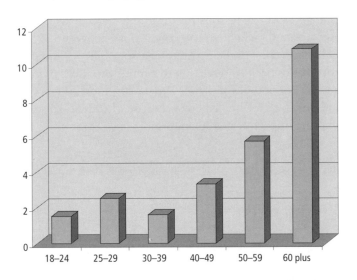

Source: NZES, 2002 (n = 4,359)

Party activism

The term 'activist' is reserved for those who are willing to become involved in a party organisation, either at the local, regional or national level, especially during election campaigns (Ware 1996, p. 67). The proportion of activists within any party is small, numbering no more than a few hundred in most of the minor parties, and 2,000 to 4,000 in the two major parties. Whereas National and Labour operate a delegate system, with the 400 to 700 who attend the annual conference having been delegated to participate on behalf of the local party members, such delegates are often simply activists who have volunteered to meet the necessary travel expenses in order to be at the conference. It is not uncommon, for example, for those attending the

National party conference as an official delegate to be the 'social companion' of a spouse or partner (Miller and Vowles 1989). In the minor parties, little or no distinction is made between the two terms—in many cases, those attending conference are unlikely to have been formally delegated by a meeting of the local party membership.

The most outstanding feature of party activism in most countries is the unmistakable pattern of decline. In their study of party activism in Britain, Seyd and Whiteley make the point that people require incentives in order to become active participants in political parties. Based on a combination of rational choice and socio-psychological approaches to participation, they argue that the incentives are much fewer and less relevant than they were a decade or more ago. They conclude that, 'Compared with 1990 members are currently less likely to feel that they influence politics, less likely to enjoy politics for its own sake, less likely to be politically ambitious, less likely to think of themselves as participants in a great social movement, and, above all, less likely to be strongly attached to the party' (2002, p. 109).

Although Labour and National continue to characterise their parties as 'broad churches', both have experienced substantial decreases in the numbers of activists since the heyday of the mass party in the 1940s, 1950s, and 1960s. During the 1980s, as a result of the pervasive influence of public choice theory, party members and activists came to be regarded with deep suspicion in the highest levels of the Labour party. According to the Finance minister, Roger Douglas, in seeking to protect their own group interests above those of the wider society, party members had contributed to New Zealand's social and economic malaise (Mulgan 1997, p. 9; Oliver 1989, p. 25). As the guardians of what some politicians regarded as the discredited Keynesian welfare state, they were viewed as obstacles to economic restructuring and social policy reform. Given the feelings of mutual distrust, it is hardly surprising that Labour lost many of its most actively committed members to small breakaway parties, especially NewLabour, a fate that also befell National during its period of radical welfare reform in the early 1990s. By the late 1990s and early 2000s, National's membership decline was the source of growing concern to party officials. However, following the party's rise in the polls under the leadership of Don Brash, many of the party's heartland electorates began to experience a sharp recovery in membership numbers, especially in seats such as Rodney, Port Waikato, Bay of Plenty, and Otago. (For further discussions on party membership trends, see chapters 1 and 4.)

Quite apart from the ideological feud within Labour in the 1980s, by adopting the role of guardians of the party ideology, members have often put themselves at odds with their political leaders, as exemplified by the tensions that exist between Tony Blair and his party's left-wing activists. The clash between the ideological commitment of members and the electoral ambitions of party leaders has come to be known as the 'law of curvilinear disparity' (May 1973). May's Law is based on the proposition that in the hierarchy of leaders, activists, and voters, the activists are the odd ones out. In May's view, since the political leaders are primarily motivated by a desire to maximise the vote, their antennae are finely tuned to the needs of the median voter. While they may pay lip service to party ideology, their views will always be broadly in line with those of the voters. In contrast, the primary motivation of party activists is to maintain the ideological purity of the party, even in the face of opposition from their leaders and the public. Indeed, their unwillingness to compromise may lead to frequent skirmishes, with the activists accusing the politicians of blatant opportunism, and the politicians responding that beliefs are all very well, but that politics is all about winning and exercising power.

While May's Law may fit the popular stereotype of party activists as the slightly odd-ball 'true believers', in New Zealand during the 1980s and 1990s the uncompromising ideologues were, in fact, the politicians (see chapter 8). This tends to be confirmed by survey data, which show that voters were significantly closer to the views of party activists on all the core issues (the economy, taxation, health, education, pensions, and so on) than of the politicians (NZES candidate, delegate and voter surveys, 1993).

Funding

The debate over party and campaign funding remains largely unresolved in New Zealand, as it does elsewhere. As part of its investigation into the merits of proportional representation, the Royal Commission on the Electoral System considered the pros and cons of state funding, whether limits should be placed on campaign spending, and what should be done about the problem of disclosure (Wallace 1986). These same issues were revisited in 2000 by parliament's MMP Review Committee as part of its inquiry into whether or not MMP should be retained. In 1995, Winston Peters introduced a private member's bill with a view to tightening existing disclosure regulations. While amendments were made to the Electoral Act the following year, disclosure laws continue to be susceptible to widespread manipulation and abuse.

Similar investigations into party funding have been conducted in Britain, the USA, Canada and elsewhere, particularly in response to public concern over rising campaign costs and the growing incidence of large, and often secret, private donations. In Britain, the Neill Committee (Neill 1998), which likened the rapid increase in campaign spending to the arms race,[3] called for spending limits and stricter rules on the disclosure of private donations. The Political Parties, Elections and Referendums Act (2000) introduced a UK£20 million limit on campaign spending and established an Electoral Commission similar to that in New Zealand to collect and monitor information on party incomes and expenditure (Butler and Kavanagh 2002, p. 18). In 2003, it began a consultation process on party funding rules with a view to setting limits on the size of donations. In the USA, where it is not uncommon for presidential candidates to grant major donors special access in the form of a private meal or game of golf, there have been many unsuccessful attempts to curb the power of big money and campaign costs. In contrast, Canada introduced spending limits and the public funding of elections in 1974, with the latter taking the form of reimbursements and tax credits for political contributions (Carty et al. 2000, pp. 137–43). More recently, there have been calls for increased regulation, including a ban on all corporate, union, and other institutional donations.[4]

Providing a backdrop for any discussion on political funding in New Zealand is the widely held belief that politicians are overpaid and underworked. In addition to a base salary of $110,000 per annum, backbench MPs are eligible for a range of allowances, including all domestic air travel, private international travel, generous living expenses, and a contributory retirement scheme. Ministers receive a significantly larger salary and allowance package, including a house in Wellington and use of a chauffeur-driven car. Although there is little evidence of widespread abuse,[5] the extent of the allowances and lack of independent monitoring help to fuel public resentment.

By the state

New Zealand has a long tradition of state involvement in the funding of campaigns and elections. Taxpayers meet all costs associated with the registration and preparation of voters, including any media campaigns to inform the public on the mechanics of the electoral system and to encourage their participation. The information function has been particularly important since the introduction of MMP and has taken the form of survey research and mass media campaigns by the Electoral Commission on such matters as proportionality, exercising the two votes, and the electoral threshold (Harris 1997). The state also bankrolls any costs incurred on polling day, including setting up booths in the 69 electorates, hiring returning officers and other staff, and counting the results.

Broadcasting allocation

More controversially, the state allocates broadcasting time and costs. At one time the process of allocating free broadcasting time was highly informal, with the final decision being left to the government. While the two major parties were generally satisfied with the outcome, since the amount of broadcasting time awarded to each side tended to be balanced, as well as extravagant by today's standards,[6] smaller parties were largely excluded from the allocation. In 1960, for example, the Social Credit Political League was given only one out of twenty-two broadcasts (Chapman et al. 1962, p. 111). In later years, while greater recognition was given to the minor parties' right to be heard, the allocation system continued to be skewed towards the interests of the two major parties.

Table 5.1   Sources of party income, 2002*

	Donations	Parliamentary Services**	Broadcasting Amount	Minutes
Labour	671,719	6,200,000	617,331	16
National	529,167	3,900,000	617,331	16
NZ First	25,000	1,600,000	166,930	10.5
ACT	88,971	1,100,000	166,930	10.5
Green	86,000	1,100,000	166,930	10.5
United Future	42,200	1,000,000	75,284	6.5
Prog. Coalition	105,000	230,000		
Alliance	10,894		100,380	8
Others			167,784	16.5
Total	**1,558,952**	**15,130,000**	**2,081,000**	

*   Totals based on 2002 election results. Figures do not include individual membership dues.
** Rounded figures based on Parliamentary Service Commission's formula on ministers', leaders' and MPs' expenses,
      party leader's funding, and funding for party group and MPs.

Source: New Zealand Electoral Commission

With the advent of MMP, the allocation of broadcasting time became the responsibility of an independent body, the newly formed Electoral Commission, although the government provided the necessary budget (unlike similar bodies involved in electoral administration in some other countries, the Electoral Commission is fully independent). Under the current legislation, the state-owned broadcasters are required to broadcast the parties' formal opening and closing addresses, although the total amount of time allocated has dropped from six hours in 1984 to one and a half hours in 2002. Any time made available by non-state broadcasters, such as TV3 and Radio Pacific, is subject to negotiation. In addition to the allocation of time, the Commission has the responsibility to provide funds, which can be used to buy advertising time on radio or television (2002 total of $2.08 million). The formula for determining allocation consists of four main requirements: whether or not the party is registered and has put forward a minimum of five electorate candidates; previous electoral support; number of MPs; and current levels of support, with the key measures being party membership numbers and opinion poll ratings (Electoral Commission 2002). In 1996, some twenty parties received broadcasting funds, although only twelve qualified for free broadcasting time. Six years later, ten parties qualified for free broadcasting time, including the small Aotearoa Legalise Cannabis, Christian Heritage, and Outdoor Recreation parties. Predictably, the small and new parties tend to feel aggrieved over the allocation, as illustrated by the objections raised to the allocation criteria by Winston Peters in 1999. Between 1996 and the pre-election period of 1999 his party had lost eight of its seventeen MPs and dropped to 3 per cent in the opinion polls. As a result, his party's allocation dropped by more than half. In 2002, the newly formed Progressive party failed to meet the criteria for funding, with the result that it was unable to run any radio or television advertisements during the campaign.

Together with partial state funding of election campaigns, spending limits have been imposed on all the candidates and registered parties. Individual candidates may spend up to a maximum of $20,000 on their own personal campaign during the three months immediately preceding an election. Registered parties are restricted to a base total of $1 million for the same three-month period, with the addition of up to $20,000 for each of the electorates in which they put up a candidate (2002 maximum $2,380,000) (Electoral Commission 2002, p. 32). These totals exclude the $20,000 maximum allowed for individual candidates, as well as the broadcasting allocation of funds made available by the state and other specified expenses, such as the cost of party polling and any travelling expenses incurred by the party leader and other candidates in the course of the campaign (Electoral Commission 2002, p. 32). Of course, candidates and parties are not limited in what they can spend outside the three-month pre-election period. Unregistered parties face no restrictions on what they can spend.

Parliamentary funding

Between elections, the state also meets the parliamentary parties' research, administrative, travel (averaging $21,000 per MP for domestic air travel in 2003, and $8,300 per partner or spouse, as well as an average of $7,540 on taxis), and electorate costs (see table 5.1). Because the line of demarcation between legitimate parliamentary activity and party organisational activity is frequently blurred, having access to these resources gives parliamentary parties a distinct financial advantage over their non-parliamentary rivals. Extra-parliamentary business being conducted in the parliamentary offices of the party leader and MPs, and parliamentary and constituency employees being deployed to assist with the party's organisational and campaign activities are but two examples of the overlap that exists between a party's organisational and political functions.[7] Although the parties are required to conduct their fund-raising and membership functions in separate offices outside of parliament's precincts, this has not always happened, as illustrated by the activities of the Alliance's Electoral Liaison Unit and the ACT party's use of electorate agents to work in parliament as researchers and press officers (see chapter 4).

The absence of clear guidelines on the use of parliamentary budgets allowed several parties to execute an extraordinary taxpayer-funded advertising blitz in 2003 and 2004. Huge campaign-style billboards began to appear throughout the country. In 2003, National's included a picture of the party leader and the words 'One standard of citizenship for all of us'. Beneath a picture of the Auckland skyline were the party's web address and the parliamentary logo. Although the New Zealand First leader refused to disclose the funding source of his party's billboards, they appeared at approximately the same time as those of National. Alongside a picture of Winston Peters was a list of the three policies on which he conducted his 2002 election campaign: immigration; law and order; and Treaty settlements. United Future's Peter Dunne used his parliamentary budget on full-page advertisements in all the major daily newspapers. Accompanying 'United Future. We Bring Something Else to the Party: Common Sense' was a full account of the party's achievements in government, together with pictures of the leader and his fellow MPs. Had the party chosen to advertise for new members it would have been required to contribute to the advertisement's cost.[8] Instead, it simply asked readers to forward their contact details in the event that they wished to either join the mailing list or receive information on the party's policies.

In February 2004, the new National party leader, Don Brash, used state funds to help pay for a nationwide advertising campaign alleging that the Labour-led government's policies were based on a commitment to 'racial separatism'. In June, the party made further use of state funds in a campaign against the government's proposed Foreshore and Seabed legislation. A full-page advertisement in the first section of the *New Zealand Herald* was entitled 'What Labour doesn't want you to find in the Foreshore and Seabed Bill'. It encouraged readers to make a submission opposing the legislation.[9] The National leader revealed that the party had spent a total of $221,643 of its state-funded parliamentary allocation on advertising during the 2003–04 financial year.[10] Labour and New Zealand First refused to disclose how much they had spent on advertising during the same period.

Party donations
As well as receiving substantial funding from the state, parties look to party members and supporters, as well as individual and institutional donors. Membership fees are small, ranging from an unspecified donation in the case of National, to a maximum of $11 for waged members of Labour ($6.60

unwaged). Several of the minor parties charge an annual fee of $5, and none charge more than $10. Thus, while members are encouraged to make additional donations, the major proportion of a party's income is likely to come from wealthy individuals, business corporations, and interest groups.

Although parties may receive donations from any source, they are required to provide the Electoral Commission with the names of all those who donated over $1,000 to an individual candidate and $10,000 to a registered party. There are no restrictions on the size or source of donations. While parties must list all anonymous donations over $10,000, they are not required to supply the Commission with the donors' names. Anonymous donations now exceed those of named donors in a number of parties, including ACT and Labour. Unlike Scotland, where there has been bitter debate between the Labour government and the Scottish Nationalists on the question of overseas donations, particularly over the sizeable donations being given to the Scottish Nationalists by an expatriate actor, Sean Connery, New Zealand places no restrictions on overseas donors—indeed, in recent times some of the largest donations have come from wealthy New Zealanders living overseas.

Table 5.2   Declared party donations, 1996,* 1999, and 2002

	Lab	Nat	NZF	ACT	Alliance
Known					
1996	39,342	156,805	90,878	62,500	62,060
1999	356,356	1,213,558	66,383	30,273	240,552
2002	291,669	329,117	25,000	38,971	10,894
Anonymous					
1996	225,000	13,621	6,300	290,000	–
1999	824,375	375,000	–	809,950	14,000
2002	380,050	200,050	–	50,000	–
Total					
1996	264,342	170,426	97,178	352,500	62,060
1999	1,180,731	1,588,558	66,383	840,223	254,552
2002	671,719	529,167	25,000	88,971	10,894

*   Disclosure regime did not come into force until 1 April 1996.

Source: New Zealand Electoral Commission

Given the opportunities for concealment, it is hardly surprising that some parties show little regard for the principles of transparency and accountability. For example, with the disclosure regime not coming into effect until 1 April 1996, several parties ensured that major donations were received in advance, as illustrated by National's receipt of a donation of $250,000 from the merchant bankers, Fay Richwhite, in March 1996 (Electoral Commission, Press Release, 17 May 2002). By so doing, it was able to reduce its declared income to a mere $170, 400, well short of the reported figure of $3 million.[11] As well as organising their affairs in advance, some parties also set up blind trusts through which anonymous donations could be filtered. In 1999, for example, National's New Zealand Free Enterprise Trust collected some $570,000 in donations towards the party's election campaign. Although ACT's declared donations in 1996 were $352,500 (see table 5.3), the party reportedly received donations totalling $2.8 million.[12] Much of its funding was channelled through trusts.[13]

Table 5.3 Campaign spending by registered parties, 1996, 1999, and 2002

	1996	*1999*	*2002*
Labour	1,946,000	2,462,000	2,089,000
National	2,909,000	3,682,000	1,668,000
NZ First	1,662,000	565,000	454,000
ACT	2,100,000	1,105,000	1,792,000
Alliance	1,349,000	1,224,000	215,000
Green	–	374,000	765,000
United (Future)	290,000	120,000	169,000
Prog. Coalition	–	–	271,000
Others	1,183,000	881,000	592,000
Total	**11,439,000**	**10,413,000**	**10,124,000**

Source: New Zealand Electoral Commission

While a number of donors, including the ANZ Bank, Natural Gas Corporation, Deloitte Touche Tohmatsu, and Westpac Trust, give to more than one party, perhaps partly to hedge their bets, but also to avoid accusations of favouritism, others are unapologetically partisan. Among Labour's declared backers in 1999 were the Engineers' Union, Lion Breweries, and, somewhat controversially, TV3 Network Services. Despite concerns within the party over the increase in anonymous donations, prior to the 2002 election the party received four anonymous donations of $50,000 or more. In 1999, National received substantial donations from Brierley Investments and businessmen Sir Roger Bhatnagar and Barry Brill.[14] Three years later, the party received sizeable donations from two trusts—$64,000 from the Holland Memorial Trust and $123,000 from the Waitemata Trust.[15] Although all of ACT's donations were received anonymously, known donors include Douglas Myers and Alan Gibbs, both residents of the United Kingdom, and property magnate Michael Friedlander.[16]

In 2002, the declared income of all the main parties was significantly lower than in 1999 and 1996 (see table 5.3). How can this be explained? Clearly the timing of the early election caught several of the opposition parties by surprise, leaving little time to raise funds. The inevitability of a Labour victory also made the traditional sources of business donations less receptive to appeals for help from National and ACT. The National president, Michelle Boag, had close links with several of the party's most important donors, including Sir Michael Fay and David Richwhite, and National was able to call on a number of proven fund-raisers, including a former Finance minister, Bill Birch. However, their impact was blunted by the size of the party's $300,000 debt and poor performance in the polls. They also found that business opinion on the leadership and policy priorities of National's Bill English was lukewarm at best.

Labour was uncharacteristically well placed to take advantage of National's difficulties, although most of its support was to come from small and medium-sized businesses rather than the ones that traditionally supported National and ACT. The party president, Mike Williams, regarded himself as an assiduous fund-raiser, who even scanned the newspapers for the names and contact details of prospective donors. One such contact included a wealthy American immigrant who had settled in Marlborough and who, on being approached by Williams, promptly donated $10,000.[17] Having secured more funding than any other party, Labour was able to launch an expensive advertising blitz in the final week of the campaign. This said, the total amount of Labour's corporate donations in 2002 was well short of that targeted by officials, with the result that the party organisation was left with a sizeable campaign debt to repay before fund-raising began for the 2005 election.

In contrast to Labour, National and ACT, the minor parties receive relatively few institutional donations. Apart from 1999, when it was widely expected to be in government, the Alliance has attracted little money from business or the unions. New Zealand First and the Greens are opposed to anonymous donations, but may also refuse known donations if they are deemed to be in conflict with the two parties' principles and policies. Most of New Zealand First's donors are from medium-sized, owner-operator businesses and are personal supporters of Winston Peters. In the first instance, the New Zealand First leader may be invited to attend a social event, such as a dinner party. Most of the prospective donors come from New Zealand First's natural constituency, being strongly nationalistic, angry, especially over high business taxes and compliancy costs, and not inclined to want things in return for their support. Party officials then follow up on those social contacts with requests for donations.

The Greens rely more heavily than the other parties on the small donations provided by party members and supporters, as well as the tithes provided from MPs' salaries. In 2002, 70 per cent of the party's total budget came from the electorates. In addition, six companies made unsolicited donations totalling $32,000. A cheque for $3,000 from a mining company was returned, and a further offer of $15,000 from a gambling organisation was declined.[18]

Arguments for state funding

Concern over the potential for abuse in any funding system that includes private donations has resulted in calls for full public funding of parties and campaigns. The case for state funding is built on the following four main arguments.

1. Cost

Given the frequency of elections in New Zealand and the pervasiveness of the new technology, campaigns are becoming too expensive for most political parties, leading to excessive dependence on large private donors and the prospect of substantial debts having to be carried over from one election cycle to the next. The decline in the number of grassroots members, coupled with the competitive pressure to make greater use of professional services, such as mail-delivery companies, polling and focus-group agencies, computer specialists, public relations and advertising firms, and so on, have increased the financial pressures on all parties. Party organisations also face rising costs in advertising production and dissemination, including billboards, commercial slots on television and radio, and in the major daily newspapers. While these trends have been discernible for decades, under MMP the pressures on available resources have intensified. Whereas parties could once concentrate their energies on a few key marginal electorates, under MMP they are also required to run a nationwide campaign for the party vote. Advocates of public funding adopt the view that only the state can ensure that all parties receive sufficient funding to execute a modern campaign. By receiving adequate funding, the parties will also be better able to devote greater attention to policy research and development, thereby helping to create a more informed electorate. Finally, it is argued that state control offers the best chance of achieving effective limits on the amount of money that is spent on election campaigns.

2. Fairness

Private funding benefits those political parties that have access to wealthy institutional and individual donations. It is no coincidence that the parties most strongly opposed to full state funding are those with a business-friendly policy agenda, notably National and ACT. Labour is also in a position of being able to supplement its union income with substantial business donations, especially during its periods in government (see tables 5.2 and 5.3). In contrast, most of the minor parties, including New Zealand First and the Greens, both of which enjoy a level of support at least equal to that of ACT, receive few donations, and mostly of small amounts. Non parliamentary parties are in an even weaker position, being forced to rely almost exclusively on the subscriptions and donations of their members. Supporters of full state funding argue that the campaign budget could be carved up to the benefit of all parties, including those emerging parties that lacked either a track record of success or a network of institutional support.

3. Transparency

The issue that resonates most strongly with the voting public is that of anonymous donations. Regardless of the way they vote, New Zealand electors are overwhelmingly of the view that political parties should be forced to disclose the sources of their donations (see figure 5.4). Prior to 1996, parliamentary candidates, but not parties, were required to disclose all sources of income. When the Royal Commission on the Electoral System considered the issue as part of its review of party finance, it recommended that candidates and parties be required to disclose the sources of all major donations, arguing that it would 'provide healthy confirmation that political parties are not dominated by big business, trade unions or overseas interests' (Wallace 1986, p. 188). The issue received wide public attention when, shortly before the 1990 election, a TVNZ Frontline programme entitled 'For the Public

Figure 5.4   Parties should disclose sources of their income, 2002 voters

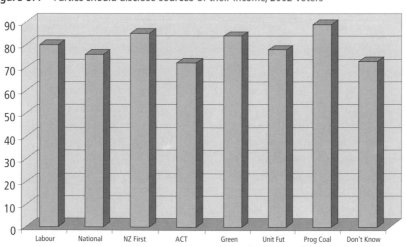

Source: NZES 2002 (n = 5,888)

Good' alleged that the Labour government was receiving anonymous dona-tions in return for political favours.[19] While the claims were found to be false, the public continued to be sceptical of the relationship between parties and their wealthy donors. A *National Business Review* poll conducted two years later found that 90 per cent of respondents believed that all donations should be publicly declared. It also found that some 57 per cent supported a com-plete ban on business donations.[20] As the results of figure 5.4 show, ten years later public opinion remains firm on the issue.

In contrast to public opinion, elite opinion on the issue is divided along party lines, with National and ACT and, to a lesser extent, United Future candidates opposing public disclosure, and the candidates for the other par-ties supporting it (see figure 5.5).

Figure 5.5 Parties should disclose sources of their income, 2002 candidates

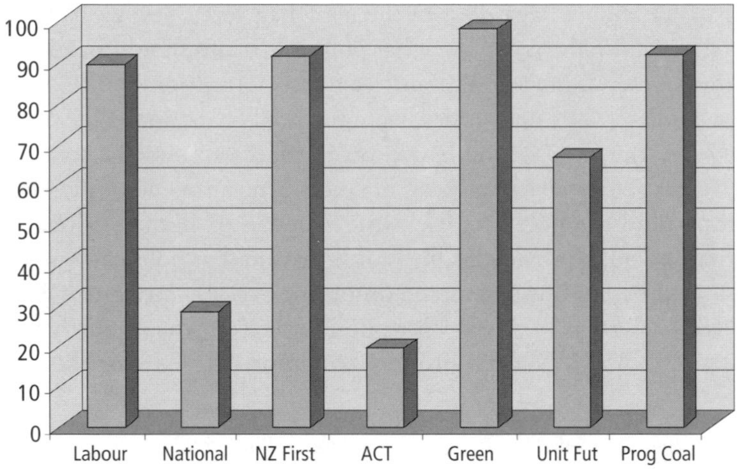

Source: NZES 2002 (n = 308)

4. Accountability

Since parties are not required to reveal their sources, and may indeed use 'filter' organisations to provide a further guarantee of anonymity, they are not well placed to refute the widely held claim that money buys political influ-ence. While there may be no evidence of a direct link between the two, perceptions are important, as illustrated by the British public's cynical response to Labour's decision to exempt Formula 1 from the ban on cigarette sponsorship around the time the party received a UK£1 million donation from the sport's chief executive, Bernie Ecclestone. Supporters of state fund-ing argue that the credibility of the democratic process is dependent upon a clear line of demarcation being maintained between political parties and their funding sources, be they wealthy individuals, corporations, or trade unions.

Arguments against state funding

1. Cost

Opponents of public funding reject the claim that the state is better placed to both limit campaign costs and improve public knowledge of the parties and their policies. Indeed, they argue that state funding will inevitably result in an increase in administrative and monitoring costs and do nothing to prevent overspending, as illustrated by the abuse of the funds currently being administered by the Parliamentary Service Commission. If spending limits are what is required, they can be achieved as effectively in the predominantly private funding regime as in a fully state-funded one, an argument supported by the data in table 5.3, which shows that overall campaign spending remained largely static in the period 1996 to 2002.

2. Fairness

Regardless of whether the funding is private or public, it is impossible to allocate resources across the entire party system without being accused of unfairness. Besides, what is fair about a system that fails to reward a party's hard work and initiative in raising its own finances? Because they will have a guaranteed source of income under a fully state-funded system, parties will further neglect their members and other stakeholders (Carty et al. 2000; Thomas 2000). In the view of the Royal Commission on the Electoral System, 'if parties no longer have a need to solicit funds from the public, the overall political process may stagnate and the natural growth and decline of political parties may be inhibited' (Wallace 1986, p. 211).

3. Transparency

Supporters of private funding concede that the scale of anonymous donations may arouse suspicions, but ask for evidence of a smoking gun. Contrary to public perceptions, they argue, there is no evidence in New Zealand of sleaze, let alone corruption. If money buys influence, as is alleged, then why has the pool of institutional donors, such as the unions and major businesses, been getting smaller rather than larger? Besides, as the examples of Italy and the USA patently show, state funding does not prevent financial scandals and corrupt practices (Thomas 2000).

4. Accountability

Finally, opponents of state funding argue that self-regulation, together with the Electoral Commission's reporting system on party income and expenditure, are sufficiently rigorous tests of accountability to allay any public concern. Should there be any need for yet another independent watchdog, then the government could explore the possibility of setting up an anti-corruption commission. Such an initiative would not be dependent on a fully state-funded system, however.

Conclusion

A number of conclusions can be drawn from this examination of party membership and funding. Since the size of a party's membership is an important guide to its health as a democratic institution, ways need to be found to make participation more meaningful. As will be discussed in future chapters, 'high-intensity' participation is best served through involving members in important decisions, such as leadership and candidate selection and policy-making, as well as in the running of election campaigns (Whiteley and Seyd 2002, p. 214). Also, as Pippa Norris has observed, parties could do more to restore the social networks and firm political convictions that once engendered in members a sense of purpose and belonging (2002a, p. 219). Engaging the young is likely to be a particularly difficult task, although the success of the 2004 US Democratic presidential contender, Howard Dean, in mobilising tens of thousands of young activists through his grassroots Internet campaign may provide a model for other parties to follow.

Despite attempts to address the issue of party funding, a number of problems remain. Changes that need to be made include the following.

1. Disclosure

In the interests of transparency and good governance, and in accordance with the wishes of a vast majority of voters, parties should be required to reveal in full the sources of all donations of $1,000 or more. This would prevent parties from either organising their affairs well in advance of an election campaign or setting up blind trusts through which anonymous donations could be filtered without detection.

2. State funding

While the move towards state funding seems inexorable, there is a danger that full state funding would remove one of the few remaining functions of party membership. To both preserve a membership culture and prevent parties from becoming complacent, state funding should be based on a dollar-for-dollar matching formula, with each party being eligible for a level of state funding equal to the total received from membership fees and donations.

3. Use of state funds for campaigning, party staffing, and administrative resources, etc.

There needs to be a full review of parliamentary budgets with a view to preventing the extensive use of parliamentary resources to finance the administrative, staffing, advertising and campaigning costs of the political parties. In other words, a clear line needs to be drawn between the parliamentary and party organisational functions.

4. MPs' allowances and entitlements

These should not be monitored and administered by the politicians, either directly or indirectly, but by an independent body, preferably the Remuneration Authority (formerly the Higher Salaries Commission). This would include such matters as the setting and overseeing of air travel costs.

5. Broadcasting allocation

In line with the recommendation of the recently retired chief executive of the Electoral Commission, Paul Harris, restrictions on broadcast advertising should be lifted, thereby allowing parties to spend up to their election limit, irrespective of size or how recently formed.[21]

Notes

1   The term 'cash-for-access' was coined in relation to Labour government advisers using their access to ministers to secure personal benefits. The 'cash-for-questions' scandal involved questions being asked in the Commons by Conservative MPs on behalf of known party donors.
2   P. Preston, *The Guardian*, 24 April 2000, p. 16.
3   D. Campbell, 'New Rules on Party Funding', *The (Glasgow) Herald*, 14 October 1998.
4   *The Globe and Mail* (Toronto), 2 December 2002.
5   One recent instance of abuse concerned an Alliance minister, Phillida Bunkle, who claimed an out-of-Wellington housing allowance while a resident of the capital. She was subsequently relieved of her ministerial responsibilities.
6   In 1960, for example, the two major parties received a total of 21 radio broadcasts. Of these, seven were scheduled to last for two hours (Chapman et al. 1962, pp. 110).
7   These problems are not unique to New Zealand. In Britain in late 2003, for example, a former Conservative party leader, Ian Duncan Smith, was found to have been paying his wife UK£18,000 per annum as his part-time diary secretary. According to staff, she was rarely seen at work.
8   Peter Dunne, personal interview, 16 July 2003, Wellington.
9   *New Zealand Herald*, 29 June 2004, p. A13.
10   'National opens up on ad spending', *New Zealand Herald*, 30 June 2004, p. A6.
11   F. O'Sullivan and V. Small, 'The Cost of Democracy', *New Zealand Herald*, 29–30 June 2002.
12   *Sunday Star Times*, 22 April 2001.
13   F. O'Sullivan and V. Small, 'The Cost of Democracy', *New Zealand Herald*, 29–30 June 2002.

14   *New Zealand Herald*, 12 May 2000.
15   G. Vaughan, 'What Sort of Business', *The Independent*, 20 August 2003.
16   F. O'Sullivan and V. Small, 'The Cost of Democracy', *New Zealand Herald*, 29–30 June 2002.
17   M. Williams, personal interview, 8 August 2003, Auckland.
18   Rod Donald, personal interview, 15 July 2003, Wellington.
19   *The Dominion*, 30 April 1990.
20   NBR-Mattingly Poll, *National Business Review*, 19 June 1992.
21   K. Taylor, 'Single Body for Elections Suggested', *New Zealand Herald*, 15 January 2004.

Further reading

Electoral Commission 2002, *The New Zealand Electoral Compendium*, 3rd edition, Electoral Commission, Wellington.

May, J.D. 1973, 'Opinion Structure of Political Parties: The Special Law of Curvilinear Disparity', *Political Studies*, 21, pp. 135–51.

Neill, Lord 1998, *Standards in Public Life: The Funding of Political Parties in the United Kingdom*, Stationery Office, London.

Norris, P. 2002, *Democratic Phoenix: Reinventing Political Activism*, Cambridge University Press, Cambridge.

Seyd, P. and P. Whiteley 2002, *New Labour's Grassroots: The Transformation of the Labour Party Membership*, Palgrave/MacMillan, Basingstoke, Hampshire.

Thomas, G.P. 2000, 'Should political parties be funded by the state?', in L. Robins and B. Jones (eds), *Debates in British Politics Today*, Manchester University Press, Manchester, pp. 158–72.

Wallace, J. (Chair) 1986, *Towards a Better Democracy: Report of the [New Zealand] Royal Commission on the Electoral System*, Government Printer, Wellington.

Selecting Candidates

6

OF the expected outcomes of MMP, a change in the way candidates are selected was always considered among the most important. Whereas the personal qualities required of candidates changed with the times, selection methods have long been resistant to reform. With the advent of MMP, especially the introduction of a new type of MP, the list member, it became necessary to rewrite the electoral and party rules on candidate selection. On an informal level, each party also had to decide what role its list candidates would play, especially with regard to campaigning and constituency-based representation.

In its report, the Royal Commission on the Electoral System had expressed a wish that party lists be 'constructed in a democratic way with genuine involvement by the party's membership' (Wallace 1986, p. 68). Borrowing from the German experience of proportional representation (PR), it suggested either a vote by party members or of delegates to a party convention (p. 239). This was endorsed by the Electoral Act (1993), which stipulated that registered parties must follow 'democratic procedures in candidate selection' (1993, p. 46). In a similar vein, Britain's Independent Commission on the

Voting System warned that public disapproval could be expected of any voting system that presupposed the power of party machines (Jenkins 1998, p. 2).

Despite the persuasiveness of the democratic argument, there were equally strong grounds for retaining a selection process that was essentially 'private and internal' (Denver 1988, p. 47). According to one line of argument, the democratic imperative had to be balanced against the need for fair representation. Unless party elites retained ultimate control, it was argued, improvements in gender and ethnic representation would be more difficult to achieve. The same rationale was applied to the protection of incumbents and the recruitment of candidates with particular qualifications and abilities. By so doing, the parties were able to defend the retention of selection mechanisms that were both highly centralised and restrictive.

In her study of legislative recruitment in advanced democracies, Norris identifies a number of 'filters' that help to determine selection outcomes. The filtering process can be quite complex, and is said to include 'party service, formal qualifications, legislative experience, speaking abilities, financial resources, political connections, name-recognition, group networks, organisational skills, ambition for office or incumbency status' (1997, p. 6). Among the filters to be explored in this chapter are the legal requirements for running for office, the official party rules, and the informal methods by which candidates are chosen for electorate and party list seats. Drawing on data from the New Zealand Election Study, it will report on the attitudes of parliamentary candidates and voters to these and other filters. Finally, the chapter will consider candidate recruitment in other countries and explore alternative methods for making the selection process more democratic and transparent.

Recruitment process

There are three formal influences on the selection of candidates: the legal system; the electoral system (which has been extensively discussed elsewhere); and the party system (Norris 1997). Unlike the more demanding legal requirements found in some countries, such as Norway, Finland, and the USA, where voters are afforded the right to participate in the selection process by way of direct primaries, there has been no attempt to legally enforce that provision in the Electoral Act requiring parties to uphold democratic selection procedures. The only other legally binding stipulation is that every candidate must be registered on the electoral role and hold New Zealand citizenship. The latter was considered to be something of a non-issue until it tripped up a United Future MP in 2002. Despite being a New Zealand resident of some six years standing, Kelly Chal failed to apply for citizenship until after being elected. The Electoral Office accepted her explanation that she had not intended to break the law when she failed to respond to the affirmation of citizenship on the candidate consent form, instead stating that she had been a New Zealand resident since 1994. When her ineligibility to be an MP was discovered, Ms Chal was forced to give up her seat and was replaced by Paul Adams, the next person on the United Future list.

As well as these legal provisions, a nominee's eligibility to stand for office is also subject to certain internal party rules. All parties have a membership requirement of up to one year, although it may be waived in the event that an outstanding candidate becomes available. Labour candidates are also required to sign a pledge to 'vote on all questions in accordance with the decisions of the Caucus of the Parliamentary Labour Party' (Labour Party Constitution, 2002). The Alliance is the only party to stipulate that candidates sign a loyalty pledge promising to resign in the event that they leave the party. The issue reached parliament's Privileges Committee following the 1997 decision of an Alliance list MP, Alamein Kopu, to leave the party but remain in parliament. The Committee's ruling that the Alliance's pledge was unenforceable resulted in the introduction by Labour of the Electoral Integrity Bill (2001),[1] which required that party defectors resign their seats.

In his study of candidate selection in twenty-four democratic countries, Ranney explores three dimensions to candidate selection: centralisation; inclusiveness; and the degree of participation (1981, pp. 75–106). Centralisation typically involves a mixture of local or regional involvement, but with party headquarters exercising ultimate control over all selection decisions. The inclusiveness dimension covers three basic levels of participation: party activists; financial members; and the voting public. As for measuring participation, some parties endorse the indirect method, which involves the use of delegates, who vote either in committees, selection meetings, or conventions. Alternatively, parties may use the direct method of conducting primaries or postal ballots among party members, activists, or supporters.

Prior to the introduction of MMP, selection procedures in New Zealand varied from the centralised to the partially inclusive. Whereas parties of the left tolerated a high degree of central control, right-wing parties generally ran a devolved selection process, with the final decision being in the hands of delegates representing local party members. In 1992, an attempt by National's senior officials to promote the claims of a former All Black captain, David Kirk, as Robert Muldoon's successor in the seat of Tamaki was famously rebuffed. National's former leader, Jim Bolger, was similarly unsuccessful in his efforts to persuade delegates throughout the country to select more women candidates.

Pre-selection

Something that has always distinguished candidate selection in New Zealand from that of many other countries, including Canada and Britain, is the absence of a formal pre-selection stage involving head office and culminating in the creation of a list of approved candidates. In New Zealand, any vetting of prospective nominees has tended to be *ad hoc* and informal. However, in recent years the parties have had second thoughts about pre-selection, particularly following the defection of a number of 'party-hopping' MPs and revelations concerning the private lives of some candidates, notably the previously undisclosed criminal convictions of a Labour minister, Dover Samuels. In 2001, the Labour party amended its rules to read 'The New Zealand Council shall have authority to withdraw the nomination of any candidate who fails to honour the terms of the Pledge or whose candidate's biographical statement includes information that is inaccurate or misleading in any material respect or omits significant relevant material'. The Pledge included a declaration concerning previous criminal convictions, including dates and the nature of any offences.[2]

In 2003, National introduced the concept of a 'candidates' college' with a view to recruiting and training prospective parliamentary candidates. Leading party officials, including the president, together with a small number of MPs, were given the task of identifying and mentoring potential parliamentarians, not only from inside the party, but also among members of the wider community. Initial preparation would include getting suitable candidates involved in party and local community activities, providing training in campaigning and use of the media, and developing the skills required of a successful legislator. While selection to the college is no guarantee of a safe seat or a high place on the party list, it does help to create a sense of professionalism and exclusivity. At the same time that it formed the candidates' college, National decided to reserve five places on the party's list for those who, by virtue of their prominence, preferred not to have their candidacy disclosed until close to the election. An example of a prominent citizen whose candidacy was not publicised in advance was the former Governor of the Reserve Bank, Dr Don Brash, in 2002. Another public figure approached with a view to standing on the 2005 party list was the chairman of the Business Roundtable, Rob McLeod.[3]

Although less high-powered, Labour's candidate training workshops prepare potential parliamentary and local body candidates with information on what makes a good candidate and campaigner, an analysis of the functions and influence of an election campaign, and the development of inter-personal and public speaking skills. The latter includes instruction on extempore speaking and how to handle questions from the media and members of the public. But the workshop also gives some basic training in the work of a legislator, with particular reference to conducting business in a party caucus or select committee.

Electorate selection

The electorate selection process has remained largely the same as that under the former electoral system. In the case of Labour, while the selection meeting is open to financial members, the final selection is made by a committee comprising up to three local representatives, one of whom is elected by members attending the selection meeting, and three from head office. Because the Labour Electorate Committee and/or local membership may be insufficiently strong to achieve their three-vote entitlement, and given that the head office representatives may include the leader or deputy leader and party president, it is relatively easy to see how the collective will of the leadership can be brought to bear on the local organisation. In the event of a tied vote, the final decision is in the hands of the party's central decision-making body, the New Zealand Council. In defending this level of influence over the selection outcome, the party leadership has been inclined to shape its arguments around the claims of ideological purity and coherency, as well as social solidarity and internal party discipline. In recent years this argument has been bolstered by an appeal to fair representation, particularly with respect to women and ethnic minorities—party officials have been able to point to the success of the top-down method in selecting candidates from hitherto underrepresented groups within the community, including trade unionists, Maori and, since 1993, Pacific Islanders.

Figure 6.1 Electorate selection

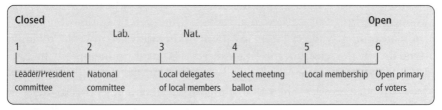

Note: Since the minor parties currently hold only 3 of the 69 electorate seats, and most contests attract limited competition for selection, they have not been included in this figure.

Fair representation has also been an overriding concern of the Alliance, which initially sought to accommodate its diverse support base by apportioning the electorates among its five constituent parties. Prospective electorate candidates had to be nominated into a candidate pool. To become eligible to contest an electorate they had to receive 75 per cent support from members of the National Council. Prior to the dismantling of its loose multiparty structure, the final choice of candidate was made by selection panels that included representatives of all the constituent parties. As with Labour, some weight was given to the results of a floor vote of all eligible party members in attendance at the selection meeting. While there is little or no competition for the candidacy in most electorate seats, by-election contests have always been an exception. At the 1992 Tamaki by-election, for example, the candidacy was expected to go to the Greens, who had polled well in the seat at the previous general election. Instead the selection panel opted for a Democrat, Chris Leitch, a decision that may have cost the Alliance the seat.

On the right, National has managed to maintain a relatively inclusive constituency selection process. Although head office retains the right to veto any decision made by the local constituency, it does so only on procedural grounds or if the candidate's personal history is likely to prove embarrassing to the party. In all other respects, the selection process remains in the hands of the local electorate and its voting delegates, who number one for every fifteen financial members (Gustafson 1997, p. 143). Incumbent MPs are generally well placed to influence, if not control, the process of choosing delegates, with the result that their re-selection is all but guaranteed. This said, in 2002 there were allegations of indirect interference by head office (specifically the party president, Michelle Boag) in the de-selection of certain 'old-guard' MPs, notably the long-serving Brian Neeson (Helensville) and Warren Kyd (Hunua) in favour of a young banker, John Key,[4] and a lawyer, Judith Collins. Boag's somewhat ingenuous reply to the accusation of head office interference was that the party simply wanted to demonstrate that it had a number of 'diverse and talented candidates'.[5]

ACT operates a similar electorate selection method to that of National, although the Board of Trustees maintains a Candidates Register of potential candidates and may intervene at any point in the selection process. Providing attendance at the selection meeting exceeds 100 paid-up members, the candidate is chosen by a vote of all members of at least three months' standing. If the attendance is less than that number, the Board reserves the right to make the final decision. A variation to this process occurred at the Taranaki-King Country by-election in 1998, when the Board issued a ballot paper to all voters in the electorate, requesting that they decide which of four nominees should become the ACT candidate. This attempt at an open primary was characterised by ACT's opponents as simply an 'expensive stunt'.[6] The results of the ballot were not made public and were treated as indicative, with the final decision being made by the Board of Trustees. In 2002, the Board made an even more controversial decision when it prevented a list MP, Rodney Hide, from mounting a serious challenge in the National-held electorate of Epsom, one of the ACT's strongest seats.

Defying all logic based on the left–right dimension, candidate selection in the small personality-driven parties, such as New Zealand First (see below), has tended to be conducted by and in the interests of the party leader. While a handful of seats may attract more than one candidate, such is the smallness of the field of available candidates in minor parties that it is not unusual for a vast majority of nominations to be unchallenged. In 2002 it was only the personal influence of the party leaders that made it possible for the Progressive and United Future parties to find sufficient numbers of volunteers to contest all sixty-nine electorate seats (the Progressives managed to find sixty-one candidates, and United Future sixty-three).

List selection

In PR systems that include party lists, the list selection process often moves from the highly centralised pre-selection stage to a more open and democratic selection of candidates. In New Zealand, on the other hand, the list selection process moves in the opposite direction. While most parties have opted for a delegate-based list selection system, the all-important ranking process is firmly in the hands of national moderating committees. This allows the parties to determine the selection outcome in a number of important ways. For the Alliance, for instance, a centralised ranking system enabled it to use quotas to both address its equity obligations and ensure that each of its former constituent parties had a reasonable chance of being represented in parliament. But it also allowed the party to make important trade-offs between the constituent parties, as occurred in 1996 when the Alliance president and NewLabour activist, Matt McCarten, attempted to secure the seventh spot on the party's list. In the face of strong opposition from the Greens, McCarten agreed to step aside on the understanding that a prominent media personality and Auckland mayoral candidate, Pam Corkery, would occupy that position on the list.

Labour's list selection process is a mixture of local and regional influence, together with a strong measure of central control. Regional conferences are assigned the task of compiling and ranking regional lists. Through an exhaustive ballot system, delegates choose the number of candidates allocated to that region by headquarters. On completion of this process, a Moderating Committee comes up with an overall ranking that reflects the party's commitment to affirmative action in preference to the less palatable fixed quotas (Street 1997, p. 151). Through this process, the party hierarchy is able to control the final outcome in a number of significant ways. Because of the sheer scale of incumbency in 2002, severe limits had to be placed on the number of high list positions reserved for new and talented candidates. All of the top 35 list rankings were filled by incumbent MPs—indeed, the first non-MP was Dave Hereora, who was ranked at 38. The 'Father of the House' and parliament's Speaker, Jonathan Hunt, was ranked third on Labour's list. This was to compensate Hunt for his having lost through merger a seat in West Auckland he had occupied for some thirty years. In an attempt to ensure that significant numbers of women and ethnic minorities represented the party in parliament, fifteen women, six Maori and two Pacific Islanders were placed in the top thirty-five. The party constitution lays down that the leader and deputy leader, both of whom are on the Moderating Committee, will occupy the top spots on the list. The overall influence of the party leader should not be underestimated, and is illustrated by the high ranking enjoyed by Clark supporters on the 1996, 1999, and 2002 party lists.

Figure 6.2 List selection

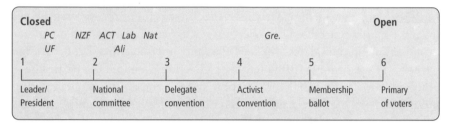

National's list selection process is similar to that of Labour, with initial responsibility for nominating regional lists residing with electorate and regional committees, culminating in a conference of each of the party's divisions. A List Standing Committee ranks the final list. While rejecting extensive use of the party list to redress its imbalance in gender and ethnic representation, National did manage to include one Maori, one Asian, and three women among its four list MPs in 2002. Protection was offered to incumbent MPs in close electorate contests, although the party's poor result made the list a less useful safety net than it had been in 1996 and 1999 (all ten defeated National MPs were too low on the list to be saved). In contrast to the inclusion of an outsider, Don Brash, at number five on the list, National's hierarchy put pressure on two ministers and senior list MPs, John Luxton and Max Bradford, to step aside in favour of some new candidates, including Hekia Parata (ranked fifteen) and Allan Peachey (eighteen). Because of the expected influx of new MPs at the 2005 election, National was able to offer attractive list rankings to a number of new and former candidates. However, the party decided to restrict the number of list-only candidates to five (including Brash). Two groups long neglected by National, women and Maori, were earmarked by Brash for high places on the list.

In contrast to the 'embarrassment of riches' confronting National and Labour, New Zealand First tried to overcome the problems associated with its small pool of available talent by requiring that all list candidates contest an electorate seat. The party also tried to create political experience by luring former and incumbent MPs away from the major parties. Between 1993 and 1996 it was able to attract one Labour and two National MPs into its ranks, partly by the leader's use of patronage politics to make policy commitments to transfer their allegiance to New Zealand First. One such deal involved the National MPs Peter Laws and Peter McCardle. The latter switched parties before the 1996 election on the understanding that his scheme to force the unemployed back into work, which had been rejected by National, be adopted by New Zealand First. In 2002 the party recruited a former National MP, Dail Jones, to a high position on its list.

Unlike Labour and National, the minor parties initially had few incumbents to protect. As a result, they were well placed to adopt a more open and democratic list selection process than the established parties. Any such opportunity was immediately squandered, however, with most adopting selection methods that were even more centralised than those of the major parties. The ultimate in centralised control was achieved by the New Zealand First leader, Winston Peters, when, in 1996, he and a close political adviser are said to have personally ranked the entire New Zealand First list (Laws 1998, p. 342). Their intervention produced a number of surprises, including the demotion of prominent candidates who had dared to disagree with Peters (e.g. Terry Heffernan) and the dramatic promotion of several relatively unknown supporters (e.g. Deborah Morris). Three years later the leadership controversially dropped two women MPs, Robyn McDonald and Jenny Bloxham, to numbers twenty and twenty-two on the list. As the party has matured, selection decisions have followed more orthodox principles, with the rankings being closely monitored by a selection committee.

Centralised coordination and control also characterises the list selection and ranking process adopted by the ACT, United Future and Progressive parties. Although ACT gives each party member the opportunity to nominate and rank a party list, 'the results of the ballot shall...be indicative only to the Board and shall not compel the Board to name any particular potential candidate on the list or at any particular place on it but shall merely provide an opportunity for the participation of the wider party membership in the selection of candidates and their ranking on the list' (ACT Constitution and Rules, May 1998). With the possible exception of New Zealand First, ACT has been the party least likely to offer full protection to incumbents, with Owen Jennings (12) and Penny Webster (13) being dropped below the cut-off point for election on the party list in 2002, and with Donna Awatere-Huata also under threat of demotion until late in the list selection process.

Adopting the same list selection process as its precursor, United New Zealand, the United Future party charges its Board with the power to collate and rank the final list, although party members are encouraged to submit an indicative list. For all practical purposes, however, the final list ranking takes place under the attentive eye of its leader, Peter Dunne. Because the Jim Anderton Progressive Coalition (later abbreviated to the Progressives) was not formed until three weeks before the 2002 election announcement, there was little opportunity to develop a candidate selection process. The party's Executive appointed a six-person list committee, including Anderton, which quickly came up with a rank-ordered list of sixty-one candidates, beginning with the four MPs that had broken away from the Alliance (Sandra Lee announced her retirement from parliament, so was not included). Although the Democrats later broke away from the new party, their two MPs, Grant Gillon and John Wright, were ranked at numbers three and four on the Progressive Coalition list.

The solitary exception to the centralised and somewhat obtuse list rank-ing methods adopted by the other political parties were the Greens, although even they adopted a form of 'guided' democracy with a view to both offering protection to incumbents and promoting their long-held commitment to regional, gender, and ethnic equity. The first stage in the process is to com-pile a list of potential candidates, all of whom are vetted to ensure that they comply with the electoral and party rules. The party's Executive and pool of potential candidates then vote preferentially, a process which involves the dis-tribution of their lists and rankings to the membership of the party. In this way, the party leadership is able to offer clear direction to members, who are free to adopt or modify their lists.

The 2001 conference of the Green party in Auckland provided an ideal opportunity to distribute biographical and other details of each candidate and to allow members the opportunity to meet prospective candidates and discuss aspects of the selection process with the party leadership. While there were some discrepancies between the overall ranking of members and those of the Executive and pool of candidates, the rank ordering of the latter groups tended to prevail. Finally, a selection committee cast an eye over the members' list with a view to ensuring that there was some balance regionally, ethnically, and in terms of gender. While the committee could make minor adjustments within a pre-set level of tolerance, this proved to be unnecessary in 2002. The final list had five women in the top ten rankings and ten in the top twenty. Although the party has not been successful in attracting significant support among Maori voters, five of the top thirty positions went to Maori candidates. All seven MPs elected in 1999 were given the top seven rankings in 2002, beginning with the co-leaders Jeanette Fitzsimons and Rod Donald.

Attitudes among candidates and voters

Drawing on the findings of the New Zealand Election Study (NZES) post-election postal surveys between 1996 and 2002,[7] it is possible to report on the attitudes of parliamentary candidates and voters to the changes in selection methods that occurred with the adoption of MMP. Voters were canvassed on who should decide the party list rankings. It is also useful to consider any changes over time in the perceptions of voters as to the way list MPs handle their jobs. But the NZES also surveyed opinion among parliamentary candidates on pre-selection, the extent to which selection methods are democratic and efficient, and whose responsibility it should be to rank the candidate lists.

As we will see in chapter 10, the public's approval of list MPs jumped dramatically in the three elections following the introduction of MMP. After some initial concern that list MPs had no mandate, no constituents, and little purpose beyond protecting their ranking on the party list, public judgments swung in the direction of being either positive or neutral. That said, respondents were clearly of the view that the voting public, not the parties, should decide which list candidates should win seats (see table 6.1). While this response may reflect a preference for open over closed lists, equally it may suggest a desire for something approximating a primary system in which voters rank their preferred party's list.

Table 6.1   Voters should decide which list candidates win seats (voters)

	1999 (%)	2002 (%)
Agree	57	56
Neutral	18	21
Disagree	15	15
Don't know	10	8
Total	**100**	**100**
	n = 4,896	n = 4,526

Source: NZES 1999, 2002

On the question of whether greater attention should be given to establishing a pre-selection process, the response of list-only candidates proved to be the most favourable (see table 6.2), perhaps reflecting either a failure on the part of their party to give sufficient attention to the pre-selection stage or disappointment that their particular strengths had not been fully appreciated. Although caution should be exercised in drawing conclusions based on the

Table 6.2   Support for a pre-selection process (candidates)

	1999		2002	
	Yes (%)	No (%)	Yes (%)	No (%)
List-only candidates	61	39	63	37
Electorate-only	45	55	41	59
List/Electorate	45	56	47	54
		n = 235		n = 246

Source: NZES 1999, 2002

small numbers of respondents per party, support for an improvement in pre-selection was strongest among the New Zealand First and ACT candidates, and weakest among those representing National and the Greens. The concern of New Zealand First is understandable, given the lack of political experience and loyalty under pressure of several of its MPs during the time it was in government between 1996 and 1998.[8]

While the candidates' faith in the democratic nature of their party's list ranking process is adequate but not strong, with the Greens being the only candidates to give their party anything approaching unqualified endorsement, the most significant change in attitudes between 1999 and 2002 was the declining confidence of National party candidates in the openness and efficiency of the list selection process. Given that the party's selection methods had not changed in the intervening years, the 2002 result may have something to do with the controversy over the de-selection or forced retirement of some long-time MPs, including Messrs Bradford, Luxton, Kyd, and Neeson. Overall, it can be said that as the candidates gained experience with MMP, their faith in the efficiency and straightforwardness of list selection began to grow.

Table 6.3 Candidate attitudes to drawing up of party lists, 1996–2002

	Per cent agreeing							
	Democratic		Complicated			Efficient		
	*1999	2002	1996	1999	2002	1996	1999	2002
Labour	60	57	23	30	31	50	41	50
National	65	42	19	35	21	61	43	29
Alliance	49	57	48	40	13	24	29	56
NZ First	52	67	25	35	8	23	28	67
ACT	51	59	14	16	24	76	51	63
Green	94	88	–	18	27	–	57	35
United Future	–	49	–	–	3	–	–	54
Prog. Coalition	–	47	–	–	6	–	–	47

Note: Question in 1996 was on 'fairness' of the process rather than how democratic.

Source: NZES 1996–2002

Given that those questioned in our surveys had successfully completed the selection process, it is perhaps hardly surprising that relatively few found the leader's influence over the ranking process to be excessive (see table 6.4). Most preferred committee decisions to those made by conference delegates or activists, even when it came to ranking the party lists (see table 6.5). Only the Greens saw a place for party members. Unlike voters, a vast majority of candidates had no use for primaries or open lists.

Table 6.4 Candidate attitudes to central versus local influence over party lists, 1996–2002

	Per cent agreeing					
	Leaders influence excessive			Local influence inadequate		
	1996	1999	2002	1996	1999	2002
Labour	16	32	35	21	23	23
National	22	30	41	16	23	18
Alliance	50	52	31	60	37	26
NZ First	22	35	25	41	35	27
ACT	15	35	26	20	40	15
Green	–	6	9	–	4	15
United Future	–	–	8	–	–	13
Prog. Coalition	–	–	24	–	–	32

Source: NZES 1996–2002

Qualities expected of candidates

What personal qualities and prior experience are considered important for a list or electorate candidate? Drawing on the NZES 2002 candidate data, we will discuss the relevance of a number of 'filters' in the selection process, specifically a parliamentary candidate's educational qualifications, work experience, community and party service, and campaign skills.

1. Personal qualifications

Before the dramatic growth in the availability of higher education in the 1960s and 1970s, few politicians had attended university or received a professional qualification. It was frequently said of the Labour party, for example, that the lack of qualified lawyers among its MPs made the position of Attorney-General a potentially fraught appointment for any incoming Labour government. Neither of the two prime ministers of the time, Keith Holyoake (1957 and 1960–72) and Norman Kirk (1972–74), had attended high school, and the number of university-educated ministers in their cabinets could be counted on the fingers of one hand. By 2002, in contrast, some 74 per cent of parliamentary candidates across all parties had attended a university or other tertiary institution, and 54 per cent held degrees (Miller 2004, p. 95). In the two main parties the proportions with degrees were even higher (Labour 63 per cent and National 71 per cent).

During the 1960s and 1970s the most highly represented occupations in New Zealand parliaments were farmers (30 per cent of all MPs and 50 per cent of National MPs), small business proprietors (20 per cent), and professionals (20 per cent) (Martin 2004, p. 265). By 2002 the professional and management occupations had come to dominate. In contrast, only 4 per cent of candidates were from the farming sector (Miller 2004, p. 96). A decline in the number of unionised manual workers was being observed as far back as the 1960s, but by 2002 they were less than 6 per cent of all candidates.

2. Party and community service

Consistent with the findings in other countries, party service is a valuable, though not necessarily essential, form of preparation for political office. As McAllister found in his study of candidate selection in Australia, for example, prior party involvement gives prospective candidates the opportunity to become familiar with the relevant people and policies, as well as demonstrating a commitment to public and community service (1997, p. 27). In New Zealand, prior party service is deemed to be more important for electorate candidates than for those on the party lists; major parties than minor parties; and parties of the left than those of the right. In the case of the Labour party, for example, prior experience in the party is considered almost essential to becoming a candidate, with almost three out of every four candidates having held party office at the local level (Miller 2004, p. 91). Unlike National and several of the minor parties, Labour has avoided recruiting prominent candidates with no previous record of party membership or involvement (a Don Brash, for example). Whereas 48 per cent of the list MPs across all parties had held local party office prior to being elected, some 88 per cent of electorate MPs could claim such experience.

Even more important than party service for aspiring candidates, however, is a proven track record of involvement in the community. Parliamentary candidates across all parties, and especially elected MPs, typically have extensive links with a wide range of organised groups, including occupational and public sector (e.g. Federated Farmers, Chambers of Commerce), public interest (e.g. Greenpeace, World Vision), and community groups (e.g. Waipareira Trust and local parent–teacher associations). While candidates for the minor parties are likely to have had relatively limited and tenuous connections with their party organisations, their record of holding office within the community is much more impressive, as illustrated by the wide network of contacts established by candidates for the Green and United Future parties (Miller 2004, p. 94).

3. Campaign skills

Despite the more 'presidential' nature of the modern campaign, with very little opportunity for individual candidates to 'strut their stuff', there is a growing expectation within party organisations that candidates should be taught some basic campaigning skills, especially in their dealings with the local media organisations. Among the abilities recognised by the candidates themselves, the personal qualities of enthusiasm, hard work, and maintaining a high profile in the electorate are deemed to be the most important. In contrast to the high expectations placed on electorate candidates, list candidates are seen to play a much more ambiguous role—they are not expected to play a major part in the local campaign, nor is it clear what their role should be in the national, leader-focused campaign.

In fact, very few voters now have any direct contact with either the local electorate candidates or the list candidates in their area. This partly reflects the decline of the campaign meeting as a forum for presenting the candidate and the message, but also the displacement of traditional forms of door-to-door contact with the mass mail-out of party propaganda, often by professional companies (see chapter 9). As a result, in 2002 only 20 per cent of voters had any contact with a candidate or other member of a political party during the course of the campaign (Miller 2004, p. 97).

Conclusion

It has been the contention of this chapter that the parties missed the opportunity provided by the advent of MMP to make their candidate selection procedures more open and democratic. Although the Electoral Act stipulates that party members and/or delegates will participate in the selection process (1993, p. 46), the influence of grassroots members has fallen well short of what some scholars were predicting (see, for example, Scarrow 2000, p. 100). While party activists may be called upon to nominate list candidates at the local or regional level, apart from the Greens the all-important ranking process is conducted by a national board or central committee, an approach to decision-making aptly summed up by Peter Dunne as 'the New Zealand way'.[9] Parties of the centre-left argue that the high level of central control over both list and electorate selection mechanisms offers the best chance of fair representation. Those of the centre-right, on the other hand, are inclined to adopt the meritocratic argument. In the end, most parties have chosen to adopt an approach to candidate selection that is best described as 'centrally determined yet decentralised' (Denver 1988, p. 48).

An alternative approach for the selection of electorate candidates, and one that is likely to have a positive effect on levels of party membership, is the one-member-one-vote (OMOV) method found in the party systems of Britain, parts of Europe, and Canada. While it may threaten the stranglehold currently enjoyed by incumbents, OMOV can be adapted in such a way as to provide the party leadership with an accurate guide to grassroots opinion. While OMOV may take the form of a postal vote of all local members, equally it can be limited to those in attendance at a candidate selection meeting. Introducing a more rigorous pre-selection stage, such as that found in the Scottish party system, would provide an important brake on the power

Table 6.5   Candidate attitudes to who should rank party list, 1999–2002

	Per cent agreeing									
	Leaders		Committee		Activists		Members		Voters	
	1999	2002	1999	2002	1999	2002	1999	2002	1999	2002
Labour	6	9	69	81	8	0	15	6	2	4
National	12	24	67	64	2	3	12	6	7	3
Alliance	13	5	57	68	15	8	13	17	2	0
NZ First	12	25	58	42	4	0	4	17	23	17
ACT	15	18	54	53	0	25	24	4	5	–
Green	2	8	8	31	6	8	82	49	2	4
United Fut.	–	46	–	36	–	3	–	10	–	5
Prog. Coal.	–	8	–	75	–	0	–	11	–	6

Source: NZES 1999, 2002

of party members. As well as ensuring that nominees comply with the party's rules, as typically happens in New Zealand, pre-selection can be used as a filter to ensure that approved candidates have shown evidence of integrity, reliability (including party loyalty and service), and effectiveness (as a potential representative and legislator).

Critics of OMOV argue that it prevents parties from achieving fair representation. This argument is based on the unproven assumption that grassroots members are less committed to gender parity and increased ethnic representation than party elites. A solution experimented with elsewhere is to *pair* or *twin* electorates, with one electorate selecting a woman candidate, the other a man (although the legality of all-female lists has been challenged in the British courts). An example of this would be to twin, say, the similarly marginal seats of Hamilton East and Hamilton West. If the selected Labour candidate in the first of these selection contests happens to be a male, then the paired seat is required to select a female. As long as there are separate Maori seats, ethnicity may not be a major issue, although it would be possible to pair seats with large Pacific Island populations to ensure that at least one Pacific candidate emerged from those two seats. In the event that National, ACT, and New Zealand First get their way, and the seven Maori seats are abolished, the same twinning could take place in seats with significant numbers of Maori voters, thereby ensuring that, in areas such as South and West Auckland and parts of Wellington, Maori candidates could be selected in winnable Maori seats.

Despite its undoubted impact on the major parties, democratising the electorate selection process leaves the smaller, predominantly list, parties largely unaffected. Combating centralised list-ranking practices can take at least three practical forms: regional and/or national conventions (perhaps the party's annual conference), at which delegates meet and rank the party list; balloting all paid-up members, a system widely used in parties with small memberships, such as the Scottish Liberal Democrats and New Zealand Greens; and the adoption of open rather than closed party lists. To ensure some protection is offered to incumbents and to achieve gender and ethnic targets, the party leadership can follow the Green party model and circulate an indicative list (better that the views of the leadership are non-binding than those of the membership).

An alternative approach would be to impose the *zipping* method on voting delegates and/or members (for example, every second place on the list goes to a woman and every fourth place goes to an ethnic minority candidate). As well as helping to achieve gender and ethnic equity, zipping can be used to ensure balanced regional representation. The open list solution is more straightforward and democratic in that it satisfies voter demands for the final say over which candidates go on to represent the party in parliament. Parliament's MMP Review Committee considered but rejected this option on practical grounds, including the problem of dual candidates, although it recognised that regional lists held some appeal (Hunt 2001, p. 52). However persuasive the open lists argument is to parties such as United Future, it fails to address the major problem confronting the modern political party, that is, how to make party membership and activism more meaningful and attractive.

Notes

1 The 'party-hopping' provision in the Electoral Integrity Act (2001) was not invoked in the highly publicised defections from their parties of Jim Anderton and his Alliance allies in 2002, and Tariana Turia (Labour) in 2004. A long-running dispute between Donna Awatere-Huata and the ACT party culminated in a Supreme Court ruling in November 2004 that the renegade MP had distorted the proportionality of parliament. The Speaker of the House then declared her seat vacant, whereupon the next candidate on ACT's list was sworn in as the party's new MP.

2 Mike Smith, general secretary, New Zealand Labour party, personal correspondence, 23 October 2001.

3 H. Tunnah, 'Wanted—new Brash-pack MPs', *New Zealand Herald*, 9 July 2004, p. A6.

4 John Key was a former head of an international banking division of Merrill Lynch. In a small 27-person caucus, he quickly rose to become finance spokesman.

5 *New Zealand Herald*, 18 March 2002, p. A3.

6 *New Zealand Herald*, 3 March 1998.

7 Background information about the New Zealand Election Study Programme, including the mass and candidate surveys, is available at http://www.nzes.org.
8 Between 1996 and 1998, eight of New Zealand First's 17 MPs defected from the party, mainly to become independents.
9 Peter Dunne, personal interview, Bowen House, Wellington, 3 July 2001.

Further reading

Gallagher, M. and M. Marsh (eds) 1988, *Candidate Selection in Comparative Perspective: The Secret Garden of Politics*, Sage, London.

McLeay, E. 2003, 'Representation, Selection, Election: The 2002 Parliament', in J. Boston, S. Church, S. Levine, E. McLeay and N.S. Roberts (eds), *New Zealand Votes: The General Election of 2002*, Victoria University Press, Wellington, pp. 283–308.

Miller, R. 2004, 'Who Stood for Office and Why? in J. Vowles, P. Aimer, S. Banducci, J. Karp and R. Miller (eds), *Voters' Veto: The 2002 Election in New Zealand and the Consolidation of Minority Government*, Auckland University Press, Auckland, pp. 85–103.

Norris, P. (ed.) 1997, *Passages to Power: Legislative Recruitment in Advanced Democracies*, Cambridge University Press, Cambridge.

Ranney, A. 1981, 'Candidate Selection', in D. Butler et al. (eds), *Democracy at the Polls: A Comparative Study of Competitive National Elections*, American Enterprise Institute, Washington D.C., pp. 75–106.

Salmond, R. 2003, 'Choosing Candidates: Labour and National in 2002', in J. Boston, S. Church, S. Levine, E. McLeay and N.S. Roberts (eds), *New Zealand Votes: The General Election of 2002*, Victoria University Press, Wellington, pp. 192–208.

Choosing and
Assessing Leaders

7

O NE of the most fascinating, if elusive, questions in the study of politics concerns the qualities of a successful leader. While it is relatively easy to name great leaders, with Mahatma Gandhi, Winston Churchill, John F. Kennedy, and Nelson Mandela being obvious examples, a more challenging task is to identify those characteristics that distinguish success from mere ordinariness or failure. The burgeoning interest in leadership reflects a number of international trends, including the decline of ideology (to be discussed in chapter 8) and the emergence of a more 'presidential' style of politics. In New Zealand, the recent advent of personality-based parties has helped to personalise politics to a degree where leadership is frequently elevated above the more established influences of policy, practice, and belief.

New Zealanders ought to know their leaders well. In a small and intimate society with a unitary system of government and a limited number of news outlets, the attention devoted to party leaders is both unrelenting and pervasive, reaching every nook and cranny of the national community. This ready public access to prominent politicians helps explain why feelings of familiarity can so easily degenerate into disparagement and open contempt. Populist sentiment demands that the country's prime minister be accessible and adopt the lifestyle of ordinary voters, as illustrated by 'Kiwi Keith' Holyoake's personal intervention in helping a railway traveller find some missing luggage, David Lange's well-known preference for fast food outlets, and the decisions of Sir Robert Muldoon and Helen Clark to have their home numbers listed in the Auckland telephone directory (a practice shared with the archetypal New Zealander, Sir Edmund Hillary).

Despite this tradition of accessibility, practiced modesty, and quaint egalitarianism, comparatively little is known about the functions and expected qualities of our political leaders. Strong central control over the selection of party leaders, together with the absence of a presidential voting system, have meant that the comparative qualities of party leaders are not subject to the same degree of public scrutiny that prevails in presidential democracies, especially the USA. Paradoxically, precisely because New Zealand is a parliamentary rather than a presidential system, its leaders are largely shielded from pressure to make their private lives public or to become the paramount citizen who personifies the highest values and aspirations of the nation. Together with the absence of any tradition of 'civics' teaching in our schools (on the mistaken assumption that political education is unnecessary) and the dearth of in-depth comparative analysis, these cultural and institutional conventions help to explain why relatively little is known about what motivates New Zealand's political leaders and representatives, or, more basic still, what they actually do.

The focus of this chapter will be on assessing the role of party leaders. Central to the particular characteristics of each party's leader are the formal and informal rules of leadership selection. With one or two notable exceptions, New Zealand's party elites have been able to resist the trend in a number of countries, including the United States, Canada, and Britain, towards greater grassroots participation in the selection of party leaders. To help measure the qualities that make leaders successful, the analysis will draw on public attitudes towards our major political figures, as measured by opinion polls and the New Zealand Election Study. After considering a range of approaches to the study of leadership, the discussion will propose a leadership typology for New Zealand.

Choosing leaders

In Western democracies, leadership selection follows one of (or some combination of) the following four methods:
1   by the party's parliamentary caucus
2   by a conference of party activists or delegates
3   by a ballot of all party members
4   by a ballot of all party identifiers or members of the general voting public (American primary system).

During the past two decades the trend internationally has been towards greater participation by party activists, supporters, and members, with the most preferred option being a ballot of party members (Hayward and Whitehorn 1991, p. 3). An obvious motivation for these reforms has been the need to revive the public's interest in joining and supporting political parties. According to a British Labour party report entitled *Partnership into Power*, moving to one-member-one-vote was intended to 'give more opportunities for a bigger cross-section of party members to get involved in the party processes and debates…' (quoted in Seyd and Whiteley 2002, p. 20). But democratic contests may have a number of other uses, including breaking up the monopolistic power of entrenched party factions, such as trade unions or the ideological left.

The American primary system, with its state-by-state 'beauty contests' or mini-elections, is on one end of the participatory model, although some states continue to restrict the vote to those attending party caucuses. Canada's parties, which traditionally used special conferences or conventions to elect their leaders, have been moving in the direction of one-member-one-vote (OMOV). An extreme example of this was Canada's Alliance party (now merged with the Progressive Conservatives), which even allowed candidates to subscribe new members during the course of the leadership campaign. According to Preston Manning, in one contest between the incumbent leader, Manning, and the successful challenger, Stockwell Day, the party's membership rose to 250,000, only to drop back to 70,000 by the end of the year.[1] To preserve a measure of influence by the parliamentary elite, the British Conservative and Liberal Democrat parties introduced a two-step selection process, with the MPs nominating a slate of leadership candidates and party members making the final decision. The British Labour party, on the other hand, convenes an electoral college in which the vote is split evenly between three sections of the party—MPs, union members, and constituency members. The Scottish National party (SNP), which is that country's main opposition party, moved from a vote of conference delegates to OMOV in 2003. At its next leadership contest, in September 2004, the party's 8,209 members were given the opportunity to vote in a three-way contest. To avoid the destabilising effects of any last-minute membership drive by the leadership aspirants, the SNP denied a vote to any new members joining the party after the start of the leadership campaign. Some 80 per cent of members participated in a postal ballot, electing Alex Salmond and Nicola Sturgeon as the party's new leader and deputy leader respectively.[2] As we will see, in retaining the oldest selection method, that of granting their MPs the exclusive right to choose, New Zealand's parties (along with the Australian federal Liberal and Labor parties) have managed to buck the international trend.

Choosing a party leader is a product of two broad requirements: the formal leadership selection rules laid down in each party's constitution; and any informal considerations that may be factored into the final decision. The formal rules may include when the leadership contest will take place—that is, whether there are fixed times for re-election (such as at the party's annual conference) or if they can happen at any time (a common occurrence in parties in which the parliamentary caucus gets to choose). The informal process often includes upholding certain conventions, such as always choosing someone with extensive parliamentary experience. However, it may also reflect the particular needs of the party at any given time, including the need to project a more youthful, metropolitan or media-savvy image, or to have a leader who is prepared to change the focus of the party's ideology or electoral appeal.

Formal requirements

Most New Zealand parties give their MPs the exclusive right to choose a leader, with a simple majority being the sole requirement. While individual MPs may consult their grassroots supporters, there is no formal provision for the participation of members or activists. In the case of Labour, this has resulted in some tight contests, with Bill Rowling repelling Lange's challenge in 1980 by a single vote (presumably his own), and Clark defeating Mike Moore by a similarly narrow margin of only 'four or five' in 1993 (Edwards 2001, p. 229). The unsuccessful informal bid by five senior MPs to persuade Clark to step down before the 1996 election (Edwards 2001, p. 247) is illustrative of the frequently cavalier attitude towards due process and accountability within Labour. In the case of National, the speed and stealth with which some leadership coups have been mounted suggests a similarly centralised and largely non-consultative process. For example, the thwarted attempt to replace Muldoon in 1980 and the defeat of Jim Bolger by Jenny Shipley in 1997 were hatched by small groups of MPs at a time when the two prime ministers were overseas. In 1986, Jim McLay refused to accept the signatures of a majority of his MPs requesting his resignation. Despite the opposition of party officials, the National caucus proceeded to replace him with Bolger (Gustafson 1986b, p. 163). In 2003, National's Don Brash won the leadership in a caucus vote of 14 to 12.[3]

With the notable exception of the Greens, who put the choice of leader to a vote of delegates attending the party's annual conference, the minor parliamentary parties largely replicate the selection procedures of Labour and National. New Zealand First's constitution gives its caucus the sole power to select the leader and deputy leader. Had there been a challenge to Winston Peters' leadership during the period 1999 to 2002, the decision is likely to have been made by the five-member caucus, which would have included the incumbent leader and deputy leader. The United Future party also gives its caucus the authority to choose the leader and deputy, in consultation with the party's Board. At the time of the party's formation in 2000, Peter Dunne and the Future New Zealand (formerly the Christian Democrats) leader, Anthony Walton, agreed informally that Dunne should become the leader and Walton the deputy leader. As Dunne himself has acknowledged, the decision was reached in the MP's parliamentary office.[4]

In the tradition of the corporate sector it claims to represent, the ACT party initially left the appointment of leader and deputy leader to its Board, which was empowered to make changes 'when it considers it appropriate so to determine' (ACT New Zealand 'Constitution and Rules' 1998, Section 12.1). However, on the first occasion the leader was replaced (following the 1996 decision of its founding leader, Roger Douglas, to step down), the Board sought the approval of the party's annual conference before confirming its choice of Richard Prebble. When Prebble retired as leader in 2004, the Board made the appointment on the recommendation of the eight-member parliamentary caucus (reduced from nine following the expulsion of Donna Awatere-Huata). The party also conducted an indicative vote (referred to as a 'primary') among its members. While it was intended that the results of the poll would be confidential to the party's caucus, it was later reported that Rodney Hide received 54 per cent of the popular vote to Stephen Franks' 46 per cent.[5] Following intense debate, the caucus recommended by a one-vote majority that the Board confirm Hide as leader (four[6] of the seven eligible caucus members had been contestants for the leadership).

Informal requirements

Among the most important informal requirements for any aspiring leader of a major party are: a proven track record of loyal service to the party organisation; substantial parliamentary experience; and an ability to earn the respect and support of the parliamentary caucus.

a. Age

Since leaders tend to retire or be replaced in opposition rather than in government, the timing of a candidate's bid for the top job is crucial, as illustrated by the tenures as party leader of two transitional figures, Labour's Arnold Nordmeyer (1963–65) and National's Jack Marshall (1972–74). Both had served long apprenticeships under their predecessors—Walter Nash (1951–63) and Keith Holyoake (1957–72)—before being elevated to the leadership. However, their age (sixty-two and sixty years of age respectively) and extensive parliamentary experience (twenty-six years in each case) proved to be liabilities, not assets. At forty-two, Nordmeyer's successor, Norman Kirk, represented a new generation of Labour leaders, and Robert Muldoon offered a vitality and aggression that were in stark contrast to the leadership style of 'gentleman Jack' Marshall.

Although Labour's eleven party leaders from Harry Holland (1918–33) to Helen Clark (1993–) averaged fifty-one years of age on assuming the leadership, there is a clear split between the first five (Holland, Savage, Fraser,

Nash, and Nordmeyer) and the second six (Kirk, Rowling, Lange, Palmer, Moore, and Clark), with the average age of the first group being fifty-nine years, and the second forty-three. Nash, for example, became leader at sixty-eight and stepped down with considerable reluctance upon turning eighty-one. In contrast, Lange was only forty when he became leader, and Moore forty-one. The age profile of National's ten incoming leaders follows a similar pattern, although the overall average of fifty-one years is somewhat lower than that for Labour, resulting from the unusually rapid turnover of National's recent leaders, with McLay, Shipley, and English averaging a mere three years in office. McLay and English were only thirty-nine years of age when they assumed the leadership. At sixty-three, English's successor, Don Brash, was the oldest incoming National party leader.

b. Political experience

The leaders of the two major parties have averaged 13.5 years in parliament at the time of their appointment. Although few of the early leaders had previous ministerial experience (Labour took nearly twenty years to gain power), typically they had given long service to the organisational and parliamentary wings of the party. Savage, for example, had been an MP for fourteen years when he became Labour leader in 1933. With the exception of Brash (sixteen months) and Lange, who had spent only six years in parliament and had no prior ministerial experience, all recent leaders have had significant legislative and executive experience. Despite his young age, Jim McLay had been an MP for nine years and was a minister for six (Attorney-General, minister of Justice, and briefly deputy prime minister) when he replaced Muldoon as party leader in 1984. He had also held many senior positions within the party organisation and was the party's deputy leader. Helen Clark's apprenticeship was even more extensive. As a young activist she had held positions at all levels in the party organisation, including the national executive. In addition to her twelve years in parliament, she had wide-ranging cabinet experience that included the portfolios of Health, Housing, Labour, and Conservation.

c. Regional and occupational backgrounds

As a party with its roots in the countryside and provincial towns, it is hardly surprising that National has shown a preference for leaders from its heartland South Island (Hamilton, Holland, Shipley, English) and rural North Island electorates (Holyoake and Bolger). National's 'country party' image has been reinforced by the fact that, prior to the election of Brash, a former banker and professional economist, its previous three leaders had been farmers (although Shipley had a background in teaching and English had been a Wellington-based public servant).[7] Indeed, in close to forty-three years in power, National has produced only one prime minister from Auckland (Muldoon 1975–84), a city with one-third of the country's population. Recognition of this weakness contributed to the move to replace English with Brash, an Auckland-based list member. Where possible, the party has tried to achieve an urban-rural and/or North Island–South Island balance between its leader and deputy leader, as illustrated by Brash's endorsement of Nick Smith, then Gerry Brownlee, as his deputy leader. Both MPs represented South Island electorates.

Whereas Labour's early leaders were from heavily unionised manual occupations (the first three were union officials) in the industrial enclaves of Wellington (Fraser and Nash) and the South Island's West Coast (Holland), recent leaders have been members of the professional middle class. Despite being a transitional figure, Arnold Nordmeyer, a Presbyterian minister, was the first of Labour's university-educated leaders (as well as being its first New Zealand-born leader). Later leaders included a secondary school teacher (Rowling), two lawyers (Lange and Palmer), and a university Politics lecturer (Clark).[8] Only Kirk and Mike Moore (one a stationary engine driver, the other a printer) shared the occupational roots of the early leaders and a vast majority of the party's supporters. While it may be an exaggeration to suggest that Labour deliberately courts politicians from the professional class, the evidence confirms that, as in social democratic parties elsewhere, it is the university-educated professionals who rise to the most senior positions of political power.

d. Ideological requirements

No doubt reflecting the pragmatic thrust of New Zealand politics, as well as the fact that most of the leadership changes have occurred during periods in opposition, a potential leader's ideology is of less importance than the range of skills that may be brought to an election campaign. There have been exceptions—Harry Holland and the early Savage, for example, were part of a radical political tradition that was not sullied by the experiences of government, and Clark's appeal to Labour's grassroots supporters in 1993 was enhanced by the perception that she was a critic of the fourth Labour government's monetary reforms. As a general rule, however, both parliamentary caucuses have preferred those candidates who occupy the largely non-ideological middle ground. This said, there is little doubt that National's preference for Muldoon over Marshall, and Labour's for Lange over Rowling, had less to do with where each politician stood on the ideological spectrum than with the conviction that one was better equipped than the other to lead the party to electoral success. Similarly, the decisions to replace Palmer with Moore and Bolger with Shipley were driven by practical, not ideological, considerations. While those National MPs who voted to replace English (a moderate) with Brash (a monetarist) were perfectly aware of the beliefs of each candidate, their primary motivation was not ideological, but practical—that is, choosing a leader capable of reversing the party's steep slide in the polls.

Assessing political leaders

A number of different approaches have been taken to the study of leadership, with some adopting the tools of psychoanalysis, while others have looked for more contextual and functional explanations. The broad range of approaches can be summarised thus:

1 *Single-actor narratives*—These provide the most common approach to the study of leadership. Single-actor studies typically provide a biographical account of the subject's life and times, together with an analysis of the overall contribution made both nationally and internationally. Among the most impressive examples of research in this genre are the Roy Jenkins' studies of Asquith (1964) and Churchill (2001), and Arthur Schlesinger's biography of Robert Kennedy (1978).

2 *Use of prototypes*—By constructing profiles of the careers of some early political leaders, exponents of this approach are able to create leadership models that can be applied to all succeeding generations of politicians. Examples of this method include James McGregor Burns' study (1965) of the American presidency, which was responsible for the creation of the 'Madisonian', 'Jeffersonian' and 'Hamiltonian' prototypes. A more modest attempt to apply the same approach to the study of British prime ministers (specifically Margaret Thatcher) produced a typology based on the careers of four leaders: Gladstone, Salisbury, and the two Chamberlains (Joseph and Neville) (Clarke 1991, 1992).

3 *Cyclical typologies*—These are based on the assumption that history repeats itself, and that different social, economic, and political conditions require contrasting styles of political leadership. In his study of the leadership of Thatcher, Dennis Kavanagh (1987) distinguishes between the mobilising and the reconciling styles of leadership in British politics, with the former having greater appeal in times of national crisis or when policies do not appear to be working, and the latter when there is a need to restore social order and harmony.

4 *Psychoanalytic method*—This approach is most controversially associated with the psycho-biographical studies of significant but flawed politicians, notably Woodrow Wilson (George and George 1956; Freud and Bullitt 1967), Richard Nixon (Mazlish 1972), and the Australian leader, Bob Hawke (Anson 1991). It is based on the assumption that, to properly understand political behaviour, it is necessary to pry into oft-repressed and unconscious psychological conflicts. The overriding objective of this developmental approach is to relate the subject's childhood and adolescent experiences to adult predispositions, values, and attitudes. James David Barber applies aspects of the psychoanalytic method in his study of American presidents (1972). His taxonomy measures both the amount of energy a leader devotes to the job (the active–passive dimension) and

the level of personal satisfaction derived (positive–negative). Barber claims to be able to use the typology to both analyse and predict political behaviour. A similar, if less rigorous, study of American women legislators by Jeane Kirkpatrick (1974) proposes a typology based on four legislative styles—the leader, the personaliser, the moraliser, and the problem-solver. It argues that each type is a product of a complex interaction between the influences of personality, political experience, and legislative behaviour.

5 *Functional approach*—Unlike the aforementioned studies of personality, the functional approach assesses leaders in relation to the governmental arrangements and expectations within which they operate. The analysis by Jean Blondel (1987) of political leadership within the British Commonwealth, for example, considers the functions of leaders under contrasting presidential and parliamentary systems. He finds, for instance, that the British legacy has resulted in a more collective and partisan style of leadership than that found in non-Commonwealth countries.

The New Zealand literature is replete with single-actor narratives on early leaders, with major works having been produced on: Julius Vogel (Dalziel 1986), William Pember-Reeves (Sinclair 1969), Joseph Ward (Bassett 1993), Gordon Coates (Bassett 1995), Michael Joseph Savage (Gustafson 1986a), Peter Fraser (Bassett 2000), Walter Nash (Sinclair 1976), and Muldoon (Gustafson 2000). Although some studies provide multiple biographies within the same volume (e.g. McMillan 1993; Clark 2001; Eunson 2001), an obvious limitation of this particular method is that leadership is seldom discussed in ways that allow for easy comparison between one category of personality or political style and another.

One of the most useful approaches to the study of political leadership in New Zealand is derived from the psychological method pioneered by Barber in his study of American presidents. John Henderson, a former student of Barber's, has adapted the latter's taxonomy to the study of New Zealand prime ministers. Although most of Henderson's early work was on Labour leaders (he once served as head of the Prime Minister's Department under Lange), subsequent research has included the leaders of other parties, notably Muldoon (e.g. Henderson 1980; 2001). The four leadership types identified by Barber and adopted by Henderson are: active–positive, active–negative, passive–positive, and passive–negative (see figure 7.1). The active–positive leader is described as being the achiever, who puts great effort into political life and derives an equal amount of personal satisfaction from it (e.g. John F. Kennedy in the context of the USA, and, according to Henderson, Geoffrey Palmer in New Zealand (1992, p. 107)). Being the most rational of the four personality types, the active–positive politician has the ability to suppress personal feelings when confronted by logical argument, even when called upon to relinquish power. In contrast, active–negative politicians are charac-terised by extreme exertion and a desire to hold on to power regardless of the cost (e.g. Richard Nixon and, in New Zealand, Mike Moore). Despite their insatiable appetite for power, active–negative politicians derive little personal satisfaction or fulfilment. The passive–positive politician relishes the role of consummate performer while avoiding activities that are personally distasteful, especially those that are monotonous, repetitive, or involve personal conflict (Ronald Reagan and David Lange). When it comes time to move on, the passive–positive leader does so without regret, as exemplified by Lange's good-humoured announcement in 1989 that he was retiring from the prime ministership forthwith. Finally, according to Henderson, the passive–negative leaders neither derive any great pleasure from the pursuit of power nor let it rule their lives (1992, p. 102). Leaders of this type may have been persuaded to assume the position through an appeal to duty, a decision they may have cause to regret. According to Henderson, a classic politician of this type was Bill Rowling, who had the leadership of the country thrust upon him following the unexpected death of Norman Kirk.

Figure 7.1   Barber and Henderson leadership typology

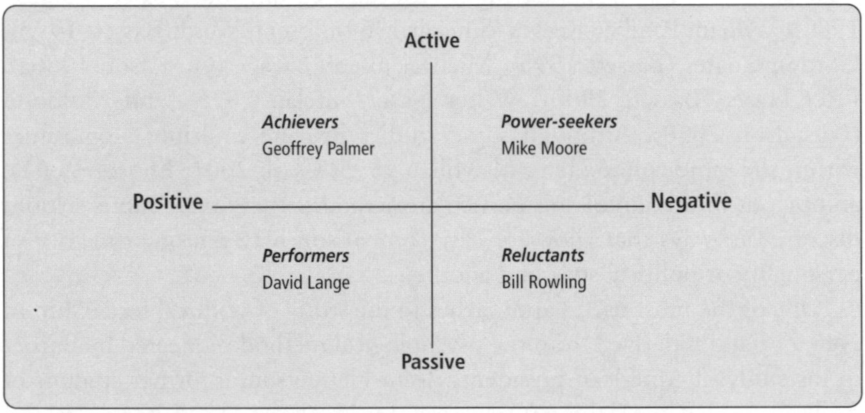

Source: J. Henderson 1991, 'Labour's Modern Prime Ministers and the Party: A Study of Contrasting Political Styles', p. 3.

As well as providing a useful tool with which to compare one New Zealand party leader with another, the Barber/Henderson typology offers ample evidence of the importance to leadership of personal qualities and attitudes. But Henderson's analysis also provides insight into the particular requirements of leadership under MMP. Whereas the inflexibility and divisiveness of an active–negative personality, such as that of Muldoon, may be well attuned to the adversarial, winner-take-all environment associated with first-past-the-post, it is less likely to succeed in circumstances that require high levels of inter-party consultation, cooperation and compromise. Henderson concludes that the active–positive politician is the one best suited to the demands of coalition government (2001, p. 114).

Despite its obvious strengths, the Barber/Henderson leadership model has a number of potentially significant limitations. Given that leaders will not willingly sit on a psychoanalyst's couch, reconstructing their motivations and emotions is a subjective process, resulting in judgments that are both speculative and imprecise (for example, who, apart from the person concerned, is capable of measuring feelings of sadness, happiness, and personal satisfaction?). While Henderson had the unique advantage of knowing his subjects well, each had to be fitted into a highly deterministic, two-dimensional and arbitrary schema that makes no allowance for gradations of activity or emotional response. Moreover, while the four categories may have relevance to the American presidency (although it is hard to imagine how a modern president can possibly remain passive), they do not fit well with the experiences of leadership in a Westminster parliamentary system, as evidenced by the fact that Geoffrey Palmer, one of the least popular and least successful prime ministers of recent times,[9] is given the 'ideal' classification of active–positive. Being prime minister is the ultimate goal of most MPs and represents the culmination of many years of intense preparation within the party and parliament. Unlike American presidents, New Zealand prime ministers play a similar, if somewhat elevated, role to that previously performed in parliament and cabinet. As a result, they are less likely to be susceptible to the negative emotional experiences that characterise two of Barber's four types.

A leadership model that avoids the psychological aspects of personality, instead focusing on the cabinet-based structure of the British parliamentary system, is the cyclical typology of Kavanagh. The bold, decisive, and polarising qualities of the mobilising leader are nicely exemplified in the political careers of Kirk and Muldoon. The latter was an uncompromising and fearless politician who refused to tolerate dissent and who regarded compromise as a form of weakness. Not surprisingly, the leader he most admired was Thatcher, who exemplified all the characteristics of the mobilising politician. In contrast, the reconciler has a commitment to consultation and cooperation, even if that involves significant compromises or trade-offs. Kavanagh notes that 'the movement between the two [types] has often been cyclical, with one style breeding a reaction in favour of the other' (1987, p. 202). Even if it could be demonstrated that leadership in New Zealand once followed a cyclical pattern, as Henderson points out the advent of MMP has significantly changed the requirements of political leadership, making it less likely that the cyclical pattern will so readily reoccur.

A functional model for New Zealand

By adapting features of the Henderson and Kavanagh typologies, but with a focus on the key functions of leadership, it is possible to propose a model for New Zealand that emphasises three distinct sets of characteristics or styles:

1 the mobiliser
2 the legislator
3 the manager.

Although leaders are likely to manifest all three functions, the typology shown in figure 7.2 is based on the assumption that every leader has one particular function that distinguishes his or her style of leadership. Deciding which function most clearly defines each politician's leadership is largely intuitive and intended to be descriptive rather than evaluative. Since all three functions are part and parcel of leadership under the Westminster system of government, the following analysis avoids overriding judgments about the superiority of one function, and of one style of politician, over another. Nor should it be assumed that New Zealand's 'ideal' political leaders are clustered in the mid-point of the triangle, that is, equidistant from all the three functions.

Mobilising leaders are the great communicators who, through the channels of public oration and television, can manipulate and inspire mass opinion, providing directional, even inspirational, leadership in times of national uncertainty or crisis. If the overused 'charismatic' has any remaining value, it should be attached to this type of leader.[10] Mobilisers have a good

Figure 7.2 Typology of New Zealand leaders

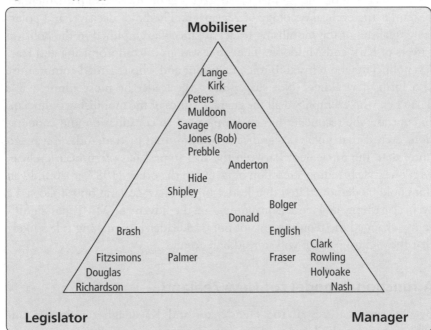

understanding of the collective psyche and derive much of their influence by personifying those values that define the national character, or, as one study has described it, being 'embodiments of national archetypes' (Foley 1993, p. 3). Some, though by no means all (Lange being an obvious exception), mobilising politicians draw on the themes of populism, including anti-elitism and anti-intellectualism, in order to appeal to the fears and frustra tions of disaffected sections of the community. In parliamentary systems, much of the mobilising leader's appeal comes from the rhetorical and debating skills displayed in the House, which has been described as 'the nation's political playhouse' (Mitchell 1966, p. 18). Parliament provides a 'stage' on which mobilising leaders can dominate their parliamentary rivals (e.g. Muldoon over Rowling, or Lange over an ageing Muldoon), thereby raising their profile and boosting morale within the party. Because they have a tendency to polarise opinion, mobilisers can find it hard to adapt the range of skills developed in opposition to the more consultative and collaborative requirements of being in government, a point made by Henderson with respect to Lange, whose reluctance to seek support from his cabinet and caucus colleagues helped account for his limited influence over the direction of government policy (1992, p. 106).

In addition to Kirk and Muldoon, examples of mobilising leaders include Lange, Moore, Winston Peters, Bob Jones, Jim Anderton, and Richard Prebble. Although broadly similar in talent and approach, Kirk and Lange were more skilled public speakers than Muldoon, who tended to 'lecture' from notes and charts, though with a keen sense of timing and clever turn of phrase. In a country that has produced precious few genuine orators, certainly in the past fifty years, Lange stood out as a mobilising politician of exceptional ability. There is no better example of the power of Lange's eloquence, self-deprecating humour, and emotional connection with an audience than his performance in the Oxford nuclear debate with the evangelical preacher and leader of America's 'Moral Majority', Jerry Falwell. But the modern leader must also perform well in the intimate atmosphere of a television studio, a lesson never properly learned by other orator-leaders, notably National's Jim McLay and Geoffrey Palmer. Muldoon was the consummate television performer—larger-than-life, authoritative to the point of being intimidating in word and voice, and with an ability to control the pace of an interview in a way that only Winston Peters has come close to imitating. In contrast, Lange relied almost entirely on his charm, intellectual and verbal skill, and rapier-like wit. As the leader of the New Zealand party, Bob Jones introduced another technique into the lexicon of television interview styles by being the first of the 'showbiz' politicians, capable of combining the blunt opinions of the wealthy entrepreneur with Wellington gossip and a politics-as-sport analysis that made him the media darling of the 1980s.

The difficulties a mobilising leader of the adversarial, winner-take-all type can have in a collaborative political environment can be illustrated with respect to Muldoon's handling of the Clyde [High] Dam Empowering Bill in 1982. The National government's razor-thin parliamentary majority was threatened following the decision of Michael Minogue, a government member, to vote with the Labour opposition to defeat National's high dam option. The two Social Credit MPs, Bruce Beetham and Garry Knapp, offered the government legislative support in exchange for certain guarantees, including electricity price controls and provisions for workers in Clyde. Beetham described the negotiations with the government as 'a good demonstration of how a third party can act as a catalyst to resolve an extremely sensitive and difficult situation'. However, having taken advantage of Social Credit's support to pass the legislation, which overrode any successful judicial appeal against the government's decision to proceed with the high dam, Muldoon stated that 'There is not one single thing I can think of that the government was not prepared to do before the Social Credit people asked us'.[11] By adopting this winner-take-all attitude, Muldoon ensured that there would be no future legislative cooperation between the government and the small party.

Given MMP's formidable 5 per cent threshold below which a party is not assured of seats in parliament, the minor parties place great store on being led by mobilising leaders, as illustrated by the indispensability of Peters to the success of New Zealand First, even though it was a style of leadership that caused numerous difficulties for the minor party after it formed a government with National in 1996. Although he commanded near-reverential respect for his radical ideas, ACT's first leader, Roger Douglas, lacked the tub-thumping skills required to raise his party's profile as an electoral organisation. In 1996 he resigned in favour of Prebble, a politician very much in the mobilising mould.

The second category of leaders, the legislators, are the analytical thinkers whose political ambitions have got less to do with persuasion than with achieving desired policy change. For the most part, legislators have little inclination or aptitude for taking personal control, preferring to work alongside those with the ability to broker the necessary deals and present the legislator's reforms to the mass public. Leaders of this type tend to be ideologues whose commitment to principle transcends that of personal popularity or ambition. Legislators are at their most influential in times of political stagnation or crisis, when old ideas are either discredited or under siege. Although Palmer used his position as deputy prime minister to successfully manage Labour's reform agenda (along with another lawyer–minister, David Caygill), he will be best remembered for his role as a cabinet minister, especially his environmental and constitutional initiatives, including the anti-nuclear legislation, Constitution Act (1986), Bill of Rights Act (1990) and, most notably, the initial recommendation that New Zealand adopt a proportional electoral system (it was Palmer who convened the Royal Commission on the Electoral System when he became Minister of Justice in 1984). As Eunson has observed, 'Geoffrey Palmer is an academic marinated in the law. The law is his life. He loves it like a mistress. He loved making law when he was in politics, and he loves teaching and practicing it now that he is away from the Legislature' (2001, p. 215). Although Lange counselled his reforming ministers after the 1987 election to take a 'cup of tea', Palmer's commitment to rapid change proved to be unrelenting. Other examples of legislator-politicians are Roger Douglas, Ruth Richardson,[12] and Jeanette Fitzsimons, who continued to defend her stance on genetic engineering long after it had cost the Greens any chance of being in government.

Managers have tended to be the longest-serving prime ministers in New Zealand. They are also the ones whose skills are most in demand in an MMP environment. Unlike mobilising leaders, who believe in the power of mass persuasion, and legislators, who are committed to transformational change, managers tend to adopt a moderate and pragmatic approach to politics, with a conception of leadership that recognises the need for hard-fought compromises or trade-offs. Because they place high value on consultation and compromise, and invariably have one eye on the next election, managers tend to have highly developed inter-personal skills, hence their ability to broker deals between competing interests and factions, and even rival party organisations. Peter Fraser, Keith Holyoake and Helen Clark, have all been technocratic managers. Another prime minister in the manager mould was Bolger, although he struggled to control his Finance minister, Ruth Richardson, between 1990 and 1993, and was subsequently accused of being outmanoeuvred by his coalition partner, Winston Peters. Shipley, who in 1997 was brought in to manage Peters, ended up dismissing him from her government. That the government went full term had less to do with Shipley's management skills, however, than the determination of her minor party and Independent allies to avoid an early election. Other examples of manager-politicians include Bill Rowling, Jack Marshall, Bill English, and Peter Dunne.

There are good reasons why prime ministers are often judged on the success of their micro and macro management skills. Unlike the leaders of much larger countries, New Zealand's prime ministers are required by convention and necessity to adopt a hands-on approach to party and governmental leadership. Although admittedly an extreme example, beginning in her days in opposition and continuing through her premiership, Clark made a habit of either writing or extensively editing her own speeches, often delivered from hand-written notes, dispensing her mobile phone number to journalists, personally responding to many of her own emails, and conducting her domestic life with minimal use of hired staff. Moreover, in contrast to Britain's Tony Blair, who in 2001 had 411 MPs from whom to select his cabinet, the pool of talent available to Clark numbered a mere fifty-one. Choosing an executive of close to thirty from such a small group inevitably results in the appointment of a number of weak ministers whose portfolios need to be kept under the continual gaze of the prime minister. Examples of high maintenance ministers in the Clark administration included George Hawkins (Police), Maori Affairs (Parekura Horomia), Mark Burton (Defence), and Annette King (Health).

Following the introduction of coalition government, even greater demands began to be made on the consultative and management skills of the prime minister. As well as maintaining a sound working relationship with the junior Progressive Coalition partner, during her second term Clark had to accommodate many of the demands of the two support parties, United Future and the Greens. These challenges notwithstanding, Clark, a keen student of New Zealand political history, aspired to a standard of leadership not seen in over three decades: 'Last time there was a stable government was during the Holyoake years...I want people to have predictability, certainty' (quoted in C. du Chateau 8–9 March 2003, p. 20).

The tentative decision to classify Brash as a legislator rather than as a manager needs to be explained. As a fourteen-year chief executive of a major public sector institution, the Reserve Bank, Brash's reputation had been built on meticulous planning and organisational management. Even before his election as party leader, however, Brash displayed signs of being an unconventional, if not enigmatic, political manager. As Audrey Young has pointed out, prior to the party leadership vote in October 2003 Brash appeared to have few strong supporters within the National caucus, and no 'identifiable team of plotters'.[13] Instead of following the familiar pattern of launching a clandestine assault on the leadership, accompanied by public denials that a challenge was underway, Brash took the unorthodox approach of announcing his candidacy through the media a week before the vote. In need of a political strategist and communications advisor, he was given the name of a young campaign organiser who was domiciled in Sydney. 'I literally rang him Saturday night [three days before the vote] when I was getting more and more desperate,' Brash told Young. 'After talking with him for quite a while on the phone I decided he would be worth a gamble. I had never met him before.' The gamble paid off, as did his first major decision as leader. Having enthusiastically endorsed the appointment of his new deputy, Nick Smith, within a matter of days Brash withdrew his support, leaving Smith with no option but to step aside.

While National's dramatic 17-point surge in the polls owed much to Brash's growing reputation as the antithesis of the career politician (to some, he had become something of an anti-politician), more important still was the potency of his ideas. During his time with the Reserve Bank, Brash had been a cerebral and wooden performer with a reputation for being an uncompromising economic 'dry'. At the time of his election as leader, it was widely anticipated that he would be a transitional figure who, following the party's expected defeat at the 2005 election, would quickly be replaced.[14] Within months these predictions had to be extensively reviewed. His attacks on the government's race relations, justice, and welfare policies promised to recast the political agenda for at least the next year to eighteen months (for a discussion on these and other Brash policies, see chapter 8). For these reasons, Brash has been classified, not as a manager, but as a legislator, although with shades of a mobilising politician to be found in his keen sense of political timing and in his populist ideas. However, as one study has observed, there is no magic formula to leadership success. In the words of Geoffrey Stern, 'In short, the leader may need to be a successful warrior or an accomplished conciliator, an innovator or a preserver of tradition, an orator or an organizer, a visionary or a pragmatic operator depending on the circumstances' (1993, p. 6).

Assessing the qualities of recent leaders

A number of criteria have been used to identify the qualities that distinguish leadership success from failure. Public opinion offers some indication as to the relative merits of individual leaders, although variations in historical context and in the recall ability of individual respondents raise doubts as to the reliability of comparisons over several generations of political leaders. Another largely unhelpful approach is to enquire of voters who they would choose as prime minister. In a country that does not elect its prime minister, such a question is too hypothetical and heavily biased in favour of the incumbent prime minister, especially if asked outside the immediate context of an election campaign.

One of the country's main polling agencies regularly measures a number of pre-selected qualities against the performances of the two main leaders. In polls conducted in the months before and after the 1999 election, the

Figure 7.3   Clark versus Shipley and English—capable leader

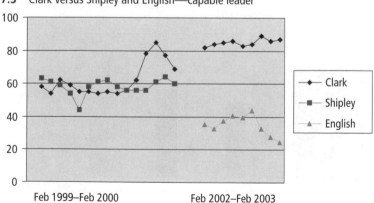

Source: TV3/CM Research

TV3/CM poll compared the abilities of the National leader (and prime minister before the election) Jenny Shipley with those of Clark. Whereas Shipley consistently out-polled Clark on the issue of personality, the latter was deemed to be more honest, have better judgment, and have superior skills in a crisis. An event that clearly damaged Shipley's reputation for integrity was the 'Hawkesby Affair'. Early in 1999, Shipley claimed in a television interview that the dismissed newsreader, John Hawkesby, had received a NZ$1 million settlement from his employer, Television New Zealand. Her comment followed a series of questions on the government's inability to prevent some departing senior public servants from receiving 'golden handshakes' from the public purse. Shipley later conceded to the interviewers, Mike Hosking and Linda Clark, that she had simply made up the claim. Although the admission was made in a private conversation held off-camera, the two journalists considered that it was in the public interest that the information be released. Under threat of being sued for defamation by Hawkesby's lawyers at Buddle Findlay, the prime minister issued a written retraction and apology.

Where the gap between Shipley and Clark was greatest, however, was in their attitude towards voters, with Shipley being regarded as patronising and out of touch with the views of ordinary voters (see figure 7.4). The high rating for Clark on the qualities of being down-to-earth and in touch with the views of ordinary voters is surprising, given her early reputation, and that of her deputy leader, Michael Cullen, for being ivory-tower intellectuals with little or no experience in the 'real world'. Although Shipley was seen to talk down to people, the same was not said of Clark—indeed, only one in four respondents saw her as being somewhat condescending and arrogant, compared with more than two out of every three in the case of Shipley.

While Shipley benefited from the exposure received as the incumbent prime minister for most of 1999, Bill English was relatively unknown at the time of his elevation to the leadership in October 2001 (despite having been

Figure 7.4 Clark versus Shipley, 1999

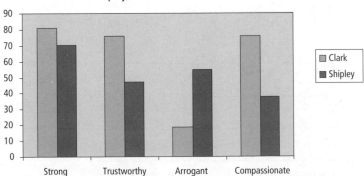

Source: NZES 1999

Finance minister in the Shipley government). Although he received wide public attention during the 2002 election campaign, English was not viewed as either competent or strong, judgments that were reinforced by National's poor performance at the polls (see figures 7.3 and 7.5). Whereas Shipley was given credit for her ebullient personality, English was deemed to be dull, even after attempts had been made to expose a macho, risk-taking side to his character, as illustrated by the decision to let him take part in a televised charity boxing tournament.

Figure 7.5   Clark versus English, 2002

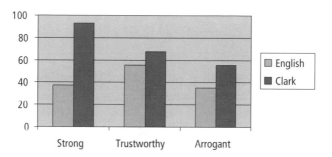

Source: NZES 2002

During 2002, Clark's integrity was the subject of unrelenting attack from political opponents and sections of the media. The incidents that became known as 'Paintergate' (based on the allegation that she forged her signature on a painting offered for a charity auction) and 'Corngate' (the claim of a cover-up over the accidental release of genetically modified materials) received extensive publicity during the campaign and appeared to tarnish her reputation as an honest and trustworthy leader (see chapter 9 for a full discussion of these incidents). It is therefore surprising to learn that her personal rating for honesty never dropped as low as that of English and averaged 55 per cent, compared with 36 per cent for the National leader (TV3/NFO New Zealand, 18 February 2002 to 16 February 2003).

The extent to which mobilising leaders polarised public opinion in 2002 is revealed in the findings of figure 7.6. While Peters enjoyed the loyal support of his party's core constituency, many of whom had come to regard him as the most able and honest politician of his generation, less devoted admirers found appeal in the panache and derring-do with which he conducted his campaigns. Having built a formidable reputation as a hard-hitting, cantankerous politician in the Muldoon mould, Peters could hardly be expected to leave many voters with a sense of indifference or neutrality, as the combined figures for and against in figure 7.6 clearly show. Though for slightly different reasons, Richard Prebble evoked a passionately negative

Figure 7.6   Attitudes towards party leaders, 2002

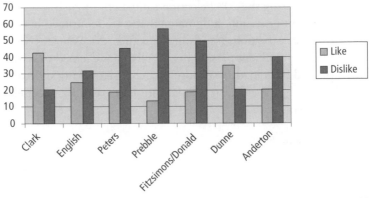

Source: NZES 2002

response, as did the previously popular leaders, Jeanette Fitzsimons and Rod Donald. The Green party's uncompromising position on genetic engineering clearly damaged the duo's reputation for being well-intentioned and harmless, if a tad naïve. Only Peter Dunne among the small party leaders attracted more sympathy than scorn. In his case, however, the dominant sentiment was one of bemusement, an understandable reaction given United Future's dramatic surge in the polls in the last few days of the campaign.

Conclusion

Despite its role in creating a more representative parliament, the advent of MMP has had no impact on leadership selection, which, with the exception of the Greens, remains under the control of each party's parliamentary caucus. Arguments for reform include the need to give party membership and activism greater meaning and to make the process of selection more open and accountable. Supporters of the status quo, on the other hand, reason that MPs are better judges of the leadership qualities of their peers than party members or activists, many of whom are unlikely to have had any direct contact with the leadership contenders. Moreover, as the supporters of the Australian Labor leader, Simon Crean, argued in response to the unsuccessful challenge from the more popular Kim Beasley in June 2003, elections are won and lost on policies, not leaders.[15] As this chapter has shown, however, the two approaches are not necessarily mutually exclusive. A possible compromise for New Zealand would be to follow the example of parties such as the British Conservatives and Liberal Democrats by giving the MPs the right to provide a shortlist of potential leaders, with delegates or members making the final selection.

Given the importance of party leadership in contemporary New Zealand politics, it is pertinent to consider whether the performances of the party leaders should not be subject to more frequent and searching peer reviews. The suggestion of a formal performance review, to be conducted by the party's Board of Directors, was first mooted by the veteran MP for Pakuranga, Maurice Williamson, on the eve of National's 2003 conference. Responding to a series of poor opinion poll results for the party and its leader, he suggested that Bill English be given a performance agreement similar to that of the chief executive of a business. 'You'd say to the leader that, "We want to have this party at 30 per cent by the end of the year and 35 per cent by midway through next year…or your contract is terminated".'[16] Apart from the distinctly undemocratic nature of the suggestion, with the power to dismiss a party leader being transferred from the parliamentary caucus to an even smaller nine-member executive committee, making the leader responsible for the party's popularity would remove any responsibility from the hands of other MPs, including Williamson. Moreover, while opinion polls provide a measure of public opinion at any given time, they have no predictive value, as evidenced by the number of party leaders who, having languished on less than 10 per cent popular support for much of their period in opposition, have gone on to be highly successful and popular prime ministers. For an example of this transformation one need go no further than Helen Clark, whose personal popularity, and that of her party, hovered at record lows for much of the mid-1990s. Whereas mobilising leaders enjoy the cut and thrust of electoral competition, manager-leaders may be relatively unsuccessful opposition politicians, who only come into their own on assuming power. Potentially outstanding prime ministers who failed to survive their period in opposition include National's Jim McLay and Labour's Arnold Nordmeyer.

While mobilising leaders will continue to have a place in the MMP environment, especially in lifting the electoral profiles of small parties, being a constructive partner in government requires an ability to adapt to the more flexible and pragmatic qualities of the manager-leader. Winston Peters showed little capacity for conciliatory leadership during his eighteen months in government between 1996 and 1998. Whether he or any other minor party leaders have the capacity to make the necessary adjustments in their leadership style if given the opportunity to form a partnership in some future coalition, time alone will tell.

Notes

1 Preston Manning, personal interview, 27 November 2002, University of Toronto, Toronto.
2 Interview with Peter Lynch, 2 September 2004, University of Stirling, Stirling.
3 *The National Business Review*, 31 October 2003, p. 10.
4 Peter Dunne, personal interview, 3 July 2001, Parliament Buildings, Wellington.
5 C. James, 'Herculean effort needed by Hide to overcome hurdles', *New Zealand Herald*, 15 June 2004, p. A11.

6 Apart from Hide, the leadership contenders were the deputy leader, Ken Shirley, Stephen Franks, and Muriel Newman. Newman was later chosen as deputy leader.

7 Although he is best known as a merchant banker and former Governor of the Reserve Bank, Brash has had extensive connections with the kiwifruit industry, both as an orchardist and administrator.

8 Clark's deputy leader, Michael Cullen, was also a university lecturer.

9 Apart from the first three months of his thirteen-month prime ministership between 1989 and 1990, Palmer was unable to reverse the government's low ratings in the polls. Three months before the 1990 election, he was persuaded by his cabinet colleagues to step down as Labour leader.

10 The term 'charisma' can be traced back to biblical times. Max Weber used the term in relation to 'the quality of leadership which appeals to non-rational motives' (Talcott Parsons, in Weber 1958, p. 281). It was adopted by political scientists in the 1950s to describe the attributes of the exceptional political leader.

11 *New Zealand Herald*, 14 July 1982, p. 1.

12 Although Ruth Richardson was a Finance minister rather than a party leader, without question she was the dominant politician of the National government of 1990–93.

13 A. Young, 'Brash's inner circle', *Weekend Herald*, 1–2 November 2003, A6.

14 G. Hunt, 'Newcomer has little time to succeed', *The National Business Review*, 31 October 2003, p. 10.

15 Quoted in Radio New Zealand's *Morning Report*, 16 June 2003.

16 *New Zealand Herald* 14 July 2003, p. A1.

Further reading

Barber, J.D. 1972, *The Presidential Character: Predicting Performance in the White House*, Prentice-Hall, Englewood Cliffs.

Clark, M. (ed.) 2001, *Three Labour Leaders: Nordmeyer, Kirk, Rowling*, The Dunmore Press, Palmerston North.

Edwards, B. 2001, *Helen: Portrait of a Prime Minister*, Exisle Publishing, Auckland.

Henderson, J. 1992, 'Labour's Modern Prime Ministers and the Party: A Study of Contrasting Political Styles', in M. Clark (ed.), *The Labour Party After 75 Years*, Victoria University of Wellington, pp. 98–117.

Henderson, J. 2001, 'Prime Minister', in R. Miller (ed.), *New Zealand Government and Politics*, Oxford University Press, Melbourne, pp. 106–16.

Johansson, J. 2003, 'Leadership and the Campaign', in J. Boston, S. Church, S. Levine, E. McLeay and N.S. Roberts (eds) 2003, *New Zealand Votes: The General Election of 2002*, Victoria University Press, Wellington, pp. 59–74.

Kavanagh, D. 1987, 'Margaret Thatcher: The Mobilizing Style of Prime Minister', in H.D. Clarke and M.M. Czudnowski (eds), *Political Elites in Anglo-American Democracies: Changes in Stable Regimes*, Northern Illinois University Press, DeKalb Ill., pp. 177–208.

part four

How Parties Compete

Ideology and Policy

'With the end of ideology, more and more parties are centre-seeking.'

Giovanni Sartori

8

IDEOLOGY is a belief system that helps us to distinguish one party from another. Every political party lays claim to its own ethos, set of doctrines, and plan of action. Whereas Labour was founded on the principles of social democracy, including social equality, the mixed economy, and universal welfare, National became the party of individual freedom, self-reliance, and the free market. Because these concepts are difficult for ordinary voters to understand, our political attachments are frequently expressed by way of signposts, such as 'socialist' and 'conservative', or 'left' and 'right'. Although such labels may appear overly simplistic, even out-of-date, they help to bring intellectual order to our assumptions, instincts, and beliefs.

From the perspective of the twenty-first century, the term 'ideology' tends to conjure up old-fashioned images of dogmatism and division, as illustrated by the rise of the Fascist parties of the 1920s and 1930s and the postwar standoff between the communist and capitalist blocs. In *The End of Ideology*

(1988), Daniel Bell makes the point that, having generated considerable passion and promise, only to be followed by disappointment, ideology lost its ability to persuade. As a result, it has been largely superseded by the term 'values', which is seen to better reflect the changing mores and styles of contemporary society. These are said to include the growth of individualism and corresponding decline in the importance of group identities, the personalisation of politics, and the politicians' appeal to voter self-interest.

But not everyone is happy with the association of values with politics. Whereas Labour places great store on its appeal to voters' values,[1] the ACT party chose to make 'Values, *not* Politics' a campaign theme. Quite how the right wing party's support for low taxes and limited government can remain unsullied by politics is not entirely clear. Detaching principle from politics has a number of practical advantages, however, not least in fostering a sense of moral rectitude by characterising politics as fundamentally unprincipled, opportunistic, and even corrupt.

This chapter will explore two starkly contrasting accounts of the importance of ideology to party politics. The first is based on the assumption that ideology still matters. According to this view, parties are best defined in relation to their underlying values and beliefs. While their actions may reflect some attentiveness to public opinion, ideology is an anchor that determines what parties say and do. Evidence for this view is not difficult to find. Despite the unpopularity of their free market reforms, successive Labour and National governments persisted with them, even in the face of near-certain electoral defeat. The second account proposes that the main purpose of ideology is to help parties win votes. According to this view, parties are not primarily concerned with implementing policy, but rather enjoying the fruits of power. To this end, each party engages in a number of pragmatic decisions, with the most important being where it should locate itself on the ideological spectrum with a view to maximising its vote. These two accounts are best summed up in Anthony Downs' famous hypothesis: 'Parties formulate policies in order to win elections, rather than win elections in order to formulate policies' (1957, p. 28).

As we will see, by following Tony Blair's dictum that 'what matters is what works' (Blair 1998, p. 4), the Clark government devised a pragmatic policy agenda that sought to strike a balance between fairness and fiscal restraint while leaving the economic reforms of the 1980s largely untouched. The acknowledged purpose behind this strategy was to reflect the interests of so-called 'middle' New Zealand. In contrast, National appeared to be signalling a lurch to the right when in late 2003 it chose Don Brash, once a poster-boy for neo-liberalism, as its leader. Subsequent policy announcements revealed that it too was pitching its message to middle New Zealand. The relevance of Downs' model to this intriguing two-party battle for the hearts and minds of voters will be the focus of our enquiry. The vote-maximising tendencies of the two major parties will be illustrated with reference to two case studies: Labour's commitment to the politics of the Third Way; and National's orchestration of the race and law-and-order debates to fuel its dramatic rise in the polls. Whereas the first involves a gradual repositioning over several years, the second is narrowly focused, immediate, and ad hoc.

Families-based approach

The most common way of comparing parties across countries is by placing them in ideological clusters or groups. The notion of ideological families is derived from the work of a number of European scholars, notably Duverger (1954) and von Beyme (1985). Their starting point was the almost self-evident assumption that similar sorts of parties can be found in many parts of the world. While von Beyme's families-based model was designed with the party systems of Europe in mind, he stressed that it could also be applied to New Zealand and Australia.[2]

Of the ideological families that are represented in New Zealand, six stand out:

1 social democratic parties
2 liberal/conservative parties
3 populist parties
4 environmental parties
5 libertarian parties
6 ethnic parties.

1. Social democratic parties

Social democratic parties believe that curbing the excesses of the market is a necessary first step towards a more equal, harmonious and productive society. While their message is targeted to the industrialised working class, social democratic movements draw support from other parts of the electorate, especially ethnic minorities, beneficiaries and, increasingly, the middle class. Despite the early presence of an international socialist movement, there have always been individual and regional variations between the various social democratic parties. While some have enjoyed a close association with the trade union movement, for instance, others have not.

Along with its counterparts in Britain and Australia, the New Zealand Labour party professed an early belief in the foundations of socialism, including the need for a fundamental restructuring of the capitalist economy towards public ownership and control. However, because it lacked a radical intellectual or unionised left-wing, but also as a result of the conservative nature of the New Zealand electorate, during the postwar period it became distinguished more for its ideological conservatism than for a commitment to social democratic reform. Indeed, it can be argued that, having both embraced Keynesian economics and created the modern welfare state, the party provided no further significant revision of the social democratic model until the 1980s (for a discussion on the economic crisis of the 1970s and early 1980s, see chapter 2).

In applying market solutions to the country's growing economic problems, the fourth Labour government (1984–90) was instrumental in transforming Labour from a social democratic party to a 'hybrid' party of the neo-liberal/ social democratic type.[3] In a series of reforms that became known as 'Rogernomics',[4] the Keynesian paradigm was deemed to be out-of-date. Some party members and activists tried to keep the party's former reputation alive with empty symbolic gestures, such as the singing of the Red Flag and quaint references to fellow members as 'comrades' and 'socialists'.[5] In reality, the government's economic agenda, especially its commitment to economic deregulation, the privatisation of state-owned assets, increased foreign investment, and initial steps towards user-pays in health and education, had little in common with traditional Labour beliefs.

While Clark consistently argued that, under her leadership, the party had returned to its natural home on the centre-left of the political spectrum, its policies in government were decidedly more centrist than left. In embracing that body of ideas that has become known as the Third Way, Labour steered a course that allowed it to defend its free market credentials with middle-income voters, while at the same time pursuing more traditional goals with respect to beneficiaries, low-income Maori, and workers' rights. (For a discussion on social democracy and the Third Way, see McKenzie 2002.)

As Gustafson has pointed out, the rise of postwar generations to positions of leadership within Labour had had a significant bearing on attitudes towards social issues (1992, p. 273). Suddenly the postmaterialist values of the young were on the ascendancy, challenging the social conservatism of more traditional members, especially those in the industrialised working class, the unions, and the Catholic Church. Liberal social initiatives included women's and Maori rights, abortion and homosexual law reform, and the environment. A ministry of Women's Affairs was established in the 1980s, efforts were made to achieve pay equity for women, the terms of reference for the Waitangi Tribunal were extended, allowing it to consider claims dating back to 1840, and there was support for affirmative action programmes to benefit Maori in areas such as health, employment, and education. As we will see, this socially liberal agenda has continued to the present time, presenting opportunities for the parties of the centre-right to exploit a growing conservative backlash, especially among racially motivated European voters.

Despite Labour's flirtation with market liberalism, the spirit, if not the substance, of the international social democratic family lived on. In an attempt to find common ground with a view to promoting a centre-left agenda, at the turn of the century President Bill Clinton formed the Progressive Governance Group. Its membership included the leaders of a number of 'social democratic' parties, including Clark and Blair, Gerhard Schroeder (Germany), Jean Chretien (Canada), and Goran Persson (Sweden). At its 2003 meeting in London, which was attended by some 400 academics, policy analysts, and advisers, the leaders of the Progressive Governance Group attempted to apply social democratic solutions to a number of contemporary problems, including global citizenship, migration, social inequality, and economic stagnation.[6]

2. Liberal/conservative parties

National generally presents itself as a hybrid party of the liberal/conservative type.[7] Although lacking the international 'family' connections of Labour, it bears a strong resemblance to liberal/conservative parties elsewhere, including the Canadian Conservatives, and Australian Liberals. Having been formed in opposition to Labour, National's ideology is strongly anti-collectivist, anti-unionist, anti-interventionist, and anti-welfare. Socialism and even social democracy are deemed to be antithetical to the principles that conservatives hold dear. These include upholding the rule of law, personal freedom and initiative, private property and enterprise, limited government, and belief in a harmonious and economically prosperous society. Although both major parties believe that reward should be based on merit, Nationalists are much more likely to believe that all are created equal and that success is best achieved through competition and individual effort. The value placed on civil and political rights has been reflected in some landmark legislation, such as the Official Information Act (1982) and the Human Rights Act (1993).

While some commentators believe that the ideologies of the two major parties 'pull in divergent...directions' (Shorter 1974, p. 348), others regard the differences to be more imagined than real. For much of the postwar period National was an efficient manager of Labour's reforms, including the mixed economy, steeply progressive tax system, and universal welfare state. Although continuing to campaign against the dangers of welfare dependency and state control, National showed levels of ideological flexibility and modernity not seen in Labour. Of the two parties, it appeared to be the more liberal and pragmatic, a perception that largely accounted for its enviable record of electoral success (between 1949 and 1984, National was in opposition for only six years). As Shorter once observed, '[National] gives its blessing, in some form or other, to virtually all the values entertained by the New Zealand public. It is in effect a gospel for all occasions' (1974, p. 364).

Beginning in the 1980s, under the leadership of Jim McLay, Jim Bolger, and Ruth Richardson, National evolved from the economics of twentieth century liberalism, which saw limited state interventionism as a necessary antidote to the excesses of capitalism, to that of neo-liberalism. However, in contrast to Labour, which spent its final years in office trying to slow down the pace of reform, National was prepared to take it to the next stage of development. On regaining power in 1990, the party substantially reduced social spending, increased the pace of privatisation, and introduced legislation to reform the labour market. Implicit in these initiatives was a willingness to abandon the centre ground for the first time in over half a century. It provided a welcome reprieve for Labour, which had suffered a landslide election defeat, and opened the way for the emergence of the anti-reform Liberal and New Zealand First parties. Some ten years later, National's senior politicians were still engaged in an internal debate over the party's precise location on the left–right spectrum, with the leader, Jenny Shipley, urging that it re-brand itself as a 'radical conservative' alternative to Labour.[8]

3. Populist parties

Populist parties fit the stereotype of the dysfunctional family, with each denying any familial relationship with the other members of their ideological group. Although strands of populism are to be found in the belief systems of a number of New Zealand parties, including the Democrats (formerly Social Credit), National, and ACT (see chapter 3), New Zealand First offers the most complete manifestation of contemporary populism. Populist parties commonly exploit feelings of powerlessness and popular discontent. Resentment and victimisation are directed at particular groups, notably immigrants, refugees, over-stayers, the media establishment, and foreign investors. Being naturally suspicious of members of the business, political, and bureaucratic elites, mainly on the grounds that they are self-serving and corrupt, populists tend to support the instruments of direct democracy, including referendums and citizens' initiatives. During his long political career, Winston Peters launched a number of anti-corruption campaigns against leading companies and their directors, as well as politicians, who were accused of a number of vices, including wasting public money and appointing cronies to statutory bodies. His repeated call for a reduction in the number and incomes of MPs proved popular with his party's voters.

While Peters has avoided the overt racism and strident nationalism of, say, Pauline Hanson's Australian One Nation movement or Haider's Austrian Freedom party, his attacks on outsiders are an almost perfect fit with classical populism. For example, during the 2002 election campaign, Peters blamed immigrants and refugees for many of the social and infrastructural problems facing New Zealanders, particularly in the main centres. His extravagant claims received extensive media coverage both domestically and overseas, especially when they linked asylum-seekers with political fanaticism, even terrorism. On one occasion, for example, he claimed that 'We have an obligation to our own people, our own emerging culture and our own creeds…before that of any Tom, Dick, Harry, Mustaq, or bin Laden who wants to come here'.[9] Given Peters' particular blend of nationalism and ethnic intolerance, it is hardly surprising that most of his support has come from late middle-aged and elderly voters in the provincial cities and towns.

Providing a local twist to the New Zealand First leader's particular brand of populism were his views on Maori development. The settlement process, in which the Waitangi Tribunal played an instrumental role, were said to threaten the social cohesion of the nation, with Maori being pitched against Maori, and Maori against European. As well as squandering precious resources, the Tribunal was accused of encouraging Maori dependency and spawning a 'grievance industry' that not only included the many claimants, but also their researchers, lawyers, and other advisors. In keeping with his belief in one standard of citizenship for all, Peters campaigned for the abolition of Maori seats and against suggestions that the 'principles' of the Treaty of Waitangi be incorporated in New Zealand's legal and constitutional system.

4. Environmental parties

The Green party is another of those hybrid parties that contains features of more than one ideological family. As the name suggests, at the core of green ideology is a commitment to environmental activism aimed at conserving the natural resources and, where a no-growth policy is unrealistic, working towards the goal of 'sustainable development'. A number of Green activists were former members of the Values party, which was established in 1972. The contemporary Green party is best known for its opposition to genetic engineering, support for consumption taxes, and solutions to the problems of pollution, traffic congestion, and water and electricity scarcity. More than any other party, the Greens exemplify the 'new politics' values that we have come to associate with 'post-materialism' (Inglehart 1977). Issues upon which postmaterialists can be expected to hold liberal views include opposition to nuclear arms and energy; the rights of women and minorities in such areas as homosexual law reform and abortion; and Maori sovereignty.

In contrast, the materialist 'old politics' has been described as placing 'a high priority on a stable economy, economic growth, fighting rising prices and, on the more personal level, on securing a high-paying job, adequate housing, and a comfortable life' (Flanagan 1987, p. 1304). Throughout the Green party's existence it has maintained contact with other environmental parties in Australia, Europe, and elsewhere. Beginning in the 1970s, for example, members of the Values party and the German Greens (Die Grunen) forged strong and enduring links. Indeed, the fledgling German Greens made extensive use of the Values party's 1975 manifesto, *Beyond Tomorrow*, in preparing their party's policy platform.

Although the Greens generally refuse to be located on the left–right dimension, research conducted shortly after their formation found that, when pressed, Green activists placed themselves and their party on the centre-left, midway between Labour and the left-wing NewLabour party, which became a founding member of the Alliance (Miller 1991, pp. 55–6). With the decline of the Alliance between 2001 and 2002, the Greens began to 'assume the mantle of the Alliance as the only serious "alternative" voice on the New Zealand political scene' (Bale 2003, p. 288). This combination of 'red' and 'green' does not sit well with some Green activists, who fear that the distinctive green ideology could become submerged within a more traditional social democratic agenda. Leading social democrats among the Greens have included the MP Sue Bradford, a former leader of the Unemployed Workers' Association, and Keith Locke, whose views on foreign policy made him the most radical member of the New Zealand parliament.

5. Libertarian parties

The ACT party was established with a view to completing the process of economic liberalisation begun by the former Finance ministers Roger Douglas (Labour) and Ruth Richardson (National). In his book *Unfinished Business* (1993), Douglas argued that, while important steps had been taken towards greater individual autonomy and limited government, fear of a voter backlash had caused the two major parties to slow down the pace and extent of reform. Among ACT's radical suggestions were calls for the abolition of income tax and substantial reductions in fiscal spending, leading to a more residualist welfare state. Its key policies were similar to those of neo-liberal parties elsewhere, notably Canada's Reform party (later renamed the Alliance) and the American Libertarian party. Douglas estimated the potential constituency for his party's views to be in the order of 15 to 20 per cent of all voters.

Following the party's failure to fulfil its leader's expectations—in 1996, its share of the party vote was 6 per cent—an internal debate took place between ACT's ideological *purists*, led by Douglas, and its *pragmatists*, notably Richard Prebble and Rodney Hide (see Reid 1999). The latter wanted to temper the party's radical economic agenda and improve its electoral prospects by mirroring some of Winston Peters' populist positions on political corruption, Treaty settlement issues, and law and order. Under the leadership of Prebble, it made its name as a perk-busting, low-tax alternative to National. To counter criticism that its policies would have drastic consequences for many middle-income families, ACT abandoned its nil-tax policy, replacing it with tax rates of 18 per cent for those on medium incomes and 28 per cent for high income earners and businesses. Despite clear evidence that its appeal was narrowly confined to men and those on high incomes, Prebble rejected the party's boutique image, preferring to try to court a broad constituency. At its 2004 conference, and following the party's decline in the polls to a mere 1 per cent, Prebble made the startling claim that ACT was the party of 'middle' New Zealand. As such, he reasoned, it belonged on the left rather than on the right of National.[10]

On Prebble's resignation as leader in June 2004, the party's members and supporters debated the relative merits of the two leading candidates, Stephen Franks, who was associated with the purists, and Rodney Hide. Against the advice of Douglas and the other leading ideologues, a bare majority of MPs endorsed Hide, a decision that was later confirmed by the party's Board. By its decision, the party appeared to be signalling its desire to continue tapping into the same rich vein of populist politics that had restored the electoral fortunes of New Zealand First and, more recently, National.

6. Ethnic parties

While there have been a large number of Maori parties, prior to the forma-tion of the 'Maori party' in 2004, none was able to appeal to mainstream Maori opinion (see chapter 3).[11] Several had their roots in tino rangatiratanga (self-determination or autonomy), while others, such as Mauri Pacific, pur-sued policies that were more inclusive. However, these parties' efforts were frustrated by a combination of tribal differences, Labour's sixty-year stran-glehold on the Maori seats, and the emergence of a distinct urban Maori perspective. Writing in the 1990s, Mason Durie observed that, while tribes were 'more strongly established and more visible than they were a decade ago…at the same time, urban power blocks have emerged, ready to compete with tribes for resources and a share in Maori decision-making' (1997, p. 378).

The issue that brought these disparate elements together, forging a common bond, was the government's response to a landmark Court of Appeal decision in 2003 on Maori customary title. The Court's ruling gave South Island Maori the right to proceed with their claim to the Maori Land Court to establish customary rights to the seabed and foreshore of the Marlborough Sounds. Despite initially expressing the view that title must reside with the Crown, the prime minister proceeded to fudge the government's position by replacing any reference to the Crown with the words 'public domain'. In a series of hui with the government, Maori grassroots opinion towards the gov-ernment became increasingly fractious and rebellious. The decision of a government minister, Tariana Turia, to resign from parliament and to force a by-election in the Te Tai Hauauru electorate, together with the extensive publicity given to a hikoi (march) of some 15,000 to 20,000 protestors on parliament, provided the necessary impetus for the formation of the first credible ethnic party since the introduction of MMP.

Beyond its assertion of Maori ownership and customary rights over the foreshore and seabed, it was not immediately obvious what the new Maori party might stand for. In a strategic document released following the Te Tai Hauauru by-election, the party signalled its commitment to some broad principles, including social solidarity and mutual respect (Manaakitanga), self-determination (Rangatiratanga), and the nurturing of a spiritual identity rooted in a strong connection with the land (Wairatanga).[12] At the time of writing, quite what these principles would mean in policy terms remained to be seen. The interim president, Whatarangi Winiata, had long argued for a separate Maori parliament, although the party's other political leaders quickly distanced themselves from any such proposal. More realistic objectives were likely to include a commitment to increased spending on Maori health, education and welfare, the promotion of Maori language and arts, and the upholding of the Treaty of Waitangi as the nation's founding document.[13] But there were also likely to be a number of ad hoc initiatives reflecting the particular interests of leading members of the movement, such as the advocacy of privately run prisons by the party's co-leader, Pita Sharples. Quite where these policies would place the party on the left–right spectrum was the subject of keen debate, especially after Turia and Winiata, among others, began speculating about the possibility of a coalition arrangement between the Maori party and National (a party not only firmly committed to rescinding all 'race-based' legislation, but also the abolition of the seven Maori seats).

While von Beyme's families-based approach provides a useful schema for discussing the ideological underpinnings of New Zealand's parties, it has a number of limitations. As the large number of hybrid parties suggests, parties are dynamic organisations that are not easily contained within the dimensions of a single ideological category or space. Being a static model, it neither recognises the ideological changes that parties undergo over time nor allows for a significant degree of overlap between one party and the next. As Ware points out, the competition for votes can, and does, cause quite dissimilar parties from different ideological traditions to look alike (1996, p. 47).

Vote-seeking approach

This brings us to the model of Anthony Downs, which is based on the assumption that parties are primarily concerned with securing votes. Instead of parties winning elections to make policy, according to Downs they make policy in order to win elections. In *An Economic Theory of Democracy* (1957), he presented a model of two-party competition that characterised voters as consumers and ideology as a product to be sold. As a starting point, Downs drew on the model of spatial competition developed by Harold Hotelling. In his study of retail competition, Hotelling asked why, in a situation where customers were evenly located along a street, two competing retail outlets set up business immediately adjacent to one another midway along the street.

On the assumption that shoppers prefer to travel to the store closest to their home, Hotelling discovered that, by locating in the mid-point, each shop was able to maximise its customer base, one from the middle to one end of the street and the other in the opposite direction. In his study, Downs applied this same principle to the nature of electoral competition. In a two-party system, he reasoned, it was in the interests of both parties to move to the middle of the left–right spectrum with a view to optimising their appeal to the median voter.

For the purposes of our discussion, we will consider the following three key propositions made by Downs with respect to parties and voters.

1. Parties choose policies to maximise their vote

Consistent with Kirchheimer's catch-all party model (see chapter 4), Downs reasoned that, since parties are primarily motivated by a desire for power, they search for policies with the greatest popular appeal. In a normal distribution, the vast majority of voters will be clustered centripetally (see figure 8.1). Whereas voters have fixed preferences, parties do not. This gives the two major parties sufficient flexibility to be able to come up with policies that, by virtue of being moderate and predictable, will appeal to a broad-based constituency (1957, p. 122). Because of the temptation to mirror one another's policies, the parties are frequently accused of being little more than 'tweedledum and tweedledee'. According to Downs, in the absence of any significant policy divergence the two parties have an incentive to stress other points of difference, such as the personality of the leader and the party's governmental experience. If one party strays too far to the left or to the right, it risks either losing support to the other major party or providing a gap for the appearance of a new party 'to cut off a large part of the support of an older party by sprouting up between it and its former voters' (1957, p. 128).

Figure 8.1   Downs' two-party distribution

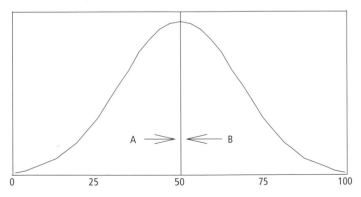

Source: Downs 1957, p. 118

2. Parties are ideologically flexible and mobile

Despite this tendency towards ideological convergence, in the view of Downs ideology remains important to voters. By using ideology as a signpost to how they should vote, they are able to short-circuit the problem of having to absorb a mass of policy details. This said, it is not the parties but the voters themselves who determine what the voters' interests and priorities will be. In other words, all that ideology does is facilitate voters in knowing whether the actions parties take in government are compatible with their own personal interests. Because the ultimate decision lies with the voter rather than the party, politicians compete by making their ideological priorities conform to those of their targeted voters. Whereas in two-party systems the movement will be towards the centre, under multiparty conditions in which the voters are widely dispersed, parties tend to be evenly distributed along the left–right scale. However, as Downs points out, their flexibility and mobility are not without constraints. For example, because parties have a responsibility to maintain a measure of integrity with the voting public, there is a need for ideological consistency, both during an election campaign and while in government. Downs also argues that parties cannot plausibly leapfrog over one another, although they may compete for votes by adopting some of their rivals' policies.

Figure 8.2   Distribution of parties on left–right economic scale

3. The number of parties reflects the distribution of votes

According to Downs, the critical factor in determining whether a party system is of the two-party or multiparty type is not the electoral system, although that may have some bearing, but rather the distribution of votes. New Zealand's recent experience of party system change would appear to contradict this hypothesis, with up to eight parliamentary parties surviving despite the centripetal distribution of votes (see figure 8.1), as discussed in chapters 2 and 3, with a number of the small parties having been formed around a strong leader and in response to a particular set of events. As a result, the high incidence of small parties winning seats has always appeared unsustainable in the medium to long term.

This leads us to the application of the vote maximisation and party mobility theories to contemporary New Zealand. There are two basic approaches to re-branding for the purpose of increasing a party's market share of the vote. The first involves a gradual repositioning over several years and may include replacing some long-held assumptions about what the party stands for, and for whom it actually speaks. An example of this first, *gradualist* approach was the attempt in the late 1980s and 1990s by a group of modernisers (notably the leaders John Smith and Tony Blair) within the British Labour party to shed its left-wing image and re-cast it as a party of moderate, middle-class British opinion. As we will see, under Clark's leadership the New Zealand Labour party embarked on the same gradualist re-branding exercise during the 1990s. Its overarching goal was to steer the public's perception of Labour away from the extremes of right-wing 'Rogernomics', on the one hand, and socialist interventionism on the other. (For a fuller discussion, see Barker 1998.)

A second approach to party repositioning is more dramatic and ad hoc, and is best described as the *shock-dose* method of vote maximisation. The leading exponent of this approach was Robert Muldoon, who, on becoming National party leader in 1974, launched a series of populist attacks on minority groups, particularly those claiming preferential treatment, illegal (Pacific Island) immigrants, criminals, and welfare dependents. His appeal to the fears and prejudices of voters lifted National to a resounding election victory the following year. A number of parallels can be drawn between National's circumstances in 1974 and those facing the party some thirty years later. After an extended period in government (1960–72 and 1990–99 respectively), culminating in a landslide defeat, a demoralised party replaced its leader at close to the mid-point in the three-year election cycle. This gave the new leader too little time to put a long-term recovery plan in place. Resisting his natural preference for free market reform, the implications of which might prove unpalatable for middle New Zealand, Brash took the same populist root that had served Muldoon so well in 1975.

The *gradualist* and *shock-dose* approaches to vote-seeking will be examined with reference to two case studies, one involving Labour, the other National.

Case study 1　Labour and the Third Way

During the 1990s, Labour struggled to dispel two contradictory images, both of which were frustrating its efforts to regain power. The first was based on the assumption that, as the architect of the free market reforms of the 1980s, the credibility of the party's social democratic message had been seriously compromised. The second image cast a much longer shadow, having been around for most of its history as an electoral organisation. According to a view happily endorsed by National, Labour was secretly committed to the implementation of a radical socialist (some would say 'socialist-feminist') agenda, the free market reforms of the 1980s notwithstanding. The politics of the Third Way provided a set of principles that could assist Labour in neutralising these two negative public images.

After almost two decades in opposition, during the early 1990s the leaders of the British Labour party began to develop a formula that would broaden the party's appeal beyond its core working-class constituency. According to Tony Blair, the Third Way provided a pathway between 'an Old Left preoccupied by state control, high taxation and producer interests; and a New Right treating public investment, and often the very notions of "society" and collective endeavour, as evils to be undone' (Blair 1998, p. 1). For social democratic governments grappling with the legacy of neo-liberal reform and the impact of globalisation on national sovereignty, inequality, and the knowledge-based economy, the promise of a modernised and revitalised version of social democracy had understandable appeal.

The Third Way has been described as upholding a number of social democracy's core values, including social justice, equality, and individual freedom. Where the Third Way and social democracy are most at odds is over the latter's antipathy to free market capitalism, its commitment to egalitarianism, and its support for rights without reference to responsibilities. According to the leading academic exponent of the Third Way, Anthony Giddens, the decline of class politics and the growth of a more affluent, consumption-oriented society have resulted in the emergence of a new individualism, built on the goals of self-reliance and fiscal restraint. In his view, the politics of left and right have since become less meaningful and important. 'We need more actively to accept responsibilities for the consequences of what we do and the lifestyle habits we adopt…We have to find a new balance between individual and collective responsibilities' (Giddens 1998, p. 37). Having carved out a position somewhere between the extremes of 'uncaring' individualism on the right and 'costly' collectivism on the left, by the late 1990s the Third Way was well positioned to exploit the moderate and meritocratic values of the burgeoning middle class.

In rejecting the collectivism of the old left, Giddens proposed a system of 'positive welfare', which is said to involve strategies for dealing with social exclusion and lack of personal responsibility and initiative. Practical proposals include 'welfare-to-work', entrepreneurial risk-taking (such as giving up the welfare benefit for a job in an unfamiliar field of employment), renewed emphasis on education and training (to achieve greater equality of access), abolition of statutory retirement and finding ways to encourage the fit elderly to remain in work, and policies designed to increase levels of personal savings and investment. To reverse the growth of voter dissatisfaction and alienation, Giddens offered a number of initiatives, including: the decentralisation and devolution of power; constitutional change aimed at providing more open and accountable political processes; and a range of voting mechanisms to encourage greater public participation, such as citizens' juries and the use of electronic referenda. In the interests of a more vibrant civil society, Giddens proposed schemes for community renewal, crime prevention, and the enhancement of family life (idealised as the 'democratic family'). Ideas for the enhancement of the family include co-parenting, greater responsibility for child-care, and the idea of reciprocal obligations between parents and children.

The New Zealand version of the Third Way shared a number of the key principles of the Giddens model, including recognition that a desire for personal independence and autonomy had largely replaced collective allegiances, including class, and that declining trust in government eased the way towards greater decentralisation and devolution. On taking office, the Clark government tried to maintain a delicate balance between the goals of limited state intervention, on the one hand, and retention of the essential features of free market reform. Examples of state intervention included the re-nationalisation of Accident Compensation, abolition of the Employment Contracts Act, and significant infrastructure investment. On the other hand, by exercising tight fiscal restraint, the government was able to avoid significant tax increases and assuage middle-class fears that Labour rewarded dependency and penalised hard work. An example of Labour's attitude to welfare can be seen in its 'Jobs Jolt' policy, the purpose of which was to force the unemployed back into work by limiting their eligibility for a benefit. The policy included work testing for those over the age of fifty-five years, increasing the work training opportunities for sole parents, and suspending the benefit for those who lived in remote areas. Although the scheme received support from the business community, the Greens described it as 'pandering to the right'.[14]

Does the Third Way represent a new paradigm or simply a re-branding exercise aimed at repositioning Labour as the party of 'middle' New Zealand? After more than a decade of reform, it was clear that many voters had grown weary of change, whether of the left or the right, preferring a government that would, in Clark's own words, 'build and unite, not…fragment and polarise'?[15] According to its critics, however, the Third Way's appeal had less to do with building an alternative ideology, or even revitalising social democracy, than the pursuit of power. As one commentator has said of Britain, '"Blairism" is not a coherent political philosophy, or a programme of political policies, or even a box of political tricks…[It] is simply what Tony Blair happens to feel at any given time…But what he feels (and herein lies the genius) is entirely conditioned by what others feel.'[16]

As well as offering some respectability by virtue of its association with the policies of Clinton, Schroeder, and Blair, the Third Way fitted with the cautious and pragmatic instincts of the New Zealand prime minister and members of her government. In supporting the Third Way, she faced criticism from those on the left, who considered it to be neo-liberalism with a human face, as well as those on the right, who likened it to a blancmange—Hillary Clinton had even made the startling claim that the Third Way could 'marry conservatism and liberalism, capitalism and statism, and tie together…the faults of man and the word of God, the end of communism and the beginning of the third millennium'.[17] As Blair himself found, however, while treading a pragmatic middle path may offend those who regard themselves to be the guardians of the party ideology, the promise of electoral success can make it all worthwhile.

Case study 2   National, Brash, and race

National's dramatic rise in the polls in the aftermath of Brash's 'racial separatism' speech provides a second opportunity to consider the relevance of the Downsian account of vote maximisation and the ideological mobility of parties. Beginning in late 2000, the polls revealed that a significant gap had opened up between National and Labour. Following the 2002 election, which produced National's worst-ever result of 21 per cent, there was increasing speculation that Bill English would be replaced as leader, although the successful challenge did not come until October 2003. Following the new leader's Orewa Rotary speech in January 2004, in which he accused the government of promoting race-based policies that had caused widespread public resentment and division, the party's support leaped 17 percentage points in the space of one month to 45 per cent.[18] It was the largest single increase in the history of polling in New Zealand.

Figure 8.3   Party support, 2001–04

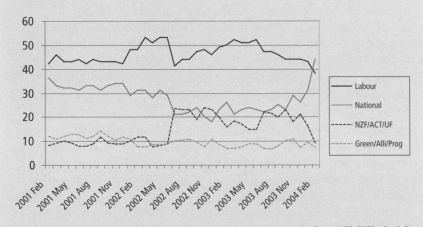

Source: NBR–Phillips Fox Poll

How can we account for this epic change in voter opinion? As the results in figure 8.3 show, support for Labour began to decline as early as mid-2003, with most of the traffic going towards the small parties. During this time, the government was responsible for some controversial legislation, especially the Supreme Court bill, which removed the right of appeal to the Privy Council and set in train the creation of a New Zealand Supreme Court, the prostitution reform bill, and a series of announcements on school amalgamations and closures. By far the most significant decision, however, was the government's response to the Court of Appeal's foreshore and seabed ruling. As we have seen, it had the effect of polarising public opinion along racial lines, with disaffected Maori supporting Tariana Turia and the incipient Maori party movement, and disaffected Pakeha accusing the government of giving away New Zealand's foreshore and beaches to radical Maori.

For some considerable time, National had been trying to come up with policies that would strike a chord with mainstream opinion. Having lost large parts of its natural constituency during the period of economic and welfare reform in the early 1990s, the party's vote remained stuck in the low 30s from the 1993 election on, only to slide to an all-time low at the 2002 election. So successful was the Labour-led government at striking an acceptable balance on economic, social, and political issues, that National was left with no popular issues with which to attack the government. The economic outlook was positive, unemployment rates were down, and the prime minister appeared to have her MPs and ministers under firm control. Besides, even as the government began to falter from mid-2003 on, National's leadership problems prevented it from exploiting the escalating mood of public concern.

The first inkling that Brash was about to take decisive action that would turn the tide of public opinion was revealed by the political journalist, John Armstrong, in an article in the *New Zealand Herald* in mid-January 2004.[19] Armstrong appeared to have been given a preview of the National party leader's speech, which would be delivered within the following fortnight. The journalist revealed that Brash's 'kitchen cabinet' of the deputy leader, Gerry Brownlee, Murray McCully (the key figure behind National's new strategy), Simon Power, and two key media advisors had devised a plan that would 'shift the [foreshore] debate away from Maori discontent and start giving Pakeha the heebie-jeebies'. Armstrong teased readers with the warning to 'Watch out Winston Peters'. While mainstream voters would never warm to Brash's brand of right-wing economics, experience had shown that they were highly susceptible to right-wing populism, especially on the potentially divisive issue of race relations.

On the surface, there was little in Brash's Orewa speech to suggest any significant departure from what other political leaders, including Prebble and Peters, had been saying for some time. In building his argument that New Zealand had become a racially divided nation, Brash alleged that the government was moving in the direction of 'two sets of laws, and two standards of citizenship'.[20] Maori, he said, had long enjoyed the same standard of citizenship as Pakeha. While conceding that injustices had occurred during the course of the nation's history, 'there is a limit to how much any generation can apologise for the sins of its great grandparents'. Gradually, a 'grievance industry' had grown up around both a Treaty-claims process that went back to 1840 and a body of legislation that upheld the 'principles' of the Treaty, a term which had never been properly defined. Brash accused the government of reversing '125 years of settled law' with its foreshore and seabed decision. Customary title could be interpreted by the government as not only giving Maori commercial development rights, but also the right of management and veto over use of the New Zealand coastline. He called for the removal of any race-based provisions in existing legislation, the abolition of the Maori seats, and a speedy end to the historical claims process.

The impact of Brash's speech owed less to its carefully reasoned argument than to the cumulative effect of the foreshore and seabed debate. The speech became the lightening-rod for unleashing deep-seated public resentment over the perceived special privileges enjoyed by Maori. Poor management of the issue by government ministers simply confirmed the view of many non-Maori that their right of access to the New Zealand coastline was in danger of being permanently lost. That the speech was delivered virtually on the eve of Waitangi Day, an occasion when Brash was splattered with mud as he approached the Treaty House at Waitangi, was significant. In the absence of other news during this holiday period, extensive media coverage was given to the attack on the National leader, thereby providing a platform for further reflection on the significance of his Orewa speech.

But the foreshore and seabed debate is not simply a case study in the ability of the opposition National party to manipulate the polls. Within days of the turnaround in National's fortunes, the prime minister admitted that a 'new balance' had to be found in its stance towards Maori.[21] The government's seeming u-turn in the face of National's assault on the electoral middle ground could hardly have been more opportunistic. Labour would review its policies with respect to affirmative action programmes for Maori, the proposed foreshore and seabed legislation would be scrutinised yet again, with the prime minister even suggesting that the place of the Treaty within New Zealand's constitutional arrangements could be the subject of an inquiry by a parliamentary committee, or even a royal commission, and a senior Pakeha minister, Trevor Mallard, was put in overall charge of the government's race relations programme. To underscore its receptiveness to public opinion, on an unrelated matter, that of school closures, Labour announced that it was putting an immediate stop to the review process.

Conclusion

This chapter has considered the merits of two very different accounts of the importance of ideology to party politics. While the families-based approach provides a useful model for considering the importance of ideology to a party's formation and development, it masks the fact that parties are dynamic organisations that are not easily contained within the boundaries of one ideological category or group. As our discussion has shown, most of New Zealand's parties are hybrid by nature. National, for example, has been described as a 'liberal-conservative party, the emphasis being on the "liberal" or the "conservative" according to the speaker' (Shorter 1974, p. 348). Labour continued to describe itself as a social democratic party, even in the midst of sweeping neo-liberal reform. Still others have shown a chameleon-like quality that allows for even more frequent adjustments to their ideological hue—United Future, for example, happily morphs between a liberal party (in the British Liberal party tradition), an ethnic party, and a socially conservative Christian party.

The second, vote-maximising explanation also has weaknesses. Firstly, contrary to what Downs claims, parties do help to shape public opinion. While it is in their interests to be receptive to the views of the voting public, there are times when parties will lead by example. During the 1980s, for example, the Lange government led, rather than followed, public opinion on a range of policy initiatives, including a ban on nuclear ship visits, economic and welfare reform, and the sale of publicly owned assets. Despite strong public opposition to some of these changes, the government forged ahead in the belief that it was capable of turning public attitudes around. Secondly, parties can and do leap-frog over one another, as illustrated by Labour's economic lurch to the right of National during the 1980s, and its swing back a decade later. Similarly, while New Zealand First brands itself as a centre party on economic and welfare policy, when it comes to its three defining issues of law and order, immigration, and the Treaty, it has been able to outflank its rivals on the moderate to extreme right.

When the institutional and vote-maximising accounts are compared, the latter appears to be the more currently relevant and persuasive. As we have seen, it is based on the assumption that the balance between winning elections to make policies and making policies to win elections leans heavily towards the latter. Ideology may not be dead, but nor can it be viewed as a reliable guide to what a party will do in government. Because party competition under MMP has remained centripetally located, the two major parties and several smaller ones are required to engage in intense competition for the support of mainstream opinion. To this end, during the late 1990s and early 2000s, Labour embraced much of what we have come to understand as the politics of the Third Way. Under Clark's leadership, the party charted a slow but deliberate course between the extremes of socialism and the free market. In contrast, the shock-dose approach adopted by National reached out to middle New Zealand with a populist agenda focusing on race, supplemented by a tough stance on crime (e.g. the abolition of parole) and welfare (e.g. the reintroduction of 'workfare'). Policies that risked alienating mainstream opinion, including the sale of further state-owned assets, support for military intervention in Iraq, and a proposed lifting of the ban on nuclear ship visits, were either shelved or fudged. Although criticised for being highly cynical and self-serving, the vote-seeking model now dominates the electoral agenda.

Notes

1   See, for example, Hon. Steve Maharey, 'Values *and* Politics: Some Reflections on the New Social Democracy in a New Zealand Context'. Speech to the Foundation for Policy Initiatives, Auckland, 26 March 2001.
2   In the view of von Beyme, his schema had little direct relevance to a number of the most well-known non-European democracies, including Canada and the USA.
3   The term 'hybrid' was adopted by Ware (1996, p. 26) to describe parties that displayed the characteristics of more than one ideological family.
4   Named after the Finance minister, Roger Douglas, it was viewed by its critics as being little different from 'Reaganomics' and 'Thatcherism'.
5   These terms are still being used. At a recent meeting between Helen Clark and Neil Kinnock, for example, the former British Labour leader described the prime minister as a 'fellow socialist'. *Sunday Star Times*, 27 April 2003, A7.
6   F. O'Sullivan, 'Seeking ideas from like minds', *New Zealand Herald*, 10 July 2003, A18.
7   Also laying claim to membership of the family of liberal parties is United Future. The party's leader, Peter Dunne, is an admirer of the British Liberal prime minister, Lloyd George, and maintains contact with members of the current British Liberal party, including the leader of the Scottish Liberal Democrats. Personal interview with Peter Dunne, Parliament Buildings, Wellington, 16 July 2003.
8   See, for example, *New Zealand Herald*, 2 May 2000, A12.
9   *New Zealand Listener*, 20–27 September 2002, p. 21.
10 R. Berry, 'Attacks on other leaders leave ACT members uneasy', *New Zealand Herald*, 10 March 2004, A5.
11 They include Mana Motuhake, Mana Maori, Indigenous People's, Nga Iwi Morehu, Aroha-Ngai-Tatou, Te Tawharau, and Mauri Pacific.
12 www.maoriparty.com.
13 J. Milne, 'Turia feisty after historic win', *Sunday Star Times,* 11 July 2004, p. A4.
14 *New Zealand Herald*, 5 August 2003, A1.

15   H. Clark, 'Address to the New Zealand Labour Party Conference', Convention Centre, Christchurch, 8 November 2003.

16   R. Harris, 'Bewitched—10 years of Blair', *New Zealand Herald*, 22 July 2004, p.B4.

17   In F. Wheen, 'The Nutty Professor: Stating the Obvious and Anthony Giddens', *The Guardian*, 1 March 2000.

18   *One News/Colmar Brunton Poll*, 13 February 2004.

19   J. Armstrong, 'Brash ready to come out swinging', *New Zealand Herald*, 17–18 January 2004, A24.

20   D. Brash, 'Nationhood', Orewa Rotary Club, 27 January 2004 (www.national.org.nz).

21   R. Berry, 'Clark to take another look', *New Zealand Herald*, 24 February 2004, A1.

Further reading

Blair, T. 1998, *The Third Way: New Politics for the New Century*, Fabian Society, London.

Downs, A. 1957, *An Economic Theory of Democracy*, Harper and Row, New York.

Eichbaum, C. 1999, 'The Politics and Economics of the Third Way', in S. Chatterjee, P. Conway, P. Dalziel, C. Eichbaum, P. Harris, B. Philpott and R. Shaw, *The New Politics: A Third Way for New Zealand*, Dunmore Press, Palmerston North, pp. 33–62.

Giddens, A. 1998, *The Third Way: The Renewal of Social Democracy*, Cambridge: Polity Press, Cambridge.

Giddens, A. 2000, *The Third Way and its Critics,* Cambridge: Polity Press, Cambridge.

McKenzie, B. 2002, 'Left Without a Choice? Labour, Social Democracy and the Third Way in New Zealand and Britain', MA thesis, Department of Political Studies, University of Auckland.

Ware, A. 1996, *Political Parties and Party Systems*, Oxford University Press, Oxford (especially chapter 1).

The Modern Campaign

9

HAVING established that political parties shape their policies to the needs of the electoral market, it is time to consider how they compete for the support of voters. Election campaigns are central to our conception of popular sovereignty. Their legitimacy is measured not only by the degree of competition and choice, but also by public involvement, with any suggestion of low participation reflecting poorly on the credibility of the entire democratic process. New Zealand has an enviable record of popular participation in campaigns, with small armies of volunteers urging voters to attend campaign meetings and cast a vote. Indeed, for much of the twentieth century New Zealand was able to boast a voter turnout ranging between 85 and 90 per cent. Given this tradition, it is important to consider what effect, if any, campaign modernisation may have had on levels of public engagement.

The modern campaign can be characterised as one in which traditional forms of campaigning have been replaced by the techniques of professional marketing. In line with developments pioneered in other Western democracies, especially the USA, television has become the primary link between politicians and voters. Whereas the focus of the pre-modern campaign was on direct face-to-face public meetings in the local workplace or community hall, today's walkabouts and media interviews are scheduled around the requirements of the 6 o'clock television news. Together with political advertisements, leaders' debates, invitation-only opening and closing addresses, and other similar media presentations, these orchestrated events constitute the *modus operandi* of the modern election campaign. To maximise their effectiveness, campaign organisations make increasing use of professional agencies and consultants, together with the party leader's paid political staff, developments that pose an obvious threat to the traditional functions of local party organisers and activists.

When combined with the intense multiparty competition that we have come to associate with MMP, the process of modernisation has given rise to a more personal, even 'presidential', style of campaign. It is a well-established fact that television is better suited to presentational than issue based politics. Media polls on the most preferred prime minister and the use of image-makers and 'spin doctors' are ubiquitous features of the modern campaign, to the extent that voters could be forgiven for assuming that they have a directly elected prime minister. When combined with the regular diet of leaders' debates and television sound bites, it is easy to see why the instruments of political marketing have largely replaced more traditional forms of campaigning. Giving unexpected impetus to this trend has been the rise of personality-based parties, such as New Zealand First, together with a shift of focus under MMP from the electorate to the nationwide party vote campaign. This said, personality and leadership still lack the prominence that they receive in genuinely presidential systems, especially that of the USA.

This chapter will trace the development of election campaigns, describing how each stage in the process has a number of distinct, if overlapping characteristics. In her book *A Virtuous Circle*, Norris (2000) identifies three stages in the development of election campaigns. The *pre-modern* stage was characterised by limited planning, direct and highly personal means of communication between local candidates and voters, selective and partisan newspaper advertising, and the use of a largely volunteer campaign workforce. The second, *modern*, stage can be dated from the arrival of television.[1] Faced with the prospect of appealing to a nationwide audience, beginning in the late 1960s the parties began to downplay dogma, preferring to focus on more presentational aspects of politics, including leadership, party positioning, and public opinion. This required a more professional approach to campaigning, with particular attention being paid to advertising, public relations, and television performance. What distinguishes the *postmodern* or *digital* campaign from earlier stages of campaign development has been the advent of the new technologies, especially in the fields of telecommunications, satellite transmission, and the Internet. Instead of simply 'selling' the party and its leader, the emphasis of the postmodern campaign has shifted to a 'marketing' strategy 'in which the product is adapted to suit the desires of voters' (Farrell 2002, p. 81).

Underlying the transition towards a more professional and presidential campaign has been the unresolved debate over control of the campaign agenda. This will be discussed with particular reference to the relationship between politicians and the media during the 2002 campaign. Finally, while it is possible to make a persuasive case for the view that public participation is in decline, this chapter will explore the merits of the view that it is not so much a question of people disengaging from campaigns, but rather of their engaging differently (Norris 2000; Norris 2002b; Farrell and Webb 2000). This claim will be discussed with reference to survey data on public interest in campaigns and when people make their voting decisions. The chapter will consider fresh opportunities for public participation, especially through the use of interactive television, email, and the World Wide Web.

Campaign modernisation[2]

Pre-modern stage (–1969)

The first stage of campaigning coincided with the era of the mass party. Through a system of vertical links, the two major parties were able to build campaign organisations capable of competing at both the local and national levels (see chapter 4). At the local level, party members worked under the direction of campaign organisers, especially in those seats that were deemed to be highly marginal. Their activities included canvassing, distributing pamphlets, and assisting with transport on polling day. In the absence of opinion polls, they were able to provide the additional service of reporting back to their local or regional organisers on what voters were saying about the politicians and issues of the day (for a fuller discussion, see chapter 5). At the national level, the party campaign was planned by a committee, which typically included the leader and president, although much of the day-to-day coordination fell to the national secretary and head office staff in Wellington. The informality with which national campaigns were conducted is perhaps best illustrated by the experience of Labour's campaign director during the course of the 1960 election. According to Austin Mitchell, 'a slight disruption was caused towards the end of the campaign when this official was called for some days of jury service, and had to carry out his work in the evening' (Chapman et al. 1962, p. 88).

During the pre-modern stage, electioneering was built around a crowded schedule of campaign meetings and whistle-stop tours. The party leaders travelled by train or car, delivering up to 20 campaign speeches to audiences typically numbering several hundred, even in the small country towns. Although heavily policy-oriented, the speeches were peppered with questions, interjections, and applause. Local candidates also had their own separate schedule of meetings, usually in public halls, but also on street corners and in workplace cafeterias. Beginning in the 1920s and 1930s, state-owned radio played an increasingly important part in campaigns. Through his friendship with the broadcaster, Colin Scrimgeour, Michael Joseph Savage, became an early enthusiast for political broadcasting (Gustafson 1976, p. 170). During the postwar period radio broadcasts became an important feature of campaigning—in 1960, for example, there were some thirty-five political broadcasts, ten of which lasted for two hours. The crude nature of these early broadcasts, with little if any scripting or other production techniques, caused Keith Jackson to comment: 'The New Zealand parties adhered to the device of inordinately long nationwide harangues from broadcast public meetings, supplemented by one-man talk shows' (Chapman et al. 1962, p. 110).

Despite the predominance of a largely volunteer campaign organisation, the pre-modern stage of campaign development was not without some of the characteristics that we have come to associate with today's campaigns. A number of the early leaders, including Richard John Seddon (premier 1893–1906) and Savage (prime minister 1935–40) ran highly personal, even 'presidential', campaigns. As early as 1925, the Reform party's campaign was highly personalised by design, with the slogans 'Coates and Confidence', 'Coats Off With Coates: The Man Who Gets Things Done', and 'Coates and Prosperity' promoting the leadership credentials of their 'young' (he was fifty years of age) prime minister, Gordon Coates.[3] As well as focusing on the personal qualities of the leader, some of the early campaigns were also subject to central control in such areas as candidate selection, party finance, and policy formulation.[4]

While the execution of campaigns was rather amateurish by today's standards, as early as the 1920s the parties were experimenting with campaign advertising, the content of which was simple, brief, and emotional, with each side accusing the other of the most extreme views imaginable. Perhaps the first of the professional campaign organisers was A.E. Davey, who was employed by the Reform party to run the 1925 campaign. A final characteristic that we associate with today's campaigns was the notion of a permanent campaign. While the formal campaign ran for a similar length of time to that of today (approximately five weeks), the genesis of the longer, quasi-permanent campaign can be traced back to before the 1935 election, when Savage is said to have campaigned for up to two years (Gustafson 1976, p. 174). Several months prior to the start of the 1938 election campaign, he reportedly addressed up to fourteen meetings a day, with audiences as large as 900 to 1,300 (Gustafson 1976, p. 216).

Modern stage (1969–)

Although television was first introduced to New Zealand in 1961, its initial impact was blunted by the high purchase price of television sets and the absence of a national web. Prior to 1968 there was no national television news, newsreels had to be sent north and south from Wellington to the four main regional stations each day, and special telecasts, such as the 1993 and 1996 election-night specials, were produced as separate programmes in each of the main centres. However, overseas experience suggested that it would not be long before the new medium threatened traditional channels of campaign communication. As television became more accessible, politicians would be able to reach directly over the heads of party members, activists, and organisers to a mass audience.

In a series of developments we have come to associate with the 'Americanization' of politics, in 1969 the opposition Labour party was responsible for the first of New Zealand's modern election campaigns. Earlier that year, a young advertising executive, Bob Harvey of McHarmons advertising agency, had travelled to the USA, where he met strategists from Richard Nixon's 1968 presidential campaign.[5] On his return, Harvey made a pitch to senior Labour party officials, including Norman Douglas, Arthur Faulkner, and the leader, Norman Kirk. His proposal was based on the concept of an integrated campaign plan involving a new logo, the introduction of slogans, jingles, television advertisements and mini-documentary slots, and efforts to create a more positive image of the leader. A film-maker, Roger Donaldson, produced a series of one and two-minute documentaries, the Hamilton Blue Grass Band performed a jingle based on the campaign slogan 'Make Things Happen', and the art critic, Hamish Keith, created a leaning 'L' (for Labour) logo that survived as the party's symbol until 1996.[6] To help soften the party's 'trade union/RSA' image, efforts were made to persuade Kirk to dress in designer clothes and be groomed by a hair stylist. A 10-page supplement to the *New Zealand Women's Weekly* entitled 'This Man Kirk' drew the readers' attention to the personal strengths and capabilities of the Labour leader. Kirk was described as an 'ordinary New Zealander' who had 'seemingly boundless energy, and works at a pace that would exhaust many men. His favourite sports, when he can spare the time, are fishing and deer-stalking. Norm Kirk regards himself as an ordinary New Zealander—

a family man who enjoys a glass of beer, a yarn with his friends, and watching a good game of football.' The eight-page supplement contained no less than 28 pictures featuring Kirk.[7] In contrast, National ran a traditional campaign featuring the collective experience of its 20-man cabinet.

Despite these innovations, by international standards the quality of the printed advertisements was poor. Writing about the 1972 campaign, Nigel Roberts expressed the view that Labour's advertisements 'contained an excessive amount of detail, and some of the supposedly "trendy" ones with psychedelic-style drawings (in brilliant black and stunning white!) ended up looking more like advertisements for a well-known brand of ice-cream than a political party' (1975, p. 106). By 1975, the flow of political advertising was moving in the direction of television. In one of the most controversial developments in the history of campaigning in New Zealand, National's Colenso agency developed a series of hard-hitting cartoons depicting Labour as a dangerously authoritarian government, and blaming particular immigrant groups for a perceived breakdown in law and order. Given the growing importance of the new medium as a source of political information, with some 91 per cent of viewers having watched some of the 1975 campaign on television (Wilkes 1978, p. 215), it is easy to see why National's advertising strategy proved to be so influential in contributing to the Labour government's landslide defeat.

One element missing from earlier campaigns was the use of focus groups or party-commissioned polls. Shortly before the 1972 election, Labour strategists persuaded a commercial pollster, Paul Heylen, to add questions on voting intentions to his regular battery of questions on trends and issues (the National Research Bureau began conducting political polls in 1970, closely followed by Heylen). National's use of market research for its 1975 campaign themes caused one commentator to observe that campaigning had 'spawned the emergence of a new elite—the political media specialists—who are directly involved in producing campaign materials, and thereby in defining political realities' (Wilkes 1978, p. 219). By the late 1970s, party-commissioned polls had become a regular feature of New Zealand elections. In 1983, for example, poll results were used to persuade the Labour caucus that David Lange had a better chance of defeating National's Robert Muldoon at the next election than the incumbent leader, Bill Rowling.[8]

Digital stage (1999–)

As with the emergence of television in the 1960s, political parties on this side of the world have been slow to embrace features of the new technology, although no more so than in Britain, which conducted its first 'Internet' election in 2001 (Ballinger 2002, p. 224). Since the turn of the century, parties and individual politicians have been able to develop a capacity for electronic messaging that is direct, immediate, easily targeted to particular groups, and cost-effective. As one study of Internet usage found, while communication travels in both directions, the flow is largely 'top-down' rather than 'bottom-up', with the main functions being concerned with conveying information; recruiting new members and supporters; keeping the local party organisation abreast of what is happening in government and parliament; and mobilising campaign workers and voters (Gibson and Ward 2000, pp. 108–10).

While it would be an exaggeration to describe the 2002 election as New Zealand's first e-campaign, it did represent significant progress in the use of the Internet. The first party web sites, which were launched in the mid-1990s, were primitive in design and elementary in content. Today they are aimed at four main groups: party members and activists; voters; the young, especially students; and journalists. For the latter two groups in particular, the most advanced web sites are a minefield of useful source material for their academic and professional research. Whereas at the 1999 election there was scant information on the candidates or the activities of the leader, and archival material was often difficult to access, by 2002 all the user-friendly sites had an abundance of up-to-date material. This included candidate profiles, party policies, photographs of past leaders, and press releases. A feature of the ACT party's front page, for example, was a constantly scrolling list of notices and events. Most parties made provision for members of the public to register their support or become a member online. Although response rates to enquiries made by email were not encouraging, a standard feature of most sites was a list of email addresses and other contact details of political candidates and MPs. Prior to United Future's sudden rise to prominence in 2002, it was not uncommon for the party leader, Peter Dunne, to personally answer email enquiries.

One of the most innovative features of Labour's web site was the opportunity to have a live 'chat' with a cabinet minister, although participants were required to submit their questions in advance. Other advances included a film clip of the prime minister's annual address to the Labour party conference and, in the case of the Greens, a compact disc track featuring an MP, Metiria Turei. As one might expect, variations in the quality of the web sites bore little relation to relative importance and size. National's web site, for example, was extremely basic, as were those of New Zealand First and United Future. Indeed, with the notable exception of Labour, the Greens, and ACT, surprisingly little effort was made to engage the web surfer with attractive imagery or to comprehensively inform and update. That most of the parties did not do more to exploit the opportunities provided by the Internet is surprising, especially since, as a relatively inexpensive method of communication, it removes much of the natural disadvantage suffered by small and modestly resourced parties vis-à-vis their main rivals (Gibson and Ward 2000, p. 111).

Clearly more needs to be done to dispel fears that the Internet is being viewed simply as a top-down method of communication. A survey of Internet use among parliamentarians conducted in 2004 revealed that only half of all MPs responded to an email request for their views on certain political issues. Labour, which had promised to 'make government more accessible' had one of the poorest response rates, with only 39 per cent of its MPs replying. Even worse was New Zealand First at 23 per cent.[9] As these results indicate, parties need to view voters less as 'consumers' and more as 'participants' in the political process (Nixon and Johansson 1999, p. 136).

Model of the professional campaign

Although the new technology is a distinguishing feature of the postmodern campaign, equally important has been the emergence of a professionally trained and highly centralised campaign elite. In this part of the chapter, we will assess their influence by constructing a model comprising five inter-related developments: the centralisation of the campaign organisation in the office of the party leader; increased use of political marketing; access to professional consultants and agencies; the commercialisation of distribution networks; and the advent of the permanent campaign (adapted from Bowler and Farrell 1992, p. 11).

a. Centralised control

In order to effectively manage today's more professional and technically complex campaigns, all of the parties have adopted organisational structures based on highly centralised planning and control. Whereas the national campaign was once largely overseen by the extra-parliamentary organisation, with much of the day-to-day coordination being conducted out of party head office by extra-parliamentary staff, power has now shifted to the party's political wing, specifically the party leader's office. Under the supervision of a clutch of senior politicians and the leaders' personal staff, including political analysts and press secretaries, the campaign committee has access to an assortment of professional agencies and consultants, together with the full range of specialist services, including those of policy analysis, speech writing, fund-raising, liaising with the media, monitoring the party's advertising campaign and media performance, and designing and maintaining the party's web site.

Under MMP, centralised planning and control can be defended on the grounds that campaigns are being transformed into national referendums on coalition government. Because voters increasingly use the campaign to weigh up the various governing options, with opinion polls providing regular cues on the likely coalition prospects of each party, it is in the interests of the party leaders to centrally plan and monitor developments with a view to achieving the most desirable outcome for their party. Late in the 1996 campaign, for example, it became clear to key National party strategists that their most preferred coalition partner, ACT, was in danger of falling short of the 5 per cent threshold above which parties are guaranteed parliamentary representation. They responded by giving implied approval to National voters in the highly marginal seat of Wellington Central to bypass the chosen National candidate and give their constituency vote to the ACT candidate, Richard Prebble.

A further example of head office intervention on behalf of a potential coalition partner occurred during the 1999 campaign. Against the wishes of the local Labour candidate, as well as local party members and officials, Helen Clark endorsed the Green candidate, Jeanette Fitzsimons, in her close race with the National candidate for the seat of Coromandel. Three years later, the Labour leader aspired to the quite different goal of governing alone, with the proviso that a cabinet seat would be reserved for the former Alliance leader, Jim Anderton. Having caught a whiff of electoral success, perhaps even a governing majority, the prime minister centred her campaign on the theme 'What sort of Labour government?' On this occasion, voters were confronted with the potential weaknesses of coalition government, especially one that included the Greens, the Alliance, or New Zealand First.

Labour's 2002 campaign was directed from the Office of the Prime Minister. This included aspects of the national party vote campaign, as well as progress in winning the key marginal electorates. Apart from Clark, the membership of Labour's campaign committee consisted of senior cabinet ministers, including Michael Cullen, Phil Goff and Trevor Mallard, together with the prime minister's key political advisers, notably Heather Simpson, Tony Timms, Mike Munro, the senior press secretary and former political editor of the *Dominion* newspaper, and Sarah Clarke, who was head of the party's parliamentary research unit. The organisational wing was represented by the party president, Mike Williams, who was also the campaign director, and general secretary Mike Smith. During the campaign the committee met every morning at 7 a.m., with the prime minister and any others who happened to be campaigning outside of the capital participating by way of a telephone link-up. As well as reviewing events of the previous day, the committee would discuss any shifts in public opinion, the issues being raised by the main media outlets, especially television, and what the leader should say by way of response.[10]

National's campaign organisation in 2002 was broadly similar to that of Labour, although without the access to public servants and technical advisors that comes from being in government. The party's campaign committee consisted of the leader, Bill English, the deputy leader, Roger Sowry, and the MPs Simon Power, and Murray McCully. It also included the leader's key advisers, notably the leader's chief advisor Tim Grafton, and press secretary

Sue Foley (formerly chief of staff for *TV3 News*), and the party president, Michelle Boag. Although the committee met every day, responsibility for the day-to-day running of the campaign was in the hands of the campaign's director-general, Allan Johnston, whose lack of political experience and personal authority, as well as limited strategic ability, are said to have contributed to the party's disappointing campaign performance.[11] Whereas previous National leaders, such as Jim Bolger, had been directly involved in the management of the campaign, Bill English largely left it to campaign officials. As we will see, this had unfortunate consequences for the party's advertising and strategic decision-making processes.

While the New Zealand First, United Future, and Progressive parties maintained electorate offices in their cornerstone seats of Tauranga, Ohariu-Belmont, and Wigram respectively, in 2002 the all-important campaign for the party vote was effectively conducted, not by a campaign committee in party headquarters, but by the party leader, with assistance from the MPs and their parliamentary staffs, together with the leader's administrative and political staff. Unlike Labour and National, both of which continue to maintain a party head office, although with reduced staffing and functions, the three minor parties conduct most of their party business within the precincts of parliament. Furthermore, whereas under the former first-past-the-post electoral system the organisational resources of the minor parties had to be spread across multiple electorates, the two list parties, ACT and the Greens, have demonstrated the advantages of having them concentrated almost exclusively on a single nationwide campaign. This removes much of the advantage formerly enjoyed by the more highly organised and better-resourced major parties, certainly in competing for the party vote.

b. Political marketing

Adopting the techniques of mass marketing has obvious spin-offs for the political parties, especially in the competitive multiparty environment of MMP. As we saw in the previous chapter, Labour's appeal to the broad centre ground has involved compromise, not least in the dilution of its traditional message with a view to appealing to the conservative instincts of 'middle' New Zealand. More than any other party, it is finely tuned to the shifting tides of public opinion on a wide range of issues, including welfare spending, Maori seabed and seashore claims, and the war in Iraq. But as well as being something of a 'catch-all' party, Labour has been able to use the tools of the new technology to tailor its message to particular segments of the voting public, including students, professionals, such as nurses and teachers, Maori, and women.

An ability to target groups of voters is also attractive to some of the smaller 'boutique' parties, such as ACT and the Greens. Developing a strong party brand is now viewed as an essential function of the modern party, so much so that media commentary on the formation of a new party is as likely to include the views of brand managers and other marketing specialists as it is those of political scientists. ACT's target constituency includes members of the business sector, high-income earners, Asian immigrants, rural dwellers, and men. The Green party, on the other hand, enjoys support among the well educated, those in urban areas, and the young. As Tim Bale points out, the party also appeals to the 'well-to-do thirty-forty-something mother concerned about safe food and a safe environment for her children' (2003, p. 284).

c. Professional consultants and agencies

In 2002, the Labour, National, and ACT parties were sufficiently well resourced to be able to conduct focus groups and tracking polls throughout the campaign. Not so the other parties, which were severely constrained in their ability to survey public opinion. Early in the year, the Greens commissioned one piece of market research, from Consumer Link, to identify and work on the soft end of their vote (that is, those who might vote for the Greens as their second or third choice).[12] The Progressives did a similar amount of market research, drawing on a $300,000 budget provided by corporate donors. This quantitative research was supplemented by focus groups in Christchurch and Auckland, which were led by party volunteers.[13] Although United Future had insufficient resources to undertake its own polling, the party was able to conduct two focus group sessions in the pre-election period.[14] New Zealand First did no market research, preferring to trust the judgment of its leader to identify the relevant issues and sources of electoral support.

The extent to which advertising and other professional agencies were used during the 2002 campaign was largely a product of the size and financial resources of each party. As the main recipients of corporate and state funding (see chapter 5), the Labour, National, and ACT parties were able to use their advertising agencies for virtually all of their television, radio, and print advertisements. However, as recent experience shows, access to professional expertise does not guarantee a successful advertising campaign. In 1999, for example, National's 60-second advertisements featuring the party's 'brat-pack' MPs were not well received by the viewing public. Similar problems occurred in 2002, requiring a major review of the advertising strategy shortly before the final week of the campaign. According to one journalist, 'the campaign committee failed to give the advertising company a brief and so the ads, not surprisingly, were scripted without reference to the committee'.[15]

In contrast to the level of professional assistance available to the major parties, the less well-funded minor parties tend to supplement their agencies' services with as much in-house expertise as they can muster. In 2002, for example, while the Progressives used a small Christchurch firm to create their newspaper advertisements and design some flyers, party employees tended to write the text.[16] United Future used Cognito, a boutique agency in Wellington for much of its advertising, but also drew on the expertise offered gratis by an American political consultant, who was put in touch with the party by the US Embassy in Wellington.[17] Perhaps the most inspired piece of political advertising of the 2002 campaign was the 'Bob the Builder' slogan adopted by New Zealand First for Winston Peters. It came, not from a professional agency, but rather from paid employees working in the leader's office.

d. Distribution networks

A recent innovation adopted by most of the parties, and reflecting the decline in the availability of party volunteers, has involved the use of commercial distribution companies to disseminate campaign literature. By using an electronic version of the electoral roll, it is possible to target mail to particular occupational and geographical groups. Stockpiling separate email address lists provides yet further possibilities in the emerging era of the e-campaign. In 2002, ACT used Kiwi Mail to deliver several hundred thousand flyers to households around the country, and United Future, which had a very small membership, also used commercial delivery for most of the 340,000 copies of the policy booklet 'The Hard Facts'.[18] A flyer produced by the Progressives in the form of a flip-card featuring a photograph of Jim Anderton was delivered to some 400,000 households by a combination of volunteers (300,000) and commercial enterprises (100,000).[19] The Greens used direct mailing for the first time in 2002. This involved the targeting of particular groups, such as health workers and teachers, with relevant policy material, together with a mail drop to more than a million homes.[20] ACT's use of commercial distributors was even more extensive, with some 750,000 households receiving several pieces of mail during the course of the campaign. In addition, the party targeted sections of the community, including Asian voters, with pamphlets explaining particular policies and directly asking for their party vote.[21] The organisational and political wings of the party also maintained their own separate if significantly overlapping email address lists of supporters and other interested voters.

e. Permanent campaign

Ready access to mass marketing and the new technology has accelerated the trend towards a permanent election campaign (Scammell 1995, p. 277; Farrell and Webb 2000). In an era when campaigns were largely the responsibility of amateurs, there was little chance of being able to maintain an organisational readiness much beyond the formal campaign period. Today, both major parties and several of the minor ones spend much of the intervening years campaigning for the next election (Hirschfeld 1997, p. 34). For example, during the early 1990s Jim Bolger took the media on the 'campaign' trail with what became known as his 'Heartland' tours, and the annual party conference provided an opportunity for open electioneering, a practice continued by Jenny Shipley and Helen Clark during their terms as prime minister. Quite apart from lifting the party's profile, the permanent campaign allows parties to give early attention to a number of tasks, including the potentially divisive selection of list and electorate candidates, attracting corporate funds, and raising the public profile of the party and its brand.

Media-politico relationship

The transition to more presidential, market-driven campaigns has led to a rekindling of the debate over who controls the campaign agenda. The politicians' natural instinct for control is bolstered by a conviction that the primary role for the media is that of a conduit through which the parties compete for the hearts and minds of voters. In two-party systems the agenda-setting capacity of each side is reasonably clear-cut. Whereas the governing party has the natural advantage of being able to draw on the prestige and resources of office, the opposition party's task is to present an alternative vision, to mobilise and galvanise discontent, and to disrupt. Multiparty systems are more complex, with the small parties frequently struggling to capture any media attention. One potentially productive response is to adopt an extreme position, as exemplified by Winston Peters' repeated success at injecting the issue of immigration onto the campaign agenda.

In recent times, the task of opposition parties has been made more difficult by the ability of the incumbent government to manipulate and obfuscate the news through the increasingly standard practice of political 'spin'. One strategy pioneered by Britain's Tony Blair is to 'govern by headline' (Rentoul 2003, p. 292). As well as diluting the ideological content of the political agenda, such an approach gives unprecedented powers of news management and control to the prime minister's chief press secretary (until recently, Alastair Campbell, in the case of Blair). While political spin is almost as commonplace in New Zealand as it is in Britain, differences of personality and style between the two prime ministers, as well as between their senior press officers, make it less likely that the culture of command and control at the heart of the Blair government will be as successful in the more intimate surroundings of the New Zealand parliament and cabinet.

But politicians and their advisors are not the only ones seeking to influence the news agenda. In recent elections, the media has played an increasingly prominent part in defining and manipulating the issues of the campaign. Much of the initiative behind the media's role originates with the Parliamentary Press Gallery,[22] a group of approximately eighty political journalists, the most prominent of whom are household names by virtue of the fact that they interview politicians and interpret the news to a nationwide audience on an almost daily basis. From the outset of the campaign, the Gallery journalists report developments either while on the road with one of the leaders or from their base in parliament. Whereas some prime ministers, including David Lange and Mike Moore, have made a habit of returning to Wellington at the end of each day's campaigning, thereby providing journalists with the opportunity to seek background information and opinion on the day's events, in 2002 Clark spent most evenings away from the capital.[23]

While the politicians generally attempt to set the day's agenda around particular events, such as a visit to a small business or a local hospital, rarely do they do so in an overt way. More and more, the daily agenda is being determined by the media, especially television and radio, or by a random event. As one reporter, Tim Watkin, explained during the 2002 campaign: 'Early each morning for the past month, as you and I have breakfasted, fought traffic and stumbled into work, Mike Munro and Sue Foley [Bill English's press secretary] have been on the phone trying to figure out what we're going to care about that day. Since before dawn they have had the radio and television going and have been poring over the papers, in print and online. Like ancient soothsayers picking over chicken entrails, they try to read in the headlines and pictures what the big issues of the day will be.'[24] As early as 9 or 10 o'clock each morning, the journalists accompanying the party leader are likely to have been made aware of the two television networks' likely agenda for the day—for example, an interview with a victim of the health system or a violent crime. Even if they are print journalists working for one of the metropolitan dailies, they may choose to adopt the same issue, especially if it is likely to feature on one of the current affairs programmes, especially the widely viewed *Holmes* show, or in a forthcoming leaders' debate. Under MMP, the ability of the media to dictate the agenda has been enhanced, partly because of the range of perspectives provided by multiparty competition, but also because the dominant theme has switched from policies and personalities to the possible configuration of the next coalition government. As the journalist Vernon Small has pointed out, 'We can talk about how Corngate and GE dominated the 2002 campaign. However, it wasn't those two issues in and of themselves that were important, but rather how they were impacting on possible coalition governments'.[25]

Because the media-politico relationship involves a complex mixture of inter-dependency, flattery, rivalry, and suspicion, reaching judgments about the relative influence of the media and the politicians on the campaign agenda is difficult, if not impossible. As one study has asked: 'Do the media simply pick up on and reflect changes in public opinion, or do they actively catalyse such changes? And what of the role of the parties themselves in all of this? How successful are they at setting or constraining the agenda?' (Webb 2000, p. 151) What can be said with some confidence is that the cumulative effect of recent trends in campaigning has been to place the politicians in an uncomfortably reactive role vis-à-vis the media, as the following examples will serve to illustrate.

The 'worm'

At the 1996 election, Television New Zealand featured the reactions of a sample of 'undecided' voters to the comments of party leaders during the televised debates. When the pre-selected studio voters disapproved of a leader's comment, an electronic worm tracked downwards on viewers' screens, and when they approved, it tracked back up. Having been informed of the presence of the worm during a commercial break, the prime minister, Jim Bolger, turned in a lacklustre performance, perhaps reflecting anxiety over the reaction of the worm to his on-screen comments. Late that night he phoned the host, Paul Holmes, to complain about his treatment at the hands of the show's producers. As it turned out, the prime minister's senior press secretary, Richard Griffin, had been forewarned of the worm's use but had chosen not to inform the prime minister. Bolger reportedly threatened to boycott the next debate, but was advised that such action would reflect badly on the credibility of his campaign. The controversy surrounding the use of the worm became a major talking point of the campaign, with journalists going so far as to describe it as the catalyst for Clark's rise in the polls (for example, see Laugeson 1997).

The worm was next used, and to even greater effect, during the 2002 campaign. Under pressure to include the deputy prime minister, Jim Anderton, in the leaders' debates (his new Progressive party was barely registering in the polls), Television New Zealand decided to extend an invitation to the leaders of all eight parliamentary parties (including Anderton, Laila Harre of the Alliance, and Peter Dunne of United Future). While the worm appeared to respond warmly to Dunne's on-screen comments, which were unfailingly moderate and sensible in tone, the post-debate analysis probably did more to lift Dunne's stature than any wriggling worm that appeared across the bottom of the viewers' screens. The *New Zealand Herald* stated that his performance had 'blitzed the political heavyweights',[26] a view that was shared by most other media sources. Within a week, United Future's support as measured by the *Herald*-Digi Poll had jumped from 1 to 7 per cent.

'Corngate'

As important as the worm undoubtedly was in improving the electoral fortunes of Dunne and United Future, it can hardly be compared with the impact on Labour's campaign of the 'Corngate' interview, in which the TV3 current affairs journalist and newsreader, John Campbell, cross-examined Helen Clark over an alleged cover-up of the accidental release of genetically contaminated corn. Drawing on charges made by Nicky Hager in his book, *Seeds of Distrust*, Campbell quizzed the prime minister on what she knew about the case. During the interview, a visibly upset prime minister promised to pull out of the next TV3 leaders' debate if the pre-recorded interview went to air. She was offered a follow-up interview, which she declined, although she did take part in the subsequent debate. She described Campbell as a 'little creep' and suggested that the interview was part of a conspiracy involving the Greens (the publisher of the book was one of the Green party's list candidates). As well as marking a low point in Labour's relationship with the Greens, with any lingering prospect of a Labour-Green coalition now well and truly buried, the interview destroyed a previously amicable relationship between Clark and TV3 (the Canwest company had made a significant donation to the Labour party prior to the 1999 campaign). The prime minister declined to be interviewed by Campbell for the remainder of 2002 and into the next year. More importantly, the interview was followed by an immediate slump in Labour's popularity (the party's own polling showed that its support plunged overnight from 46 per cent to 38 per cent)[27] and raised questions about Clark's integrity and ability to work with the Greens in any future Labour-led government.

The reaction to the Corngate interview by government ministers and some senior journalists and media commentators was highly critical of Campbell's performance. The prime minister complained that she should have been informed of the nature of the interview in advance and that the interview was one-sided, only providing the Hager viewpoint, and in a manner that suggested that the allegations were true.[28] She denied that there had been a cover-up, pointing out that the Environment minister, Marion Hobbs had admitted that some imported corn seed might have been contaminated as far back as 2000. Fran O'Sullivan of the *New Zealand Herald* described Campbell's introduction to the interview as 'fatuously overdone' and claimed that he had taken Hager's assertions 'at face value and failed to apply sufficiently rigorous questioning to the greenie spinmeister before his inquisition of Clark'.[29] Joe Atkinson accused Campbell of resorting to 'harangue and bluster' (2004, p. 55) and observed more generally that he and other interviewers of his type were 'self-important studio moderators asking cynical questions…either interrupting and speaking over responses to their questions or failing to moderate similar behaviour by others' (2004, p. 56). In a similar vein, Tim Bale described Campbell as a 'man on a mission, a self-appointed people's plenipotentiary so utterly convinced of his role and his cause that he simply didn't know when to stop' (2003a, p. 225).

The prime minister's criticism of TV3, together with the network's response, make 'seeds of distrust' as descriptive of the prevailing culture of suspicion between journalists and politicians as of the debate over genetic modification (GM). Having been subject to heavy 'spinning' by successive governments and their advisors, it is hardly surprising that some predominantly younger journalists have begun to respond in ways that are best described as cynical and aggressive. Campbell expressed disbelief that a 'bright, formidably bright' politician claimed to have no recollection of matters raised in the interview. What was an interviewer supposed to do when a 'hands-on prime minister' who 'runs cabinet and drives it hard' suffers from a lapse of memory? 'When a politician says they can't remember we are meant to cease the exchange, put down our pen and say "thanks", I'm terribly sorry about that, refresh your memory and possibly prepare your spin and get to me when it's convenient? If that was the case democracy and journalism would be no more than the regurgitation of press releases.'[30]

TV3's failure to forewarn the prime minister of the nature of the interview was a deliberate ploy to ensure her appearance—in the view of the network, had she been told in advance of the topic, she would have refused to be interviewed. While the Broadcasting Standards Authority subsequently judged TV3's coverage to have breached standards of fairness and balance, it rejected the allegation of ambush journalism. In TV3's defence, the *New Zealand Listener's* Gordon Campbell recalled Clark telling a press conference that, 'Had an interview been properly sought on the matter, it would have been referred to the minister who handled it at the time, the Honourable Marion Hobbs'. In his view, this comment provided proof that, 'if TV3 had played by the rules, it might have got an interview, but not with Clark' (2003).

A second mitigating factor concerns the increasingly common government tactic of running issue-less campaigns. In 2002, Labour's campaign committee decided that the best way to achieve victory was to conduct a bland campaign. This involved a plan to steer clear of matters that might cause unnecessary controversy, including the highly topical issue of GM. Such tactics may help explain Clark's uncharacteristic reluctance to debate the GM issue with Campbell, even though the Greens had made their intentions clear three months earlier by staging a walk-out from parliament, a move that put paid to any lingering hopes they might have had of being part of the next government. It is easy to see how the Corngate interview damaged public confidence in Clark, her government, and the Greens. However, in as much as there is anything to be learned from the interview and its aftermath, it is the danger of allowing the media to determine the campaign agenda by default.

Figure 9.1 When voters decided, 1999 and 2002

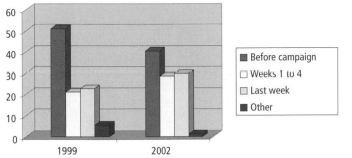

Source: NZES 1999, 2002

Participation

Having discussed the process and consequences of campaign modernisation, let us return to the issue of public participation. In her analysis of the impact of professional political marketing on civic engagement, Norris argues that 'the new forms of electioneering essentially supplement, rather than replace, older techniques' (2000, p. 312). According to this view, the tools of the new technology, including talkback radio and the World Wide Web, have the potential to rekindle the public's involvement in politics. In a follow-up study, *Democratic Phoenix: Reinventing Political Activism* (2002a), Norris explores cross-national trends in voter turnout, party membership, and political activism. Her general conclusion confirms the view that, while traditional party loyalties are in decline, citizens are finding alternative ways of expressing an interest in politics and in the political process.

Voter turnout

Norris found that, whereas trends in voter turnout in developing countries are moving steadily upwards, in post-industrial societies they have either flattened or declined. (2002a, p. 44). In the period between 1984 and 2002, turnout in New Zealand dropped by a dramatic 17 percentage points to 77 per cent (see figure 1.3). The decline is even more marked when measured against the estimated voting age population rather than the registered vote (while registration is compulsory, there are always those who do not register), with the low point being the 2002 turnout of 72.5 per cent (*New Zealand Electoral Compendium* 2002, p. 174).

Reasons for the decline in turnout may include a range of societal changes, such as growing income disparity, with a high incidence of non-voting among those on low incomes. Voting is low among immigrant groups and some ethnic minorities, perhaps because they share a sense of being

Figure 9.2 Media exposure 2002, voters

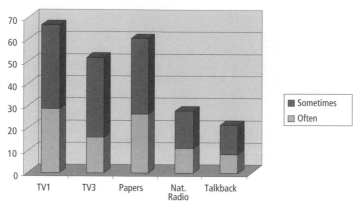

Source: NZES

marginalised (Vowles et al. 2002). What can be said with some confidence, however, is that public disenchantment with successive governments certainly took its toll on the New Zealand public from the mid-1980s on. It is interesting to observe that, contrary to the view that 'voting participation is maximised in elections using proportional representation' (Norris 2002a, p. 217), the advent of MMP failed to arrest the decline, although the low turnout in 2002 may be due to other factors, such as the predictable nature of the outcome, with Labour posturing as a certain winner from the very outset of the campaign. Be that as it may, the overall results are clearly at odds with the argument that participation is not in decline—the 72.5 per cent turnout for New Zealand, a country with a long tradition of public involvement, is virtually identical to the 72.7 per cent mean figure for post-industrial societies in general (Norris 2002, p. 45).

Figure 9.3 Internet use during 1999 and 2002 campaigns

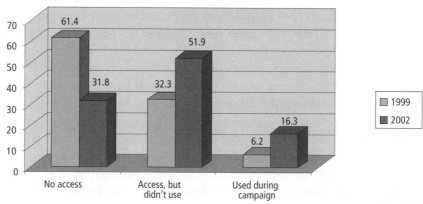

Source: NZES

Interest in politics

Another way of looking at participation is through the prism of public interest in the campaign. On the assumption that late deciders are more likely than stable voters to be influenced by campaign events, one approach is to determine when people made their final decision as to which way they were going to vote. As the results of figure 9.1 show, in 2002 a clear majority of respondents made up their minds during the campaign, with almost one in three postponing their final decision until the last week of the campaign. Given the volatile nature of the vote, it is hardly surprising that late deciders are more likely to support the minor parties, with the main beneficiary in 2002 being the late-rising United Future, followed by ACT and New Zealand First.

Despite the trend towards more professional and commercial campaigns, the level of interest in politics among survey respondents is strong (for relevant data, see figure 5.1). Given the lack of opportunity to attend public meetings or other campaign events, interest is clearly being satisfied through more sedentary forms of participation, the most important of which is television—Television New Zealand commands the largest campaign audience, with two-thirds of all 2002 respondents receiving their news from the state-owned network (see figure 9.2).

Internet

Of greater relevance to the postmodernist argument than the influence of television, however, is the recent rapid rise in access to the Internet, with one in six survey respondents (or approximately 335,000 voters) making use of the Internet to get news or other information during the course of the 2002 campaign (see figure 9.3).[31] Groups with the greatest Internet usage include the young (over 80 per cent of the eighteen- to twenty-nine-year age group have access), university graduates (92 per cent), males (71 per cent), and supporters of the ACT (85 per cent) and Green (79 per cent) parties. Partly reflecting their affluence and youthfulness, the ACT (30 per cent) and Green (22 per cent) voters are the heaviest users of the Internet for the purpose of receiving political information and news. In contrast, middle aged and elderly voters, especially those who support New Zealand First, are least likely to get their political news from the Internet.[32]

Figure 9.4 Attended campaign meetings or rallies, 2002 voters

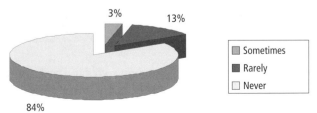

3%
13%
84%

Sometimes
Rarely
Never

Source: NZES

Conclusion

Has campaign modernisation resulted in a decline in public engagement, or are twenty-first century voters simply engaging differently? On the positive side, interest in politics is strong, a significant proportion of voters are attentive to campaign developments, with increasing numbers postponing their voting decision until late in the campaign, and use of the Internet to access and exchange political information is on the rise. While there are fewer campaign volunteers, parties now have the capacity to compile vast email directories and directly target particular segments of the electorate. Even those parties that lack an activist base are able to draw on other resources, including free broadcasting time and publicly funded parliamentary staff, to spread their message to a nationwide audience (for a fuller discussion, see chapter 5).

In so far as these developments represent a re-engagement in campaigns, their vicariousness makes them fundamentally different from earlier forms of participation. Despite the optimistic claim that traditional forms of campaigning have been 'supplemented, but not replaced' (Norris 2000, p. 142), the New Zealand evidence suggests otherwise. Party membership and activism have declined to a point where some parties no longer have the numbers to conduct campaign business at the local level, including fundraising, attending local meetings, distributing pamphlets and other party material, and providing transportation on polling day (see table 9.1). While it is possible to blame these developments on the pressures of modern society, including growing affluence and reduced leisure time (Scarrow 2000; Norris 2002a), some of the responsibility actually lies with the parties themselves. The emphasis on professional political marketing and the centralisation of campaign planning in the office of the party leader have shifted the focus of attention away from the local campaign. While the two major parties continue to compete for the electorate seats, under MMP the minor parties deliberately downplay the local contests, preferring to concentrate on the nationwide campaign for the party vote.[33]

Table 9.1 Percentage of party members who have participated in the following campaign activities

	New Zealand 2002	Canada* 2000	Britain (Labour)** 1999
Put up poster	32	–	76
Contributed money	54	89	68
Attended meetings	24	–	48
Canvassed	31	72	32

Sources: * Cross and Young 2004, p. 440 ** Seyd and Whiteley 2004, p. 360.

It is always possible that the new campaign styles and techniques will lead to the revival of party activism, especially once the interactive capabilities of online campaigning are more fully developed (Gibson et al. 2003; Norris

2003). An example of how the Internet can be used to engender participation can be found in the grassroots organisation of the 2004 American presidential nominee, Howard Dean. By the end of the previous year, more than 500,000 campaign volunteers and 280,000 financial contributors had been recruited online. Information provided on the candidate's web site included how to become an activist or team leader, where to attend house parties and other campaign events, and how to join one of the 'coalition groups', including environmental voters, African Americans, and seniors (www.deanforamerica.com). During the course of his unsuccessful bid for the presidency, the Democratic challenger, John Kerry, raised some $US80 million online, mostly in small increments from individual supporters.[34] Similar approaches, although on a smaller scale, have been adopted by a number of Green parties, including the 2000 presidential candidacy of the American consumer affairs guru, Ralph Nader, and the 2002 election campaign of the Green party of Aotearoa/New Zealand.

Even allowing for the possibility that the new technology will contribute to the gradual re-engagement of voters in campaigns, an even more testing challenge is how to address the decline in election turnout, a problem New Zealand shares with a number of other post-industrial societies.

Notes

1   David Farrell (2002) distinguishes between the 'newspaper', 'television', and 'digital' stages of development. In their study of the local constituency campaign in Britain, David Denver and Gordon Hands (2002) adopt the Fordist/post-Fordist distinction.
2   This part of the discussion elaborates on issues raised in R. Miller 2004, 'Parties and Electioneering' in Hayward and Rudd 2004, pp. 2–19.
3   Interview with Robert Chapman, 14 August 2003, Auckland.
4   Interview with Robert Chapman, 14 August 2003, Auckland.
5   Interview with Bob Harvey, 10 August 2003, Auckland.
6   Interview with Bob Harvey, 10 August 2003, Auckland.
7   'This Man Kirk', New Zealand Labour Party, Wellington, October 1969.
8   Interview with Bob Harvey, 10 August 2003, Auckland.
9   E. Watt, 'Email: MPs fail to click on', *Sunday Star Times*, 11 July 2004, p.A7.
10   Interview with Mike Williams, 8 August 2003, Auckland.
11   Interview with Murray McCully, 17 July 2003, Parliament Buildings, Wellington.
12   Interview with Rod Donald, 15 July 2003, Parliament Buildings, Wellington.
13   Interview with John Pagani, 15 July 2003, Wellington.
14   Interview with Peter Dunne, 16 July 2003, Parliament Buildings, Wellington.
15   Audrey Young, 'Into the Valley of Electoral Death', *Weekend Herald*, 3–4 August 2002, B3.
16   Interview with John Pagani, 15 July 2003, Wellington.
17   Interview with Peter Dunne, 16 July 2003, Parliament Buildings, Wellington.
18   Interview with Peter Dunne, 16 July 2003, Parliament Buildings, Wellington.
19   Interview with John Pagani, 15 July 2003, Wellington.
20   Interview with Rod Donald, 15 July 2003, Parliament Buildings, Wellington.

21 Interview with Graham Watson, 28 July 2003, Auckland.
22 The Gallery was formed sometime before 1870 (Garnier 1978), although little is known about its origins or early role.
23 Interview with Vernon Small, 17 July 2003, Wellington.
24 Tim Watkin, 'In the Spin Cycle', *Weekend Herald*, 20–21 July 2002, G1.
25 Interview with Vernon Small, 17 July 2003, Wellington.
26 Bernard Orsman, 'The Man For Whom the Worm Turned Up Trumps', *New Zealand Herald*, 17 July 2002, A5.
27 Interview with Mike Williams, 8 August 2003, Auckland.
28 In July 2003, the Broadcasting Standards Authority upheld Labour's complaint that the interview had failed to meet acceptable standards of accuracy, balance and fairness. In particular, it criticised TV3 for failing to inform the prime minister of the source of the allegations (*New Zealand Herald*, 7 July 2003).
29 Fran O'Sullivan, 'Empress is Losing Her Clothes', *New Zealand Herald*, 15 July 2002, D2.
30 Quoted in Donna Chisholm, 'The Aftermath of the Ambush', *Sunday Star Times*, 14 July 2002, A11.
31 Pippa Norris (2003, p. 43) found that approximately one in ten Internet users in Europe visited the party web sites in the periods immediately before and during an election campaign.
32 New Zealand's Ministry of Social Development has found that, in 2004, 40.3 per cent of the population had internet access. Low access was found among those over the age of 65 years (11.8 per cent), Pacific Families (16.4 per cent), and Maori families (28.3 per cent) (Ministry of Social Development, 'The Social Report, 2004', http://socialreport.msd.govt.nz).
33 Exceptions include New Zealand First in Tauranga, United Future in Ohariu-Belmont, and the Progressives in Wigram.
34 CNN News, 3 November 2004.

Further reading

Boston, J., S. Church, S. Levine, E. McLeay and N.S. Roberts (eds) 2003, *New Zealand Votes: The General Election of 2002*, Victoria University Press, Wellington.

Farrell, D.M. and R. Schmitt-Beck (eds) 2002, *Do Political Campaigns Matter? Campaign Effects in Elections and Referendums*, Routledge, London.

Farrell, D.M. and P. Webb 2000, 'Political Parties as Campaign Organizations', in Dalton, R.J. and M.P. Wattenberg (eds), *Parties Without Partisans: Political Change in Advanced Industrial Democracies*, Oxford University Press, Oxford, pp. 102–28.

Hayward, J. and C. Rudd (eds) 2004, *Political Communications in New Zealand*, Pearson/Prentice Hall, Auckland.

Norris, P. 2000, *A Virtuous Circle: Political Communications in Postindustrial Societies*, Cambridge University Press, Cambridge.

Norris, P. 2003, 'Preaching to the Converted? Pluralism, Participation and Party Websites', in *Party Politics*, 9/1, pp. 21–45.

Vowles, J., P. Aimer, S. Banducci, J. Karp and R. Miller (eds) 2004, *Voters' Veto: The 2002 Election in New Zealand and the Consolidation of Minority Government*, Auckland University Press, Auckland.

Who Are the
Representatives?

10

WRITING nearly four decades ago, Austin Mitchell characterised the New Zealand political system as 'government by party' (1966), a description that is as apt today as it was then. Apart from Winston Peters' by-election success as an independent in the seat of Tauranga in 1993 (he formed the New Zealand First party some four months later) no independent has been elected to the New Zealand parliament since 1943.[1] As representatives of one or other of the parliamentary parties, all MPs are subject to party rules and the collective decisions of their parliamentary caucus (see chapter 4), as well as to the management requirements of the party leader, deputy leader, and whips. Should they let their party down, MPs face the ultimate sanction of being either expelled from the caucus and party or de-selected at the next election.

Balancing an MP's party and parliamentary obligations against the commitments made to constituents has never been easy or widely understood. However, with the introduction of MMP in 1996, the possible role and independence of the new type of parliamentarian, the list member, came in for special attention. Speculation centred on whether the functions of list MPs were different from those traditionally carried out by electorate MPs. As in Germany, most candidates have shown a preference for safe electorate seats over a high place on the party list. As well as reflecting concern that list members will be unduly beholden to party officials, the preference for an electorate seat may have something to do with the ambiguity surrounding the constituency function of list members, specifically the question of who they actually represent. Do they serve as delegates of their party, or do they represent a particular constituency, perhaps a geographical electorate or even a designated social or ethnic group? In choosing the list option over an electorate seat, some prominent politicians have expressed a preference for ministerial and parliamentary responsibilities over the conventional constituency role.[2] Does this view coincide with that of other list MPs? If so, perhaps it reflects a growing recognition that the careers of electorate and list members are on somewhat divergent paths.

Having discussed how parties go about selecting their parliamentary candidates (chapter 6), this chapter will take the theme of representation one step further by considering the social characteristics and functions of MPs, focusing on any differences in the responsibilities of list and electorate members. But first, let us consider the nature of parliamentary representation, including any possible friction between an MP's constituency and party roles.

Nature of representation

New Zealand enjoys a strong tradition of democratically elected party government. The first election for the House of Representatives took place in 1853 and consisted of simple plurality (first-past-the-post) elections in twenty-four electorates for a total of thirty-seven legislators (eleven districts had multiple members). A property qualification restricted the early participation of Maori men, but in 1867 the vote was extended to all males over the age of twenty-one years, and in 1893 the franchise was further extended to include women.[3] Prior to the development of the party system, MPs were either complete independents or were organised into factions representing various regional and sectional groups. By the late 1800s and early 1900s, however, a rudimentary party system was beginning to take shape (see chapter 2).

As MPs began to align themselves with one or other of the emerging parties, it became necessary to impose a measure of party loyalty and discipline. During the premiership of Richard John Seddon (1893–1906), Liberal MPs began to meet together, or caucus, on a regular basis, as well as submitting to the authority of party whips (Martin 2004, p. 109).[4] Rather than simply representing themselves or their constituents' interests, they were becoming answerable to a party organisation, both inside and outside parliament, with the result that crossing the floor of parliament and voting with the other side became an increasingly rare and dangerous option, especially for those with ambitions of a career in politics. Although National was more willing to brook dissent than Labour, choosing a career in politics was described as 'not unlike joining the army, with less security of tenure' (Jackson 1987, p. 55). Labour even required that its candidates sign a pledge agreeing 'to vote on all questions in accordance with the decisions of the caucus of the parliamentary Labour party'.[5] To do otherwise was to invite expulsion from the caucus and party.

This transition to a system of government by party raises questions about the nature of representation and how to strike a balance between MPs' responsibilities to themselves, their party, and their constituents. Political representation is frequently described as being of two distinct types.

Trustee model

The *trustee* model can be traced back to the British politician and political theorist, Edmund Burke. Writing in the eighteenth century, Burke argued that, while MPs were elected to represent a particular geographical area, decisions should be based on an MP's own independent judgment rather than the opinions of constituents. As well as lacking wisdom and civic responsibility, the general populace were deemed to have no understanding of what constituted the national interest. As a result, they were ill equipped to influence parliament's decisions. The role of ordinary citizens must therefore be restricted to electing representatives capable of exercising sound judgment and protecting the interests of the nation. In short, the role of the elected representative was to act 'on behalf, not at the behest, of the people' (Judge 1999, p. 51).

This belief in the right of the political elite to rule without reference to public opinion might have made some sense in pre-democratic Britain, where standards of literacy and political awareness were low. But does the trustee model have any relevance to representation in contemporary New Zealand? Survey results show that a vast majority of parliamentary candidates (83 per cent in 1999 and 74 per cent in 2002) are of the view that parliament, not voters, should make final decisions on all matters of law and policy (New Zealand Election Study). Although an MP's opinion will often reflect those of the local constituents, clearly there are times when the two are in conflict. This was recognised by the New Zealand First party when, early in its existence, it promised that its MPs would be free to vote according to the wishes of their constituents where they were at odds with those of the party. More pertinent still, however, is the generally accepted convention within the New Zealand parliament that, on a narrow range of issues, MPs should be permitted to exercise a 'conscience' vote. (Where a member crosses the floor in defiance of the party whip, the vote is referred to as a 'cross vote'.)

'Conscience' voting

Throughout the history of party government in New Zealand, MPs have been granted leave by their party to cast a conscience or 'free' vote on issues that are deemed to impinge on an individual member's moral values. These include the consumption of alcohol, gambling, Sunday trading, abortion, prostitution, and gay rights. In 1910, for example, MPs were granted a free vote on prohibition, the arguments around which were said to have occupied the attention of MPs for several months (Martin 2004, p. 141). In 1950, a majority of MPs decided in a free vote to support the reintroduction of capital punishment. More recently, the Contraception, Sterilization and Abortion Amendment Bill (1990) stirred up a national debate, not simply on the rights and wrongs of abortion, but also on the question of whether it was appropriate to legislate values. Recent issues on which a conscience vote was permitted include: reducing the drinking age from twenty to eighteen years (Sale of Liquor Amendment Act, 2000); decriminalising prostitution and safeguarding the human rights of sex workers (Prostitution Reform Act, 2003); and allowing same-sex and de facto couples to legally register their relationships (Civil Union Bill, 2004).

Contrary to the spirit of the free vote, individual MPs are frequently subjected to overwhelming pressure, both formally and informally, to vote with other members of their party. So divisive was the 1977 debate on abortion within the National party that 'for some time afterwards prominent ministers were not on speaking terms' (Jackson 1987, p. 56). On the first reading of the 2004 Civil Union Bill, the Green, United Future, and Progressive parties refused to withdraw the party whip. Their decision was based on the view that, since the issue of same-sex and de facto relationships was the subject of party policy, granting MPs a free vote was tantamount to sanctioning the right to oppose party policy. As a result, all the Green and Progressive party MPs voted for the Bill and all United Future MPs voted against it. The outcome of the vote on the Prostitution Reform Bill followed a similar pattern, with all of the Green MPs voting to decriminalise prostitution and all of the United Future MPs voting against. Even where a party does not whip its members, a mixture of shared values and informal pressure from party colleagues can contribute to a heavily one-sided vote. In the 1950 vote on capital punishment, for example, only one MP crossed the floor of parliament to support the other side (Jackson 1987, p. 50). Shortly before the Civil Union Bill vote, a Labour minister and parliament's first openly gay MP, Chris Carter, publicly demanded that every Labour MP support the Civil Union Bill, arguing that the legal recognition of gay couples was Labour party policy.[6]

On the prostitution question, 76 per cent of Labour MPs voted in favour of decriminalisation and 78 per cent of National MPs voted against. The result of the vote on a first reading of the Civil Union vote was remarkably similar, with 78 per cent of Labour MPs voting for reform and 81 per cent of National MPs voting against. Notable exceptions to this trend were the National leader Don Brash, who voted with the Labour majority on both bills, and Labour's Clayton Cosgrove (Waimakariri), who voted against. Parliament's first South Asian MP, Ashraf Choudhary (Labour), a list member, was confronted by a dilemma not unfamiliar to MPs who attempt to reconcile their personal views with those of their constituents—Choudhary was the sole representative in parliament of New Zealand's socially conservative Muslim community. Despite sustained pressure from his party colleagues, as well as from the press, Choudhary abstained from voting on both the Prostitution Bill and the first reading of the Civil Union Bill. His decision was crucial to the outcome of the Prostitution Bill, which passed with a vote of sixty to fifty-nine.

Delegate model

Whereas the trustee model recognises the right of individual representatives to exercise their own independent judgment, the delegate model is based on the assumption that representatives will act at the behest of their constituents. The most obvious constituencies are those in New Zealand's sixty-two general and seven Maori geographical seats. With the introduction of MMP, several parties encouraged their list members to set up offices in electorate seats, thereby creating multi-member districts in all but name. Alternatively, parties can make their list members MPs-at-large, in which case they assume responsibility for a national constituency of party members and supporters. Still others are designated to represent a particular social or ethnic group. On becoming a list MP in 1999, for example, the sole ethnic Chinese MP, Pansy Wong (National), became spokesperson for the growing Asian community. Georgina Te Heuheu acted on behalf of National's Maori constituency, and Nandor Tanczos (Green) assumed responsibility for nurturing his party's ties with the young.

As well as representing a particular geographical or social constituency, MPs are delegated members of their party in parliament and government. This can produce friction between an MP's constituency and party roles. There are a number of reasons why the influence of the latter usually wins out. Unlike weak party systems, such as that of the USA, the New Zealand system of party government was built on each major party's ability to simplify the community's diverse demands, enforce discipline on MPs by claiming an electoral mandate for its policies, and build a sense of unity and belonging through regular meetings of cabinet and caucus. Where disagreements occur between members of the same party, as they frequently do, they can be hammered out in the weekly caucus or cabinet meeting, thereby preventing the more drastic step of either abstaining or crossing the floor of parliament.

Local constituency opinion, on the other hand, is notoriously difficult to quantify, let alone harness or direct. Some MPs conduct informal surveys among their constituents, often by including questions on topical issues in the weekly electorate newsletter. Apart from the problems that stem from poor sampling and design, such polls are subject to manipulation by the media or community groups with a vested interest in the outcome. A more common approach is for the local member to act as a sounding board by inviting individuals and groups to either write to the MP or attend a weekly constituency clinic. In the end, however, the strictness with which most parties observe standards of internal party discipline means that MPs often find themselves supporting a party policy which is 'contrary to the apparent interests of his [sic] constituents, contrary to the prevailing opinion in his constituency, and contrary to his own personal judgment about what is best for the country' (A.H. Birch, quoted in Judge 1999, p. 71).

The potential for conflict between an MP's constituency and party obligations can be illustrated with reference to Labour's Foreshore and Seabed legislation, which was introduced to parliament in May 2004 (for background discussions on this issue, see chapters 3 and 8). Early in the year, the prime minister stated that Labour's ten Maori MPs would be required to vote for the introduction of the legislation (even with the support of its Maori MPs, the government had only a two-vote majority). Three electorate MPs, Tariana Turia (Te Tai Hauauru), Nanaia Mahuta (Tainui), and Georgina Beyer (Wairarapa) refused to confirm their support. Turia, who is of Ngati Apa, Nga Rauru, and Tuwharetoa descent, embarked on a process of consultation with tribal leaders inside and outside her Te Tai Hauauru electorate. In the event that she voted against the legislation, the prime minister had warned that the principle of collective cabinet responsibility required that Turia be stripped of her ministerial portfolios (she was an associate minister for Health, Housing, and Social Services). In the view of Turia and Mahuta, as delegates of their people their first loyalty was to their constituents, not to the party or to the government.

A delegation of senior government ministers was dispatched to the Waikato to attempt to persuade senior Tainui executives that Mahuta should support the government. Having promised not to join Turia in resigning from the party, Mahuta was given permission by the prime minister to vote against the legislation. As the representative of a general rather than a Maori electorate, Beyer's position was less clear-cut, although she indicated that her Maori ancestry dictated that she should abstain from supporting the bill. Upon being reminded by her local executive that she was not delegated to represent Maori, but rather the electorate of Wairarapa, Beyer decided to support the legislation, the first reading of which was passed with the support of New Zealand First.

Social characteristics of MPs

In the event that a voter feels powerless to influence what an MP does, that person may decide to 'choose someone who is like me in some way, based on the idea that a person like me will share my concerns' (Catt 1999, p. 84). The importance of a sense of group identity was implicit in the Electoral Commission's argument that MMP would result in a fairer system of representation. As well as providing greater opportunity for minority viewpoints to be expressed, the adoption of MMP improved the electoral prospects of a number of hitherto under-represented social groups, notably women, Maori, and non-indigenous ethnic minorities (Wallace 1986, pp. 50–1). So convinced was the Commission by the strength of its own argument that it recommended the abolition of separate Maori seats, subject to approval of the Maori community.

Giving some early impetus to the process of change was the high turnover of MPs. Although the average length of parliamentary experience among the 2002 intake of MPs was 6.6 years, two-thirds of them entered parliament for the first time following an MMP election (see table 10.1). The high turnover was unevenly spread, however, with the bulk of it resulting from the rise and continuing volatility of the minor party vote—thirteen of the twenty-nine new MPs elected in 2002, for example, came from just two parties, New Zealand First and United Future, with a combined vote of only 17 per cent. In contrast, Labour contributed just six of the new MPs elected in 2002.

Table 10.1 Parliamentary experience of MPs, 2002

First elected	Pre-1981	1981–87	1990–93	1996–99	2002
Labour	1	9	17	19	7
National		5	5	12	5
NZ First	2			4	7
ACT	1	1		5	2
Greens				7	2
United Future		1			6
Prog. Coalition		1		1	
Total	**4**	**17**	**22**	**48**	**29**

Gender

While the proportion of women MPs had been rising prior to the introduction of MMP, partly because of pressure from the women's movement, but also as a result of the marked increase in the number of women entering and remaining in the workforce, it nevertheless rose quite sharply in response to the pressure put on the parties' selectors following the introduction of party lists (see figure 10.1), although some parties clearly demonstrated a stronger commitment to the recruitment of women than others (see table 10.2). Despite these initial gains, New Zealand soon began to lag behind other countries in its recruitment of women MPs (table 10.3). How can New Zealand's failure to build on the initial progress towards gender parity be explained?

Incumbency has been a significant barrier to the recruitment of women, especially in the electorate seats (see chapter 6). Unlike the new Scottish parliament and Welsh national assembly, both of which started with a clean slate of seats, National and Labour had a surplus of electorate MPs in 1996, when the number of electorate seats was reduced from ninety-nine to sixty-five. Loyalty, fairness, and the need for political experience gave incumbents a decided edge over their challengers, making it difficult for the two major parties to create a substantial number of vacancies in the electorate seats. By 2004, 34 per cent of Labour-held electorate seats and 10 per cent of National-held electorate seats were occupied by women. At 28 per cent overall, this was well short of the proportions found in Wales (55 per cent) and Scotland (44 per cent) (see table 10.4). While the alternative strategy of using the party list worked well for some of the small parties, specifically the Alliance, ACT, and the Greens, the two major parties won too few list seats to make any real impression on the log-jam of male incumbents. In 2002, only two of Labour's seven list MPs were women. Although National did slightly better, with three

Figure 10.1 Women candidates and MPs, 1981–2002

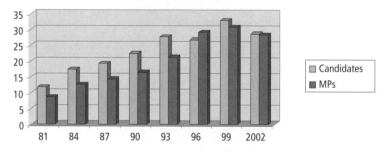

Figure 10.2 Women MPs, 1981–2002

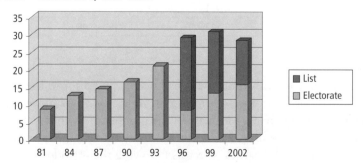

Table 10.2 Representation by gender and ethnicity

	1984 n	1990 n	1996 n	2002 n
Women				
Labour	10	8	13	18
National	2	8	8	6
NZ First			3	1
ACT			3	4
Alliance			8	0
Greens				4
United Fut.				1
Total	12 (12.6%)	16 (16.5%)	35 (29.2%)	34 (28.3%)
Maori/*Pacific/Asian**				
Labour	4	4	5 (*2)	10 (* **14)
National	2	1	1 (* **3)	1 (**2)
NZ First			8	6
ACT			1	1
Alliance			2	
Greens				1
Total	(Maori) 6 (6.3%)	5 (5.2%)	17 (14.25%)	19 (15.8%)
Total (All)	**6 (6.3%)**	**5 (5.2%)**	**21 (17.5%)**	**24 (20.0%)**

Table 10.3 Women in parliaments, 2004

Rank	Country	Per cent
1.	Wales	50.0
2.	Rwanda	48.8
3.	Sweden	45.3
4.	Scotland	39.5
5.	Denmark	38.0
6.	Finland	37.5
7.	Netherlands	36.7
8.	Norway	36.4
9.	Cuba	36.0
10.	Costa Rica	35.1
11.	Argentina	34.0
12.	Austria	33.9
13.	South Africa	32.8
14.	Germany	32.2
15.	Iceland	30.2
16.	Mozambique	30.0
17.	Seychelles	29.4
18.	**New Zealand (8th in 2001)**	**28.3**
Others		
37.	Canada	20.6
49.	United Kingdom	17.9
59.	USA	14.3

Source: www.ipu.org/wmn-e/classif.htm

Table 10.4 Women's representation in New Zealand, Scotland and Wales, 2004

	Electorate			List			Total		
	Fem.	Total	%	Fem.	Total	%	Fem.	Total	%
New Zealand	19	69	27.5	15	51	29.4	34	120	28.3
Scotland	32	46	43.8	19	56	33.9	51	129	39.5
Wales	22	40	55.0	8	20	40.0	30	60	50.0

Source: Scottish and Welsh data, Fiona McKay, University of Edinburgh.

out of six, it failed to protect two high-profile women MPs, Belinda Vernon (down thirteen places to number twenty-three) and Annabel Young (down fifteen places to number thirty-three), both of whom were defeated.[7]

A second barrier to gender parity has been complacency on the part of each party's selectors. Having made some significant gains in the first two MMP elections, there was a tendency for some of the more progressive parties, including Labour, to rest on their laurels. In the view of Helen Clark, for example, by the late 1990s the glass ceiling that prevented women from gaining representative parity with men had been broken. Despite appearances, with women occupying a number of the most prominent positions, including governor general, prime minister (since 1997), chief justice, attorney-general, and CEO of the country's largest publicly listed company, a significant gender gap persisted. In 2004, only four of parliament's nineteen select committees had women chairs. Of the twenty cabinet ministers, only five were women, and of the six ministers outside of cabinet, only one was a woman.[8] In 2002, New Zealand First had only one woman in its allocation of twelve list seats and United Future had one out of seven list seats. While it is easy to rush to judgment with respect to the lack of women MPs representing these minor parties, as Elizabeth McLeay points out, lack of supply may have been a contributing factor (2003, p. 299).

Ethnicity

Even more significant than the initial increase in the representation of women under MMP, was that of ethnic minorities, especially Maori. The strong support for electoral reform among Maori leaders in the early 1990s reflected their historically low level of representation. Although Labour had benefited from strong Maori electoral support since the 1930s, winning all four Maori seats at every election until 1993, when Tau Henare (New Zealand First) defeated Bruce Gregory in Northern Maori, there had never been any attempt to put up Maori candidates in winnable general seats. As a result, Maori representation was limited to the four Labour MPs representing the Northern, Eastern, Western, and Southern Maori electorates. The first major breakthrough came in 1975, when National selected Maori candidates in two winnable general seats. The election of Ben Couch (1975–84) in Wairarapa and Rex Austin (1975–87) was followed by the nomination of a young lawyer, Winston Peters, in the Auckland seat of Hunua in 1979. The second major advance in the representation of Maori occurred with the introduction of MMP. Of the 80 Maori to have served in the New Zealand parliament since 1868, the first two thirds were elected in the 128-year period to 1996, and the other third were elected in the six years from 1996 to 2002.[9]

The sharp increase in Maori representation can be put down to two developments: the introduction under MMP of list seats; and the provision in the Electoral Act (1993) which ties the number of electorate seats to the number of Maori opting to go on the Maori role (this boosted the number of Maori seats from four in 1993 to seven in 2002) (see figure 10.3). New Zealand First won all the Maori seats in 1996, a remarkable achievement given the stranglehold traditionally held by Labour. After Labour won them all back at the next election, New Zealand First decided not to put up candidates on the grounds that separate Maori seats were no longer necessary and should be abolished; most of the Maori elected under MMP have been members of the New Zealand First (ten) and Labour (eleven) parties. Between 1996 and 2005 National had but one Maori MP (Georgina Te Heuheu). ACT's sole Maori MP, Donna Awatere-Huata, was suspended from its caucus in 2003.

Figure 10.3   Maori MPs, 1981–2002

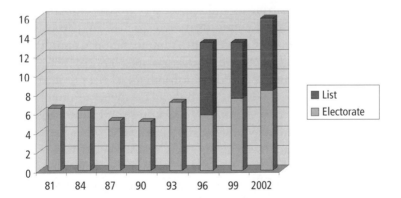

Although Maori representation is keeping pace with the Maori population, which comprises approximately 15 per cent of the total population, the same cannot be said for other significant minority groups. Those of Pacific ethnicity make up some 7 per cent of the population, which, if translated into parliamentary representation, would give them approximately nine seats. New Zealand's first Pacific MPs, Taito Field (Mangere) and Mark

Gosche (list) were elected by the Labour party in 1996. A third, Arthur Anae, became a National list member in 1996, although he was dropped down the list and out of parliament in 1999. The addition by Labour of a third Pacific member, Winnie Laban, in 1999 gave Pacific people a total of three MPs. Even more under-represented are those of Asian ethnicity, who make up 7 per cent of the national population and almost 13 per cent of those living in Auckland. While it is generally recognised that they are a potentially important constituency—Asians are expected to be over 13 per cent of the population by 2021[10]—there has been little effort on the part of the party elites to increase their level of political representation, with only two ethnic Chinese and one South Asian MP in the 2002–05 parliament.

Functions of MPs

Given the early uncertainty over the expected role of a list MP, it is useful to evaluate the priorities of list and electorate MPs in the three main areas of responsibility for any MP, that is, the constituency, parliamentary, and party functions. This part of the discussion draws on the findings of the New Zealand Election Study (NZES) post-election postal surveys of elected MPs (as distinct from all parliamentary candidates) between 1993 and 2002.

When the attitudes of MPs before and after the introduction of MMP are compared, it is clear that the role of parliament, especially the work of select committees, has become more important under MMP. The multiparty nature of select committees has increased the opportunities for individual MPs to scrutinise departments and oppose government initiatives. By 2002 five of the fourteen select committees were chaired by parties other than Labour, and only on the Government Administration Committee did the government members enjoy a majority (Martin 2004, p. 332). There was also greater opportunity under MMP for individual MPs to introduce their own legislative initiatives (Members' Bills). The advent of minority government provided further opportunities to scrutinise and frustrate government action. Ministers were now obliged to consult with other parties, as illustrated by the negotiations involving the Greens, United Future, and New Zealand First over introduction of the Foreshore and Seabed legislation.

Unlike the growing importance of the parliamentary function (with the exception of the debating chamber), the advent of the list member raises questions about the commitment of MPs to their constituency work. The local MP has two basic functions. *Pastoral care* covers a range of activities and includes helping individual constituents who have come upon hard times, advising the local primary school on zoning laws or decile ratings, advising sports club and voluntary service organisations on government funding, and performing a variety of ceremonial duties within the community. The second, *advocacy* function enables MPs to use their access to government departments and private sector organisations to help solve problems encountered by individual constituents and community groups. This may include helping a constituent with an immigration issue, housing a low-income family in state housing, trying to resolve a taxation problem with the Inland Revenue Department, or a schooling issue with the local primary or secondary school.

Table 10.5 compares the views of list and electorate members on a range of parliamentary, constituency, and party functions. As we might expect, electorate MPs highly value their constituency work, with between two-thirds and three-quarters considering their time with individual constituents to be very important. On the other hand, list MPs are seen to place greater importance on their work in parliament, both in the debating chamber and in select committees. Perhaps reflecting a stronger interest in the public role of an MP than the more private inter-personal work traditionally carried out by electorate representatives, list MPs show greater enthusiasm than do their electorate counterparts about working with the media and other non-party organisations, such as interest groups.

Table 10.5 Parts of an MP's job, 1993–2002

| | Very Important | | Important | | Not Important | |
	List MP (%)	Elect.MP (%)	List MP (%)	Elect. MP (%)	List MP (%)	Elect. MP (%)
Parliament						
Speaking in Parliament	28	21	65	60	7	19
Select committees	77	61	23	35		5
Working with interest groups	46	34	49	56	4	10
Constituency						
Electorate clinics	43	79	46	19	11	2
Dealing with individuals	46	66	42	34	12	1
Representing elect. in Parl.	40	71	45	29	15	
Local community function	35	48	53	46	12	
Representing region	30	36	51	50	18	14
Party						
Local party meetings	29	43	62	51	9	6
Developing party policy	52	40	46	53	2	6
Interviewed by media	38	29	53	53	10	18

Source: NZES 1993, 1996, 1999, 2002   n = 220.

Public attitudes towards list MPs

One of the features of MMP most heavily criticised by opponents of electoral reform was the introduction of the list member. In the view of one prominent New Zealand opponent of MMP, writing on the prospect of closed party lists for Europe, 'voters are restricted to voting for a party; the choice of candidates is left to party central committees—very European and very un-British' (Hunt 2000, p. 16). As the results of the NZES surveys of mass opinion indicate, public approval of list MPs jumped dramatically from 7 per cent to 36 per cent in the three-year period between 1999 and 2002. After some initial concern that list MPs had no mandate, no constituents, and little purpose beyond protecting their ranking on the party list, public judgments swung in the direction of being either positive or neutral (total 63 per cent), with only 10 per cent of respondents disapproving of the way list MPs handled their jobs. While some of the early scepticism was no doubt due to lack of knowledge about the likely role of this new category of MP, much adverse publicity was given to the political inexperience of some list members, as well as their inclination to party-hop (although not all those who defected from their party were list MPs). Around the time of the 1999 general election, when all of the offending MPs were defeated, the similarity in the functions and roles of list and electorate MPs began to be more clearly appreciated by voters (Karp 2001, p. 140).

Table 10.6 Attitudes to way list MPs have handled their job (voters)

Per cent	1999	2002
Approve	7	36
Neutral	36	27
Disapprove	29	10
Don't know	28	27
Total	**100**	**100**
	n = 4719	n = 1092

Source: NZES

Conclusion

The delegate model of representation is based on the assumption that MPs act at the behest of their constituents. While it would be unwise for the local MP to ignore an emphatic expression of constituency opinion, under New Zealand's system of party government it is the party, not the constituency, that determines how an MP votes. Apart from the conscience vote, the exceptions to this rule are extremely rare. In 2000, Labour's Damien O'Connor was granted a rare dispensation to oppose the government's ban on the logging of native timber on the West Coast. The ban was greeted with overwhelming opposition among the residents of the South Island electorate. Even more significant was the decision of Tariana Turia and Nanaia Mahuta to cross the floor on the Foreshore and Seabed legislation. Their decision was based on a belief that, as the delegates of their local iwi (tribes) and hapu (sub-tribes), they must act at the behest of their constituents, not their colleagues in the Labour party. Having defied their party's conventions of collective decision-making and strict internal discipline, a decision the party reluctantly acknowledged by granting permission for Mahuta to cross the floor, it will be less difficult for Mahuta, other Maori members, and Labour MPs in general to make the same case in the future.

This chapter has shown that some positive steps have been taken towards achieving the breadth of representation found in many other PR systems. However, while the proportion of Maori MPs now equals that of the Maori population as a whole, the same cannot be said for the Pacific and Asian communities, which continue to be significantly under-represented. Of the remaining threats to wider representation, three stand out.

Despite early advances towards gender parity, progress has been stalled. Contributing factors include the decision of party elites to offer protection to incumbents, both in the electorates and on the list, as well as feelings of complacency resulting from the rise of a small number of prominent women, including successive women prime ministers, to positions of political influence and power. A second threat is the possible abolition of the Maori seats. National, ACT, and New Zealand First have pledged to end separate representation for Maori. Without the protection of these seats (seven at present), and with no guarantee of compensation by way of high positions on the party lists, being able to maintain current levels of Maori representation is by no means guaranteed. A third factor relates to the electoral cycle. Because the proportions of women and ethnic minority MPs are unevenly spread across the parties, the inevitable decline in support for the reforming parties, notably Labour and the Greens, is likely to threaten the initial gains made under MMP, especially with respect to women, Maori and Pacific representation.

Notes

1   Harry Atmore served as the independent MP for Nelson from 1911 until the time of his death in 1946. He has been described as 'the last in a tradition of independent local constituency members' (Martin 2004, p. 222). While Tariana Turia contested the Te Tai Hauauru by-election as an independent in July 2004, to all intents and purposes she was the candidate for the Maori party, which was officially launched on polling day.

2   Examples include the minister of Finance and deputy prime minister, Michael Cullen, and the National party leader, Don Brash.

3   Although women received the vote in 1893, they were not able to contest a parliamentary seat until 1919.
4   Keith Jackson has noted that the use of whips in the New Zealand parliament pre-dated the era of political parties. As early as 1876 the premier, Sir Julius Vogel, reportedly used whips to keep his government members in line (1987, p. 50).
5   Labour party 'Constitution', 1981.
6   'Labour MPs should support Civil Union Bill says Carter', *New Zealand Herald*, 22 June 2004, p. 6.
7   A total of four National list MPs failed to be returned in 2002. In addition to Vernon and Young were Marie Hasler (number thirty-two on the list) and Anne Tolley (twenty-four).
8   Muriel Newman, 'Newman Online', 21 June 2004 (www.act.org.nz).
9   *Mana* Magazine, no. 59, August/September 2004.
10 New Zealand Census 2001, Statistics New Zealand (www.stats.govt.nz)

Further reading

Catt, H. 1999, *Democracy in Practice*, Routledge, London (especially chapter 5).

Catt, H. 1997a, 'New Zealand', in P. Norris (ed.), *Passages to Power: Legislative Recruitment in Advanced Democracies*, Cambridge University Press, Cambridge, pp. 137–57.

Karp, J. 2001, 'Members of Parliament and Representation', in J. Vowles, P. Aimer, J. Karp, S. Banducci, R. Miller and A. Sullivan, *Proportional Representation on Trial: The 1999 New Zealand General Election and the Fate of MMP*, Auckland University Press, Auckland, pp. 130–45.

McLeay, E. 2003, 'Representation, Selection, Election: The 2002 Parliament', in J. Boston, S. Church, S. Levine, E. McLeay and N.S. Roberts (eds), *New Zealand Votes: The General Election of 2002*, Victoria University Press, Wellington, pp. 283–308.

McLeay, E. 2000, 'The New Parliament', in J. Boston, S. Church, S. Levine, E. McLeay and N.S. Roberts (eds), *Left Turn: The New Zealand General Election of 1999*, Victoria University Press, Wellington, pp. 203–16.

Miller, R. 2004, 'Who Stood for Office and Why? in J. Vowles, P. Aimer, S. Banducci, J. Karp and R. Miller (eds), *Voters' Veto: The 2002 Election in New Zealand and the Consolidation of Minority Government*, Auckland University Press, Auckland, pp. 85–103.

Sullivan, A. and D. Margaritis, 'Maori Voting Patterns in 1999', in J. Boston, S. Church, S. Levine, E. McLeay and N.S. Roberts (eds), *Left Turn: The New Zealand General Election of 1999*, Victoria University Press, Wellington, pp. 175–83.

Wallace, J. (Chair) 1986, *Towards a Better Democracy: Report of the [New Zealand] Royal Commission on the Electoral System*, Government Printer, Wellington.

Parties in Power

11

NOTHING reveals more about the motives of political parties than their attitude to being in government. Politicians have been described as being driven by a 'desire for power, prestige and income, and by the love of conflict' (Downs 1957, p. 30). They not only compete for the people's vote, but also for legislative and governmental power. Whereas the combative 'winner-takes-all' approach is well suited to single party government, under coalition arrangements the competitive urge must be tempered and the spoils of office shared. Tangible benefits include cabinet appointments and their associated largesse, notably a ministerial salary, house and car, access to expert opinion and advice, and influence over the public policy agenda. Given the powers of the New Zealand executive, it is easy to see why the lure of office proves so irresistible, especially for small parties that hitherto have been marginalised and ignored.

But joining a coalition may also incur agonising costs. As studies of coalition government in other countries have found, these tend to be unevenly shared, with major parties incurring low costs and minor parties high costs (e.g. Mershon 2002). As one analysis of Irish coalitions found: 'It is extraordinarily difficult for a small party in government with a large rival to get noticed, implement some of its policies, and avoid a serious flogging at the next election' (Mitchell 2003, p. 217). New Zealand's minor parties have suffered a similar fate, as illustrated by the dramatic fall-off in support for New Zealand First after it formed a coalition with National in 1996. In more recent years, while the government has enjoyed high public esteem, the policy and electoral beneficiary has been Labour, not its coalition partners, the Alliance, followed by the Progressives.

Unlike most coalition studies, which are primarily concerned with attitudes among the core parties, this chapter will focus on the choices that coalitions impose on the minor parties. Adopting the analytical framework of Muller and Strom (1999), we will explore the three principal goals of governing parties, namely office, policies, and votes. As the premature termination of two out of the first four MMP coalitions illustrates, minor parties largely determine whether a coalition is stable, cohesive, and durable. Electoral slippage suffered by the junior coalition partner can place immense pressure on intra-governmental relations, particularly if it involves conflict between the junior partner's ministers and its party grassroots, and may even result in the coalition's collapse.

In light of New Zealand's difficult transition to coalition government, it is appropriate to ask whether voter rejection is simply a cross the minor parties must bear in return for the spoils of office. Can any small party survive the experience of coalition government? If it can, then what steps can be taken to ensure that the electoral benefits outweigh the costs? Comparisons will be drawn with Scotland and the Irish Republic, two small democracies that share New Zealand's Westminster tradition, multiparty system, and recent experience of coalition government under proportional representation.

Governing alternatives

Four types of government are possible under MMP:
- majority government (sixty-one +)
  - single-party
  - coalition
- minority government (– sixty)
  - single-party
  - coalition.

Even prior to the first MMP election, there was a general expectation that single-party majority government was a highly improbable outcome of proportional representation. With neither major party having managed to achieve 50 per cent of the vote since 1951, there was little prospect that it would be repeated under MMP. The popularity of the Alliance and New Zealand First prior to the 1996 election suggested that either or both might play a pivotal role in the formation of the first MMP government. But there were other possible coalition partners as well, including United, which, following its formation in 1995, was the third largest parliamentary party with eight MPs (three of whom had defected from Labour and five from National). Nor could the new ACT party be ruled out as a possible partner, especially given the scale of its campaign resources and prominence of its founding leaders—Roger Douglas and Richard Prebble had been senior ministers in the 1984–90 Labour government.

Despite the dominance of the coalition model under MMP, with the only exception being the minority National administration of Jenny Shipley between 1998 and 1999 (see figure 11.1), both major parties continued to express a marked preference for single-party government. Of the impediments to coalition government, four stand out:

1 A continuing distrust of coalition government by the elites of both major parties. This is based on the assumption of a 'natural dualism' in politics, which sees multiparty government as inherently unstable and ineffective (see Duverger 1957, p. 215).

2 Underlying animus between the major parties and several of their potential junior coalition partners. Although the debate over economic liberalisation no longer resonates with many voters, it has continued to cause bitterness among the splintered offshoots of the two major parties.

3 Intense electoral and policy competition between the minor parties themselves, largely precluding a coalition of more than two parties.

4 The potential for instability resulting from a coalition partnership between a strongly (e.g. National 1996–98) and a weakly (e.g. New Zealand First) organised party. As Panebianco (1988, p. 219) and Maor (1998, p. 13) point out, the less organised and disciplined the party, the greater the likelihood of unstable coalition.

Coalition 1: National-New Zealand First (1996–98)

Prior to the first MMP election, the parties were in a highly experimental stage of inter-party competition. As a result, voters were given no clear indication as to whether a majority or a minority coalition might be the preferred model, or indeed whether National and Labour wanted a partnership with the parties on their right and left flanks respectively or with those in the centre. Labour refused to make any pre-election coalition commitments to the Alliance, causing the Alliance leader to reply that the absence of a coalition agreement before the election meant no agreement after the election (Miller 1998a, p. 122). While National's relations with ACT were less strained, any

Figure 11.1 Timeline of New Zealand governments under MMP

12 October 1996	First election under MMP. National having won 44 and Labour 37 seats, New Zealand First (17) holds balance of power.
21 October 1996	Parallel negotiations begin between New Zealand First and the two major parties.
10 December 1996	The New Zealand First leader, Winston Peters, announces his decision to form a majority coalition with National (combined total of 61 out of 120 seats).
16 December 1996	The new National/New Zealand First government is sworn in. Peters becomes deputy prime minister and chief Finance minister ('Treasurer').
4 December 1997	Jim Bolger steps down as prime minister and is replaced by Jenny Shipley.
28 July 1998	Government loses its majority when a New Zealand First MP, Neil Kirton, becomes an Independent.
14 August 1998	Peters expelled from cabinet by the prime minister, Jenny Shipley. Eight New Zealand First MPs break ranks with their leader. They help to prop up a minority National government.
Aug 1998–Oct 1999	National minority government survives with support of ACT (8), Alamein Kopu (Independent), and former New Zealand First MPs.
27 November 1999	Second election under MMP. Total number of seats for Labour (49) and Alliance (10) one short of 61-seat majority.
6 December 1999	Minority Labour/Alliance government formed. Greens (7 seats) offer support on confidence and supply.
3 October 2001	Alliance MPs endorse US response to terrorist attack of 11 September.
25 October 2001	Alliance conference delegates attack Anderton for supporting government policy on US-led invasion of Afghanistan.
22 May 2002	Following dispute with Labour over its stance on genetic engineering, Greens say that they will no longer give support on confidence and supply.
11 June 2002	Prime minister calls an early election.
27 July 2002	Election results give Labour 52 seats, the new Jim Anderton Progressive Coalition party 2, and United Future 8.
9 August 2002	Minority Labour/Progressive government formed. Labour also signs support agreement with United Future's Peter Dunne.

prospect of a coalition of the two parties was virtually extinguished by New Zealand First's insistence that it would not support any government that included ACT. Despite refusing to rule out a deal with either of the two major parties, Peters' preferred partner appeared to be Labour, although the disdain with which he treated the Alliance and its leader, Jim Anderton, effectively ruled out a three-party coalition on the centre-left. To complicate matters still further, the National leader proposed a grand coalition with Labour, an offer that was firmly rejected by Helen Clark.

Even before the negotiating process was complete, public perceptions of coalition government were tarnished by a series of events, including the parallel and patently self-serving bargaining tactics of Winston Peters, which lasted for almost two months, and the intense media speculation over possible outcomes. The new government, which was of the 'minimal winning' type, enjoyed a paper-thin majority of sixty-one out of 120 seats (see table 11.1).

Table 11.1 Governing alternatives 1996, 1999, and 2002

Options	Seats (n)	Govt Type	Duration
1996			
Nat.	44		
Nat./NZF	*61*	*Majority coalition*	*20 months*
Nat./NZF/ACT	69		
Lab.	37		
Lab./Allia.	50		
Lab./NZF	54		
Lab./NZF/Allia.	67		
1999			
Lab.	49		
Lab./Allia.	*59*	*Minority coalition*	*31 months*
Lab./Allia./Gr.	66		
Lab./Allia./NZF	64		
2002			
Lab.	52		
Lab./Prog.	*54*	*Minority coalition*	
Lab./Prog./Gr.	63		
Lab./Prog./UF	62		
Lab./Prog./Gr./UF	71		

As this account suggests, the lack of any relevant experience was not the only obstacle to a smooth transition to coalition government in 1996. While it is fair to say that none of the parties 'were so radical or extremist as to be non-coalitionable' (Boston 1997, p. 96), it is equally clear that personal animosity threatened to have a corrosive and ultimately destructive effect on each and every one of the possible combinations, as illustrated by the disharmony within the National-New Zealand First government. Despite the initial promise of a constructive working relationship, the junior partner was the victim of damaging attacks from anti-MMP forces within the government. Suspicion that the prime minister, Jim Bolger, enjoyed an excessively close working relationship with the New Zealand First leader led to his replacement by Jenny Shipley in late 1997. Thereafter, it was only a matter of time before Shipley confronted Peters. The resulting dismissal of Peters from the cabinet not only collapsed the coalition, but also split the minor party's already fragile and ill-disciplined organisation. National was able to retain its legislative majority by drawing on the support of several party-hopping MPs, including seven defectors from New Zealand First, together with the eight ACT members and Peter Dunne. Sensing a high level of public dissatisfaction with coalition government, Shipley turned her attention to the campaign for a binding referendum on the future of MMP.

Coalition 2: Labour-Alliance (1999–2002)

Following the 1999 election, Labour (forty-nine seats) had the opportunity to form a majority coalition with the Alliance (ten) and Greens (seven). During the preceding three years, there had been attempts to patch up any differences between Labour and the five-party[1] Alliance with a view to reaching a workable coalition arrangement. This included a symbolically important appearance at the Alliance's 1998 conference by the Labour leader and joint meetings of the two parties' key politicians and advisors. Both parties wanted to avoid a repeat of the impasse of 1996, which had frustrated the coalition preferences of their voters. The leaders of the two parties recognised the importance of promoting a united front in the run-up to the election, something the deeply divided parties of the centre-right could not do. As we will see, while this rapprochement required some ideological flexibility on the part of the Alliance, it was a step the leaders of the small party were prepared to take in exchange for a role in government.

Ironically, the party most likely to upset the Alliance's plans was not New Zealand First, which had been repositioning itself as a potential partner for Labour, but the Greens, who, following an eight-year stint with the Alliance, had decided to stand on their own in 1999. Relations between the Greens and the NewLabour part of the Alliance had been deteriorating for some time, partly because of ideological and sociological differences (the Greens were seen to be too middle class), but also over conflicting styles of leadership, with the Greens regarding Anderton to be excessively domineering, even autocratic. Behind Anderton's assertion that the Greens were incapable of providing stable government, a claim he repeated during the 2002 campaign, was an understandable concern that a coalition with the Greens would reduce his own influence and that of the Alliance. To frustrate the Greens' coalition ambitions, even before the special votes had been counted and the small party's status as a parliamentary party confirmed,[2] Anderton had agreed to the terms of a Labour-Alliance minority government.

Given the tactical advantages to be gained from playing one junior coalition partner against the other, why did Labour agree to the exclusion of the Greens? While clearly acknowledging that they were a more promising long-term partner than the Alliance, which had yet to reconcile the pragmatism of its political leadership with the radicalism of its extra-parliamentary left wing, Clark shared some of Anderton's concerns about how to rein in the Greens in the event that they chose to ignore the convention of cabinet collective responsibility. Besides, the Greens could be guaranteed to support the bulk of Labour's legislative agenda whether or not they were in government. More than anything else, however, the decision reflected the growing respect for Anderton within Labour's senior political ranks.

Coalition 3: Labour-Progressives (2002–05)

At the outset of the 2002 campaign, Labour attempted to secure a mandate to govern alone, with the prime minister arguing that single party government provided the best guarantee of stable and effective government (although Clark had made it clear that there would be a space at the cabinet table for Anderton, who, along with several of his parliamentary colleagues, had broken away from the Alliance on the eve of the campaign).[3] It seemed unlikely that Labour would agree to a coalition with either New Zealand First or the Greens—Winston Peters' combative personality and shrill anti-system agenda instilled a sense of foreboding among members of the government, as did the Greens' walkout from parliament and uncompromising position over the lifting of the moratorium on the release of genetically modified crops—although neither possibility could be ruled out. A party with absolutely no chance of wooing Labour was the remnant of the Alliance, a group Clark partly blamed for her decision to call an early election.

No one could have predicted the dramatic ebbs and flows in party preferences that occurred during the course of the 2002 campaign, with the two major parties suffering significant losses and some of the minor parties making dramatic gains (Miller and Karp 2004). Although Labour failed to win its vaunted majority, the outcome was as close to ideal for the major party as minority government could hope to deliver. In addition to having a largely compliant partner in the form of the two-member Progressive Coalition (renamed the Progressives after the election), the prime minister was assured of a legislative majority from either United Future or the Greens. Each small party provided a distinctive range of legislative opportunities for the new government—whereas United Future could be relied upon to support the government's conservative economic agenda, the Greens would help to safeguard its liberal social and constitutional reforms. In the event that tensions between the two small parties threatened to boil over, the new government would be able to take comfort in the dual relationship, which, if properly managed, would help it to survive a full three-year term. However, because United Future was deemed to offer greater stability than the Greens, who, during the campaign had threatened to bring the government down, its leader received the first post-election call from the prime minister.

Coalition costs

According to Muller and Strom (1999), parties engaging in coalition bargaining do so in the full knowledge that they will receive benefits and incur costs. While some of the costs can be anticipated, others may not be known until the next election. Muller and Strom identify three broad objectives that are at the forefront of any negotiations:

1 *Office-seeking goal.* This involves the pursuit of positions within the administration, including cabinet and other ministerial appointments, influential portfolios, especially in the areas of finance and social policy, and membership of key cabinet and parliamentary committees.

2 *Policy-making goal.* This may take many different forms, such as bargaining over a full range of policies, or adopting a non-negotiable position on just one or two defining issues. There are also variations in the timing of the policy negotiations, with some coalitions being ratified without any bargaining having taken place.

3 *Vote-seeking goal.* As discussed in chapter 9, Anthony Downs (1957) is credited with the view that the primary goal of political parties is to maximise their vote. An extreme version of this position is that parties will adopt only those policies that help them win votes.

Depending on how pivotal they are to the formation of the government, parties are prepared to make compromises or trade-offs. In order to ensure that the office-seeking goals are achieved, for example, it may be necessary to trade off some valued policies. While it is possible to imagine circumstances in which politicians place greatest value on the pursuit of office, equally plausible are the factors that lead parties to remain committed to policy—Marsh and Mitchell found, for example, that where party activists were given a role in the negotiations process, policy took precedence over office and votes (1999, p. 43).

In his analysis of party participation in government, Michael Laver identifies at least three bargaining 'weights' that help to measure a party's coalition costs (1989, p. 312):

1 size

2 strategic importance—that is, whether or not a party enjoys a pivotal position

3 anticipated electoral results.

While the bargaining powers of the minor parties tend to be much weaker than those of the major parties, this is not always the case. The pivotal position enjoyed by New Zealand First in 1996, for example, gave it superior bargaining power to either National or Labour. While the electoral costs of participation are difficult to predict, it is not uncommon for junior partners to resign early if their chances of re-election are in danger of being harmed.

New Zealand's first three elections under MMP provide interesting parallels and contrasts in the costs of coalition for those parties involved.

Coalition 1 (1996–98): Office versus votes

For New Zealand First, the most costly coalition trade-offs occurred between the office-seeking and vote-seeking goals. The volatile nature of the party's support in the lead-up to the 1996 election provided warning of the dangers ahead. In February, the party's electoral support stood at 6 per cent. Within two months, and following a series of anti-immigration comments by Peters, which were directed towards business-investment migrants and refugees from Asia, the party enjoyed a sudden surge to 28 per cent (eight percentage points ahead of Labour). By the time of the October election it had dropped back to 13 per cent. This dramatic rise and fall is best explained by the largely protest nature of New Zealand First's vote. The two main sources of appeal were the elderly (most of whom enjoyed a good standard of living and were attracted by Peters' tough stand on immigration, law and order, and race relations), and low-income Maori. These groups soon proved to be an irreconcilable mix.

Given that two-thirds of New Zealand First's voters wanted a coalition with Labour, a centre-left government was a potentially popular option, with or without the Alliance. Before the election, Peters and his deputy, Tau Henare, had pledged that they would not serve under a Bolger administration. On the eve of the election, Peters repeated the promise by assuring voters that the only way to remove National from power was to vote for New Zealand First. In light of the party's subsequent decision, these commitments constitute a highly cynical form of electioneering, making a mockery of Peters' oft-vaunted pledge to make politics more democratic and accountable.

Bearing in mind the volatile nature of the New Zealand First vote, a less costly alternative might have been to return to the opposition, thereby providing the opportunity for a consolidation of electoral support. The choice of coalition partner notwithstanding, for a populist party such as New Zealand First, simply being in government can be interpreted as a violation of its commitment to voters. As Peters would soon find, accepting appointment to cabinet, including the position of deputy prime minister, seriously compromised the party's *raison d'être*, particularly its appeal to the powerless and forgotten. Following the coalition announcement the party's popularity slumped, with the greatest losses coming from Maori and those on low incomes. By mid-1997, only a year after achieving its best-ever poll result of 28 per cent, support had dropped to less than 4 per cent.

Having extracted significant concessions from National, Peters hoped that his party's office-seeking and policy-making payoffs would result in an electoral recovery at the next election.[4] By any measure, his office-seeking achievements were quite remarkable. In addition to receiving the second most powerful position in the government, that of Treasurer, Peters successfully negotiated for five appointments to the twenty-member cabinet, with the promise of three more within two years. He also received four of the six ministerial appointments outside of cabinet. Apart from Peters, none of the New Zealand First ministers had any previous executive experience. Even more remarkable, five of the nine new ministers were completely new to parliament.

But what Peters had failed to predict was the scale of the electoral costs that flowed from these office-seeking achievements. In exposing his inexperienced ministers to the rigours of government, especially in competition with their highly skilled and cynical National counterparts, Peters was placing the cohesiveness of the party under unnecessary strain, as well as opening it up to media scrutiny, and worse, public ridicule. Of the many instances of ministerial inexperience and disunity, two stand out. Beginning in 1997, there were repeated clashes between the party's associate minister, Neil Kirton, and his senior minister, National's Bill English, over implementation of parts of the coalition's health policy. The situation became so untenable that Kirton had to be relieved of his ministerial responsibilities, a decision that led to his departure from the party, thereby depriving the coalition of its one-seat majority. At about the same time, a simmering dispute between Peters and his deputy leader, Tau Henare, came to a head over the rumour that Henare and four other Maori MPs were planning to launch a separate Maori party. Henare was removed from the deputy leadership by his leader, a decision that contributed to the split within the party and the collapse of the coalition.

Coalition 2 (1999–2002): Office versus policy and votes

Whereas New Zealand First's problems were largely confined to the trade-off between office and votes, those of the Alliance were concerned with the link between office, policy and votes. NewLabour's guardianship of traditional Labour values was seen by its members to be the primary reason for its existence. Thus it was with some concern that they observed the growing rapprochement between the Alliance MPs and Labour in the months leading up to the 1999 election, especially since it involved the dilution of party policy in a number of areas, including taxation, workers' rights, and welfare spending. While most accepted the inevitability of a coalition, there were reservations about the strength of Labour's commitment to the principles of social democracy, as well as to consultative multiparty government.

Of more immediate concern, however, were the consequences of a negotiating process that was completed in only five days. As well as the need to finalise coalition arrangements before the parliamentary status of the Greens had been confirmed, the two parties wanted to allay public concern about their ability to set aside long-standing differences in the interests of stable and harmonious government. At one-and-a-half pages, the resulting agreement was remarkably brief and devoid of any reference to policy, apart from a mutually agreed declaration of intent. While the 72-page New Zealand First-National document can be criticised for its pedantic preoccupation with the minutiae of government policy, the absence of any reference to specific policies in the Labour-Alliance agreement set an equally dangerous precedent. The costs of this omission became clear within a matter of months, when doubts began to be raised about the Alliance's ability to influence government policy.

In mid-2000, an anti-government campaign by a number of business leaders and organisations resulted in a review of several Alliance proposals, including plans for four weeks' annual leave for workers and employer-funded parental leave provisions. The government's decision to shelve these initiatives could be justified on several grounds, including the need to restore business confidence and boost the public's faith in coalition government and MMP (at the time, a parliamentary committee was holding public hearings on the future of MMP). Not surprisingly, these policy backdowns, together with consistently poor poll ratings, were beginning to rankle with Alliance members and senior party officials, several of whom had set their sights on a seat in parliament after the next election. Despite the leader's impregnable majority in the seat of Wigram, poll results were suggesting that the party could lose most of its list seats at the next election, an unsettling prospect for future candidates, as well as some low-ranking incumbent MPs.

It is difficult to unravel the relative influence of power, policy, and votes on the progress of the dispute. What is clear, however, is that the flashpoint occurred following the terrorist attack on New York's twin towers in September 2001. Cabinet's decision to offer military support for the war in Afghanistan, which had been endorsed by the Alliance caucus, provoked a heated debate at the party's annual conference. However, while the battle lines were drawn over the issue of Afghanistan, a more fundamental debate concerned who should control Alliance policy. A majority of the party's MPs argued that policy decisions such as the one on Afghanistan were the responsibility of cabinet and caucus, while council members and a high proportion of the activists believed that ultimate responsibility should lie with the party organisation. Anderton's critics claimed that he had been seduced by power (ironically, a charge also levelled at Peters some three years earlier) to a point where he had become Labour's lapdog and was no longer interested in promoting the Alliance's radical policy agenda. While admitting that the party's policy gains might have been greater, Anderton argued that significant progress had been made on several fronts, including the creation of Kiwibank and the introduction of paid parental leave. He rejected as impractical any suggestion that ultimate control of policy should lie with the Alliance council. In the end, he knew that he held the trump card in the form of his safe seat of Wigram. Having overplayed their hand, Anderton's opponents, notably the president, Matt McCarten, and a cabinet minister, Laila Harre, gave assurances that the rift could be patched up. But it was too late, with Anderton and several of his parliamentary colleagues already having decided to form a rival electoral organisation.

Coalition 3 (2002–05): Office versus votes

Having vigorously defended government policy throughout his dispute with the Alliance, and having been promised a cabinet posting by the prime minister, an offer he had effectively accepted in advance, there was little left for Anderton to trade off in any coalition negotiations between his tiny Progressive party and Labour in the aftermath of the 2002 election. It would have been unrealistic for Anderton to expect to retain the position of deputy prime minister (a job that went to Labour's deputy leader, Michael Cullen), and there was little prospect of a second ministerial appointment for the Progressive's other MP, Matt Robson. Nor were there any real electoral costs to be weighed up, since Anderton was assured of retaining Wigram for as long as he chose to remain in politics. At the time of the Alliance dispute, Labour must surely have considered welcoming him back into their fold, a decision that would have created a net benefit for Labour of one additional seat. However, there was always the chance that one or more list MPs might be elected on Anderton's coat-tails. Besides, with Labour wishing to create an illusion that it was presiding over a coalition as opposed to a single-party government, and with the Progressives asking for almost nothing in return, it was an arrangement that met with Labour's unqualified support.

Where trade-offs were involved was in United Future's negotiations over the decision to offer the government confidence and supply. Dunne's view that 'all options were on the table'[5] in his bargaining with Labour would suggest that a formal coalition was a serious option. Dunne had previous experience as a coalition minister in the lead-up to the 1996 election, when the United party propped up a National administration. However, the circumstances in 2002 were vastly different, with United Future's seven list MPs having had no previous experience in parliament, let alone government. Having seen what had happened to New Zealand First, there was no way that he wanted to expose his MPs, none of whom had been expecting to enter parliament, to the pressures of being in government. Dunne had also weighed up the potential risks of being too closely associated with a centre-left government whose liberal social values were at odds with those of his party. Most important of all, however, was the need to avoid a repeat of the electoral costs that had torn the heart out of New Zealand First and the Alliance. Having seen his party's electoral support more than triple in a period of three weeks, Dunne knew that it could just as quickly collapse. Since consolidating these gains was essential to the party's future as a parliamentary party, Dunne concluded that, while he should help to provide stable government, he should do so from a safe distance.[6] As well as guaranteeing implementation of a modest policy agenda, including a Commission for the Family, cooperating from outside of government would allow him to exploit criticisms of the government on a range of social and constitutional issues, including the Prostitution Reform Bill (2003), Civil Union Bill (2004), and the removal of the right of appeal to Britain's Privy Council and the creation of a New Zealand Supreme Court (2003).

Surviving in government

Having discussed the challenges and costs of being in coalition, let us now turn to the question of whether any small party can survive the experience of coalition government with its reputation and electoral support intact. What if any measures can be taken to ensure that the electoral benefits of being in office outweigh the costs?

The experiences of coalition government in Ireland and Scotland are instructive, offering pointers to what junior coalition partners should or should not do to enhance their chances of electoral success. In Ireland, which has had a similar pattern of minority coalitions to that of New Zealand, small parties have tended to make electoral gains in opposition and suffer electoral losses in government (Gallagher 2003, p. 97). In circumstances similar to those experienced by New Zealand First, in 1992 the small Irish Labour party was deemed to have 'betrayed the expectations of its voters' by using its pivotal position to form a coalition with Fianna Fáil, a party it had long criticised, rather than with the preferred Fine Gael (Mair 1999, p. 146). Faced with growing voter disillusionment, the coalition survived only two years before Labour reversed its decision and formed a government with Fine Gael. At the 1997 election it lost half its seats. Another small governing party, the Progressive Democrats, spent half its existence in government. From an initial high of 12 per cent, the party lost votes at every subsequent election (Gallagher 2003, p. 98). At the 2002 election, for example, its senior partner, Fianna Fáil, benefited from the popularity of the government by increasing its support. On the other hand, the Progressive Democrat vote declined, although the losses would have been much greater were it not for the small party's ability to carve out its own separate identity by distancing itself from some of the major party's big-spending initiatives. The small party mounted a strongly anti-government campaign with the slogan 'Vote for us—it's the only way to keep the Fianna Fáil in check' ringing in the ears of voters. As its leader declared, the purpose of the strategy was to remind voters of 'the bad old days of [single party] Fianna Fáil power, without the Progressive Democrats here to keep them honest' (Mitchell 2003, p. 218). The senior partner was willing to tolerate this approach mainly because the two parties were not competing for the same votes.[7]

Unlike the extensive experience of coalition government found in Ireland, Scotland got its first coalition in 1999.[8] Following the inaugural election for a devolved parliament, Scottish Labour and the Liberal Democrats began to negotiate the terms of a majority government. Although Labour was primarily concerned with the allocation of cabinet portfolios and seats, the small Liberal Democrat party presented a comprehensive policy programme, the centrepiece of which was a non-negotiable demand that the government abolish tertiary student fees. In the face of strong opposition from the British Labour government, which was committed to the principle of user-pays in university education, the two parties agreed to the formation of a committee to explore the implications of the Liberal Democrat proposal. As Scotland's Liberal Democrat leader, Jim Wallace, explained, intense pressure was brought to bear by the party's federal leader, Paddy Ashdown,[9] and the prime minister, Tony Blair, to 'be flexible' and to 'get a deal'.[10] Wallace refused to make the abolition of fees a pre-condition of coalition, a decision that was derided as 'naïve' and a 'sell-out' by members of the Scottish media (Hassan and Warhurst 2000).

Of particular relevance to the present analysis are the reasons why, in light of this uncertain start to its term in government, Scotland's junior coalition partner managed to retain its popular support throughout its first term in government (at the 2003 election the Liberal Democrats retained all thirteen seats, whereas the senior partner, Labour, dropped from fifty-six to fifty). First, unlike New Zealand's junior coalition partners, the Liberal Democrats built their identity around one core issue, the abolition of university fees, which resonated strongly with middle class voters (low-income students were either exempt or paid a reduced fee). Because of Labour's well-known opposition to abolition, this became a defining issue of the minor party's term in government. Second, in contrast to Scottish Labour, which had three leaders in the space of two years and was tainted by scandal and accusations of being the lapdog of the Blair government, according to John Curtice, the Liberal Democrats appeared to be 'the more stable bit'.[11] The small party was able to maintain internal unity by keeping in regular contact with its membership and by allowing its parliamentarians to cross the floor on matters of strong disagreement with the government. And third, the junior coalition partner was able to avoid much of the tension and conflict that tends to characterise relations between governing parties, especially at election time, because the two parties were not in competition for the same votes. Whereas Labour draws most of its support from Scotland's highly populated central belt, especially around Glasgow, the Liberal Democrats' strongholds are in the Borders and northern regions, including the Orkney and Shetland Islands (Bennie et al. 1997).

Survival kit for small parties

What do these examples of coalition government tell us about the possible role of minor parties in New Zealand? A 'Survival Kit' for small parties in government might well include the following elements:

Don't mislead voters over a party's coalition plans

While there may be sound tactical grounds for not naming a preferred coalition partner in advance, the experiences of the Irish Labour party (1992) and New Zealand First (1996) point to the dangers of choosing a coalition partner the party's voters neither want nor expect. The 'wait-and-see' approach to coalition preferences is common among centre parties. At every election since 1996, Winston Peters has refused to declare a preference until after the election results have been announced, and United Future's Peter Dunne has consistently stated that he would talk first to the party winning the most seats. On the other hand, because the options available to flank parties are so limited, with one or other (but not both) of the major parties as the only credible partner, there may be little to lose in reaching a coalition understanding in advance—approximately 80 per cent of voters believe that a party should reveal its coalition plans prior to the election (New Zealand Election Study 1996–2002). In 2004, for example, the Greens were planning their 2005 campaign around the theme of 'A vote for the Greens is a vote for a Labour-led government' (following the damaging breakdown in their relationship with Labour over genetic engineering (G.E.) in 2002, the Greens decided that they would set no pre-conditions to a coalition with Labour in 2005).[12] In contrast, from the time it was formed, the Maori party, an offshoot from Labour, argued that it could form a coalition with either of the two major parties (despite the fact that National had promised to abolish the Maori seats and had adopted an even tougher stand on the foreshore and seabed legislation than Labour).

Even before going into government, establish a high public profile based on the themes of moderation and stability

As the previously discussed examples clearly illustrate, the Achilles heel of coalition government is its reputation for unstable government. The major parties in all three countries have been able to exploit the public's fear that small parties are inexperienced and unreliable coalition partners, and that they have an unhealthy ambition to be the 'tail that wags the dog'. Minor parties can counter these claims by limiting their demands and by stressing the weaknesses of single party government, particularly its association with the abuse of power. In an age of cynicism and distrust, keeping the government honest can provide prospective coalition partners with a potent campaign theme.

All else being equal, always choose the major party with the most divergent electoral support

As the recent successes of the Irish Progressive Democrats and the Scottish Liberal Democrats serve to illustrate, coalition partners enjoy a more constructive relationship when they are not competing for the same votes. Tensions between Labour and the Alliance were aggravated by the fact that both parties were fishing in the same electoral pool. The drift of low-income Alliance voters back to Labour from the mid-1990s made the party increasingly dependent on its leader, who provided a safety net in the form of his safe Wigram seat. In contrast, the confidence agreement struck with United Future in 2002 posed no real electoral threat to either Labour or United Future, since the two parties appealed to quite different constituencies.

Have a short but substantive shopping list of policies, preferably with one defining policy upon which the junior coalition partner can stake its reputation

By making at least one policy 'an issue of faith',[13] the minor party is able to establish its own identity, and in a manner likely to enhance its reputation as a party of principle. What should be avoided, however, is a non-negotiable stand that leaves no 'wriggle-room' for either side. In Scotland, the 'non-negotiable' position adopted by the Liberal Democrats on the abolition of student fees was compromised by its willingness to respect the recommendations of an independent review committee. The Alliance made a similarly unsuccessful attempt to enforce an eight-point policy agenda on Labour in 1996. More costly still was the Greens' uncompromising position on G.E. in 2002. In each case, the options were limited to either an embarrassing backdown or three more years in opposition. Conversely, in 2002 the Progressive Coalition failed to come up with a single defining policy proposal, an omission that threatened to prove costly at the next election.

Policy commitments should be made during, not after, the bargaining process

As the Alliance found over its flagship policies on paid parental leave and the establishment of Kiwibank, a minor party's bargaining power is greatly reduced once the coalition agreement has been ratified. Had the government decided not to proceed with the Kiwibank proposal (Clark and her Finance minister, Michael Cullen, were decidedly lukewarm), the Alliance would have been left with no substantive policy gains in close to three years in government.[14]

Limit the politicians' office-holding demands to the conventions of coalition government

Personal ambition is not always easy to suppress, especially on those rare occasions when the minor party holds a pivotal position between the two major parties. However, it is important to avoid creating an impression of 'unprincipled wheeler-dealing' (Hassan and Warhurst 2000, p. 20). The allocation of cabinet positions is best handled on a *pro rata* basis, with the pre-eminent posts of prime minister and Finance minister going to the senior coalition partner, and the middling and junior portfolios being split between the senior and junior partners. Significant portfolios that the junior partner might aspire to hold include Justice (as in Scotland), Transport, and Energy. Despite the attractiveness of the post of deputy prime minister, it places the leader of a minor party in the highly vulnerable position of being the official mouthpiece of the government. As the examples of Peters and Anderton show, this can cause resentment among members and compromise the identity of the party as a whole.

Insist on some flexibility on whipping

Because minor parties are often comprised of highly individualistic and comparatively inexperienced politicians, a measure of latitude may be needed to prevent internal disunity, and further party-hopping once the Electoral (Integrity) Amendment Act lapsed after the 2005 election. The importance of flexibility was acknowledged in the 'agree to disagree' provision in the Labour-Alliance agreement of 1999. Three years later, the Labour-Progressive agreement conceded 'the need for distinctive party political identities within government, especially in relation to the smaller party being able to maintain a separate but responsible identity'.[15] However, maintaining a separate identity places a reciprocal obligation on the junior coalition partner to honour a 'good faith and no surprises' commitment in the event that any of its members should choose to cross the floor.

As a precaution against falling below the 5 per cent threshold at the following election, list-only junior coalition partners should try to negotiate some form of electoral accommodation, such as the transfer of a safe constituency seat

Although there is no precedent in New Zealand for the transfer of a safe seat, it has been widely discussed, especially following ACT's dramatic decline during 2004 to approximately 2 per cent. Speculation centred on the affluent Auckland electorates of Tamaki and Epsom, although the National party leader was publicly opposed to any such deal. However, this did not preclude the possibility of a different sort of electoral trade-off either before or during the 2005 campaign. In 1996 National's strategists made the party's Wellington Central voters aware that they would not be at all unhappy if they chose to give their electorate vote to the ACT candidate, Richard Prebble, thereby ensuring that ACT would have seats in parliament, even if it did not make the 5 per cent threshold. Helen Clark conveyed a similar message to Labour voters in Coromandel in 1999, with the result that the Green candidate, Jeanette Fitzsimons, narrowly won the seat (the Greens' party vote on election night was 4.7 per cent)).

Conclusion

This chapter began by asking if any minor party can survive coalition government. As we have seen, New Zealand's early experience of coalition government is hardly encouraging. As with any party seeking power, the office-seeking and policy-making instincts of the minor parties have had to be balanced against the need for votes. Mitigating against an easy resolution of these competing goals have been: a lack of governmental experience among the minor parties; a long tradition of single party government, with the two major parties taking turns to monopolise power; continuing animosity between the major parties and their splintered offshoots; and intense competition among the minor parties themselves, largely precluding a coalition of more than two parties. While voters express a growing preference for coalition over single party government, public confusion over the perceived role and influence of the junior coalition partner persists (Miller and Karp 2004).

A further impediment to stable government has been the weakly institutionalised nature of the junior coalition parties. The absence of either a strong internal party organisation or shared sense of institutional identity and loyalty has had a corrosive effect on the effectiveness, as well as the credibility, of coalition government. Despite being a 'minimal winning coalition'— according to coalition theorists, a bare majority is the most stable of the governing alternatives (see, for example, Budge and Kenan 1990)—the National/New Zealand First government was beset by ill-discipline and eventually collapsed under the combined weight of inter-party suspicion and irreconcilable divisions within New Zealand First. Whereas New Zealand First's problems originated in the parliamentary caucus, the Alliance's organisational breakdown occurred in the relationship between the politicians and the grassroots party members and activists.

While United Future and New Zealand First can exploit their centrality by bargaining with both major parties, thereby extracting the best possible terms, flank parties, notably the Greens and ACT, are restricted to negotiating with only one.[16] Having been excluded from the 1999 and 2002 governments, the Greens are in the most vulnerable position, although, as we have seen, their bargaining position has been further weakened by a tendency to overplay their hand. Apart from declaring in 1999 that it would not work with Peters and New Zealand First, ACT has managed to avoid the pitfalls that come from taking a non-negotiable stand. As the party's leaders well know, however, any failure to meet National's coalition terms may either open the door for another minor party or produce another period of minority government.

Despite its pivotal position, New Zealand First demonstrated how easy it is to miscalculate the costs of coalition. Maximising his office-seeking and policy-making goals required that Peters go with National rather than Labour, a decision that had profound and largely unanticipated electoral consequences. Tantalising though the posts of deputy prime minister and Treasurer undoubtedly were, when combined with the decision to keep National in power, they created an impression of hypocrisy and betrayal. Whether a party of New Zealand First's populist ilk can ever hold office without shedding votes remains to be seen. To a greater extent than all the other minor parties, its success in government will depend on its ability to learn from the mistakes of other small parties, both in New Zealand and overseas.

This raises the question of whether voter rejection is simply a cross that minor parties must bear in return for the spoils of office. Experience tends to suggest that it is. What may prove interesting, however, is whether Peter Dunne's decision to stay out of government while playing the role of support party is a model other small parties may choose to imitate. Clearly there are advantages to be had, at least in the short term, in gaining further political experience and consolidating the party's membership base and electoral support. Guaranteeing the government a 'good faith and no surprises' relationship allowed United Future to claim two major achievements: stable government; and protection against the abuse of power. It also ensured passage of a policy agenda, including a Commission for the Family and a comprehensive drug strategy for the young. Although modest, these policies were no less significant than those achieved by the Alliance during its three years in government. Finally, by remaining independent, even critical of the government on a number of important matters, United Future was better able to protect and nurture its own separate identity. Since the natural instinct of politicians is to gain political office with a view to exercising power, this exercise in self-restraint may prove to be short-lived. However, in the event that the costs of coalition continue to be high, overall it may prove to be a more attractive option for a number of New Zealand's small parties than being in government.

Notes

1   The Greens announced that they would be leaving the Alliance at the 1999 election. The Liberals, under their leader Frank Grover MP, had also withdrawn from the Alliance by the time of the 1999 election (Grover stood unsuccessfully as a Christian Heritage candidate in the seat of Tauranga).

2   On election night, the Green vote fell just short of the 5 per cent threshold. It also failed to win a plurality of the votes in the seat of Coromandel. After special votes were counted, the party ended up with 5.2 per cent of the party vote and Jeanette Fitzsimons carried Coromandel by 250 votes.

3   Anderton was joined by fellow cabinet ministers Sandra Lee and Matt Robson, together with John Wright, Grant Gillon, Phillida Bunkle, and Kevin Campbell. Lee, Bunkle, and Campbell retired from politics at the 2002 election. The others went on to form the Progressive Coalition party.

4   However, as Boston has pointed out, despite winning a raft of policy concessions from National, New Zealand First was unable to convince the major party to endorse its major campaign commitments, including those on overseas investment and immigration (1997, p. 104).

5   Interview with Peter Dunne, Parliament Buildings, Wellington, 16 July 2003.

6   Interview with Peter Dunne, Parliament Buildings, Wellington, 16 July 2003.

7   Interview with Simon King, Constitution Unit, University of London, 19 November 2002.

8   For discussions on coalition government in Scotland, see Bradbury and Mitchell (2001), Finnie and McLeish (1999), Hassan and Warhurst (2000), and Winetrobe (2001).

9   Catherine MacLeod, 'Coalition Feels the Strain', *The (Glasgow) Herald*, 11 December 1998, p. 11. McLeod quotes a senior Liberal Democrat, who said: 'Few know how much time Tony Blair and Paddy Ashdown spent getting this coalition off the ground. They wanted to demonstrate that new politics were possible.'

10   Interview with Jim Wallace (leader of the Liberal Democrats), Auckland, 23 December 2002.

11   Interview with John Curtice, University of Strathclyde, Glasgow, 12 September 2002.

12   Interview with Rod Donald, 17 May 2004, University of Auckland.

13   *The Scotsman*, 10 May 1999, p. 8.

14   Paid parental leave had long been on Labour's wish-list of policies.

15   'Coalition Agreement between the Labour and Progressive Coalition Parties in Parliament', Wellington, 8 August 2002.

16   In 2004, the new Maori party stated that, in the event that it won seats at the 2005 election, it was prepared to negotiate with either major party.

Further reading

Boston, J. 2003, 'Forming a Government' in R. Miller (ed.), *New Zealand Government and Politics*, Oxford University Press, Melbourne, 3rd edition, pp. 117–34.

Maor, M. 1998, *Parties, Conflicts and Coalitions in Western Europe: Organisational Determinants of Coalition Bargaining*, Routledge, London.

Mershon, C. 2002, *The Costs of Coalition*, Stanford University Press, Stanford, California.

Miller, R. and J. Karp 2004, 'A Vote for Coalition Government', in J. Vowles, P. Aimer, S. Banducci, J. Karp and R. Miller (eds), *Voters' Veto: The 2002 Election in New Zealand and the Consolidation of Minority Government*, Auckland University Press, Auckland, pp. 134–49.

Mitchell, P. 2003, 'Government Formation in 2002: 'You can have any kind of government as long as it's Fianna Fail', in M. Gallagher, M. Marsh and P. Mitchell (eds), *How Ireland Voted 2002*, Palgrave MacMillan, Houndmills, Basingstoke, Hampshire, pp. 214–29.

| part five |

Conclusion

Future of Participation and the Party System

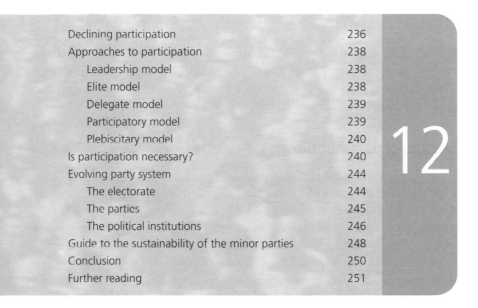

12

THERE has never been greater cause for interest in the party system than at the present time. The referendum vote in favour of a proportional electoral system led to the formation of new parties and the consolidation of others. A decade later, the party system remained in a state of flux. The collapse of the Alliance and decline in support for the right-wing ACT party paved the way for an intensification of two-party competition in the fertile middle ground. National's 17-point rise in support in the space of one month was a record, prompting ACT to survey its members and supporters on the possibility of a merger. But the popularity of National also had implications for Labour. Renewed competition between the two major parties for the support of 'middle' New Zealand had an indirect affect on Labour's previously close relationship with Maori. The subsequent formation of a grassroots Maori party rekindled speculation about the viability of separate ethnic representation and, more generally, the changing dynamics of multi-party politics under MMP.

This final chapter will consider the implications of the dramatic ebbs and flows in the fortunes of the political parties for the future of the party system. However tempting it may be to view New Zealand's experience of change as unique, the evidence from Europe and elsewhere suggests otherwise. What were the causes of change? How do the changes compare with those in other countries? And do they constitute a 'transformation' of the party system or something more modest? But first, let us consider the question of public participation, reviewing arguments for the view that the public is becoming increasingly disengaged from political parties and election campaigns. While the neoliberal reforms made a profound impact on the political system and culture of New Zealand, the internal practices of the major parties and a number of the smaller parties have remained largely impervious to change. Their failure to provide opportunities for meaningful participation raises questions about the future of parties as democratic institutions.

Declining participation

Declining participation has become a significant feature of party politics in New Zealand. For most of the last century, the mass party reigned supreme. At its peak, National reputedly had a membership of close to 300,000, making it on a per capita basis the most successful mass party in the Western world. Not far behind was Labour, with a combined affiliated and active branch membership approaching 200,000 (Gustafson 1989, p. 208). Over time, however, the two major parties took on a number of the characteristics of the 'catch-all' and 'electoral-professional' party models (see chapter 4). Spurred on by the growth of the mass media, especially television, and the increased availability of professional expertise, they began to reach over the heads of their members to a mass electorate. Features of the American 'presidential' style of campaigning that have become commonplace in New Zealand include the increased use of mass marketing, with an emphasis on party branding and style, a preoccupation with personality and leadership, and a dilution of the policy agenda with a view to appealing to the burgeoning middle class. As a result of these trends, the traditional roles of party members have become less valued and important.

While the rapid increase in the number of parties immediately before and after the introduction of the MMP electoral system might have been expected to revive interest in participation, with a few notable exceptions this has not occurred (see table 1.1). Instead, most of the new parties have assumed the character of Katz and Mair's 'cartel' party (1994). Whereas the mass party was founded on a large grassroots membership and the catch-all party pays lip-service to party membership while removing most of its functions, the cartel party finds no substantive purpose in party membership, preferring to pin its future success on increased access to the vastly superior resources and powers of the state. The suggestion that parties no longer value participation to the extent that they once did is part of what Scarrow refers to as the 'demand-side' explanation for party membership decline (2000).

Although their impact is more difficult to assess, the 'supply-side' constraints on participation should not be overlooked. Put simply, the rewards of participation are either no longer available or hold little personal appeal. Active involvement in a political party once provided a range of tangible benefits, including a ready source of political education, socialisation and recruitment, important links with the local community, and, for a privileged few, political patronage and other forms of largesse. In today's busy and highly individualistic society, few members of the public are likely to have the time to attend a political meeting, let alone the inclination to donate money or devote time to a party organisation. Moreover, with the growth of television and access to the Internet, the incentive to turn politics into a mere spectacle is increasing. Whether the particularly low levels of participation among the young is due to the life-cycle effect or reflects a more profound process of generational change (see chapter 5) remains an open question.

But what about the 'high-intensity participation' that Whiteley and Seyd associate with more active forms of party involvement (2002)? Whereas party activists were once valued for their role in disseminating party propaganda, monitoring public opinion, and mobilising the vote, they are gradually being replaced by an array of professionals, including market researchers, opinion pollsters, press secretaries, web designers, and political analysts and advisors. As we have seen, among the inevitable consequences of this transition from an amateur to a largely professional approach to politics has been a significant shift in the balance of financial power and responsibility away from individual party members and activists and towards wealthy individuals, corporations, and the state.

Does declining participation suggest a lack of interest in politics? The evidence would tend to suggest not. As this study has shown, most voters keep an eye on public affairs, with two out of every three expressing either a keen or a moderate interest in politics (see figure 5.1). A good indication of the public's willingness to be informed can be seen in the popularity of television news (Television New Zealand's evening news is consistently the top-rated show). There is also growing evidence that a significant number of voters keep abreast of campaign events and issues by way of the Internet (figure 9.3). Voters are likely to remain attentive until the final days of the campaign, when close to a third of voters finalise their voting choices (figure 9.1). Thus, while members of the public are failing to engage in the more traditional forms of participation, they appear to be maintaining an interest in what is going on.

Approaches to participation

Now let us return to a somewhat modified version of the models of participation identified by Whiteley and Seyd (2002) and outlined in the opening
chapter, assessing their appropriateness as explanations for the internal practices of the political parties in New Zealand.[1]

Leadership model

Features of this model include a dominant leader, weak party organisation,
and small core of 'supporters', as distinct from 'activists', whose commitment
is to the leader rather than the party (Whiteley and Seyd 2002). The party
leader makes all the major decisions, although often in consultation with a few
trusted friends and advisers. New Zealand First offers the most complete contemporary manifestation of the leadership model. Winston Peters became the
personification of the movement, so much so that he developed an almost
messianic reputation, with his followers frequently referring to him as the only
honest politician in the country. However, facets of the leadership model can
also be found in some of the other minor parties, including Peter Dunne's
United Future, Jim Anderton's Progressives, and Pastor Brian Tamaki's fledgling Christian party, Destiny New Zealand. Former parties that were based on
the leadership model include John A. Lee's Democratic (Soldier) Labour party
(1943) and Bob Jones' New Zealand party (1983–84).

What contribution does the leadership model make to the future of party
participation in New Zealand? Given their focus on leadership and, in many
instances, a populist agenda, parties of this type are likely to appeal to voters
with no previous attachment to a political party. Some may even regard
themselves to be political outcasts, part of a sub-group within society whose
interests have been ignored by the mainstream parties. Because of their devo-
tion to their leader and the leader's cause, supporters of such parties generally
have low expectations of their role in the party's decision-making process.
This may help explain why personality-based parties have a reputation for
being internally unstable, unreliable coalition partners, and generally short-
lived. The sheer dominance of the leader tends to preclude either the
grooming of a successor or the existence of a second tier of command. As a
result, the departure of the founding leader is likely to precipitate a vacuum
of power, causing the party to either fracture or implode.

Elite model

The elite-based party has a number of the characteristics of the 'catch-all'
party, including the promotion of a new class of professional politicians and
advisors and a corresponding decline in the influence of extra-parliamentary
party officials and headquarters' staff. While elite parties may continue to
acknowledge grassroots' involvement by maintaining membership lists and

giving their activists a limited say in such areas as policy formation, candidate selection, and campaigning, the decisions that really count are those made by the politicians and their advisors, with most being made out of the parliamentary office of the party leader. Features of the elite model can be found in most of the parties, although Labour, National (apart from its selection of constituency or electorate candidates), and ACT are predominantly of this type. For example, all three parties leave the choice of leader to their MPs. In 2003, this resulted in a mere twenty-six National MPs (two of whom were candidates) deciding by a bare majority to replace the incumbent leader, Bill English. The following year, an even smaller group of eight MPs (four of whom were leadership candidates) chose the new ACT leader, Rodney Hide. It reportedly took several ballots before they were able to reach a final decision. While nominations for the parliamentary candidate lists may include some input from party activists, in all three parties the all-important ranking process is made by a small central committee. Finally, with the decline of the party conference as a forum for genuine policy debate, responsibility for policy-making is largely in the hands of the party leadership.

Delegate model

Under this model, which tends to be associated with the mass membership party, members choose delegates to speak and vote on their behalf. Delegates are not chosen to make their own independent judgments, but rather to represent the interests of their particular group. If the model is applied as intended, then the party's national conference will be something of a microcosm of the membership at large. While the delegate model limits the role of individual members, it has the potential to hold the party leadership to account. Both Labour and National adopt the delegate method for their regional and national conferences. Of course, their failure to give these same bodies significant decision-making powers tends to undermine the premises upon which the delegate model is based. For example, despite National's commitment to a large membership and significant grassroots involvement, a series of organisational reforms introduced in 2003 placed significant executive powers in the hands of its Board of Directors. These included the right to choose the president, a decision previously made by delegates attending the party's annual conference. There was also a reduction in the role of the party's regions and the disestablishment of several elected committees, with a number of their powers being transferred to the Board of Directors.

Participatory model

This is based on the assumption that each and every party member has a right to contribute to all major decisions. Although it can be applied to parties of any size, for obvious reasons the model works best in relatively small organisations of approximately 2,000 to 5,000 active members. Parties based on the participatory model typically consult widely before reaching a majority vote of all those involved. A more difficult approach involves decision by consensus. The leading exponent of the participatory model in New Zealand is the Green party, which uses its annual conference to debate party policy, confirm the choice of party leaders, and discuss the overall tactics and strategies to be adopted in the next election campaign. There is also provision in the party constitution for a special post-election conference to consider whether the party should join a coalition and, if so, under what terms. To maximise the participation of its members, the Green party will occasionally resort to postal ballots on such matters as the composition and ranking of the party's candidate list.

Plebiscitary model

Some politicians are inherently suspicious of the delegate and participatory models on the grounds that the decisions of party members and activists are likely to be based on narrow self-interest. As the guardians of the party's doctrine and policies, they are regarded as having a predisposition to want to impose their dogma on others. Plebiscites, on the other hand, allow the politicians to reach out to a wider, and perhaps more malleable, community. In the opinion of their critics, plebiscites are used to rubber-stamp decisions made by the politicians. As a result, they provide only an illusion of participation (Whitely and Seyd 2002, p. 213). While the plebiscite model is widely used in political parties in Canada and Britain, it is new to New Zealand. An early experiment was the indicative ballot conducted by the ACT party during the course of its 2004 contest to replace Richard Prebble as leader. Although members were limited to an indicative vote (the final decision was made by the eight-member parliamentary caucus), the leadership contenders tried to sign up new members with a view to increasing support for their leadership. One unsuccessful candidate, Stephen Franks, even asked the 3,500 recipients[.] of his online legal-issues newsletter, including some lawyers, to join the party with a view to casting an indicative vote for him as the next party leader.[2] During the course of the campaign, the party almost doubled its total membership. ACT also conducts regular online polls on a range of policy issues, although there is no suggestion that the results will have any bearing on the policy decisions of the party leadership.

Is participation necessary?

Should we simply accept as unimportant the low levels of participation in political parties, or do they reflect poorly on the state of our democracy? The case for participation is built on two main claims: first, that it enables individual citizens to assert greater control over the 'public' dimension of their lives; and second, that it helps to energise parties and frustrate the natural inclination of the ruling elite towards an 'elective dictatorship'. In the tradition of the theories of direct participation made famous by the ancient Greeks and reinforced by the writings of Jean Jacques Rousseau, John Stuart Mill, and others, the sovereignty of the people is capable of being expressed in many different ways, some directly, while others may take a more indirect form. As David Held has observed, in the ideal world of these democrats, 'the "active citizen" could once again return to the centre of public life, involving himself or herself in the realms of both state and civil society' (1993, p. 25). These two arguments for participation are deserving of some attention.

First, there are many different reasons why individuals may wish to exercise some control over their public lives. The reasons can be classified into two groups: selective incentives and collective incentives (Scarrow 2000; Katz 2002). The selective incentives relate to the personal rewards of participation, including a range of material and social benefits. Quite apart from the tangible benefits discussed earlier in the chapter, participants can derive considerable emotional satisfaction from being with like-minded party members, as well as having the chance to rub shoulders with prominent politicians. Collective incentives, on the other hand, include a personal identification with a party's ethos and goals, as well as a sense of idealism about what constitutes the good society. Achieving these goals may require a commitment to either run for elective office or work for the election of others. While recruiting new members is far from easy, and is likely to become even more difficult in the future, research has shown that providing citizens with incentives can have the desired effect of increasing the levels of party membership and activism (see, for example, Seyd and Whiteley 2004).

But does participation have any continuing relevance for the parties themselves? The emergence of a more professional electoral organisation notwithstanding, party members still have an important, if not always indispensable, role to play in the modern party. For the smaller and less-well-funded parties, membership fees and donations still provide the bulk of their income. Compared with the major parties, small parties are more likely to look to their activists to distribute leaflets, knock on doors, raise funds, recruit new members, and help mobilise the vote. Party members also provide a pool of potential parliamentary candidates. Under MMP, minor parties feel an obligation to put up a full slate of list candidates, as well as to contest most, if not all, the electorate seats. Given that finding as many as sixty or seventy credible candidates can place a tremendous burden on the resources of a small party, it is important that they maintain a solid core of committed support.

Perhaps most important of all, however, is the sense of political legitimacy that members bring to party organisations. It has been said that members 'are testament to the fact that a party has support in the community and is rooted in the concerns and values of real people' (Seyd and Whiteley 2004, p. 361). There is no better example of the importance of this function than the lengths to which most New Zealand parties go to withhold their membership numbers from researchers, journalists, and members of the general public. In so doing, they are effectively conceding that the number of party members reflects on the legitimacy of the entire movement.

Second, although political leaders are frequently slow to recognise it, party organisations that fail to nurture their members tend to stagnate. Members help to reinvigorate parties by questioning unpopular assumptions, policies and ideas, and by helping to restore the link between the state and civil society. Governing parties are especially susceptible to 'groupthink', a malady that strikes at those who feel that they are being unfairly attacked and who turn to others, notably their cabinet colleagues, professional advisors and consultants, and members of the civil service, for the necessary approval and support. A vibrant membership can help to hold their politicians to account. Should they fail in their attempts to persuade, members can always challenge the political incumbents by standing for office themselves.

For evidence of the benefits of participation, we need go no further than the 2004 US presidential election campaign. Among the concerns facing party strategists was what to do about declining voter turnout and the growing fragmentation of the mass media audience. Despite offering more choice, a fragmented media market gives voters a greater excuse for opting out. Among the notable developments of 2004 was a more sophisticated voter mobilisation technology, including direct dialling and comprehensive voter data systems. More important still, however, was the ability of the two major parties to activate their grassroots support. In Ohio alone, the successful Republican candidate, George W. Bush, had four times as many workers on the ground as in 2000. These efforts were matched by those of his Democratic challenger, John Kerry, who mobilised over a million campaign activists nationwide. As well as helping with door-to-door canvassing, attending campaign rallies, and getting out the vote, the party activists were a ready source of donations and other campaign funds. Their efforts were rewarded with a significant lift in voter turnout, from approximately 50 per cent in 2000 to 60 per cent in 2004. But the 2004 campaign is instructive in another important sense: the growing influence of professional think tanks and advocacy groups, such as the liberal New Democrat Network (www.newdem.org) and the conservative Christian Coalition of America (www.cc.org) and Focus on the Family (www.family.org), each of which has its own policies, funding, and activist base, points to the potential dangers in store for any party that fails to listen to or nurture its grassroots support.

To conclude this part of the discussion, while there is a range of different approaches to participation, the leadership and elite models are the ones most commonly found in New Zealand at the present time. Neither offers any real prospect of direct, unmediated participation in important decisions, such as leadership and candidate selection, policy formulation, and campaign planning and execution. The ACT party's experiment with online plebiscites can be interpreted as signalling a willingness to consult more widely. However, the indicative nature of the polls does nothing to threaten the hegemony of the party elite. As Whiteley and Seyd have observed in relation to party participation in Britain, the plebiscitary model 'is characterized by a veneer of democracy overlaid by centralization and control' (2002, p. 216). In contrast, the delegate and participatory models provide an opportunity for parties of all sizes to mix and match the two approaches to participation. For example, while there are grounds for giving every member the right to vote for the party leader, either alone or in combination with the party's MPs (see chapter 7), the selection and ranking of parliamentary candidates may be better suited to the more controlled environment of a delegate conference or electoral college, where the relative merits of the various candidates can be more adequately discussed. Policy discussion and debate are also better suited to a general conference or specialist policy forum, the latter of which is becoming popular in other party systems. As the high level of public interest in controversial legislation coming before parliament's select committees clearly indicates (for example, in 2004 there were over 4,000 public submissions with respect to the Foreshore and Seabed Bill), members of the public are interested in public policy and want to be involved.

There is continuing speculation about the value of the Internet as a 'bottom-up' source of public feedback and debate. While Internet usage is growing, reaching sixteen per cent of all voters in 2002, access remains a problem, especially for the elderly and those on low incomes. Despite the best intentions of web designers and some senior party officials, party web sites reflect a marked tendency to focus almost exclusively on the 'top-down' approach, with the result that Internet users are treated largely as 'passive consumers' rather than active participants in the political process. As one study of chat rooms has observed, 'whilst [they] give the impression of a democratic interchange of ideas, one has to question the value that the party places on the content' (Nixon and Johansson 1999, pp. 147–8). In short, the Internet has yet to fulfil its early promise as a mass-based source of political communication and accountability.

Finally, in the event that parliament decides that parties should be fully funded by the state (see chapter 5), then one of the last remaining functions of party membership will be in danger of being lost. To both preserve a membership culture and prevent parties from becoming complacent, this study has suggested that state funding be based on a dollar-for-dollar matching formula, with each party being eligible for a level of state funding equal to the total received from membership fees and private donations. It has also called for a full review of parliamentary budgets with a view to preventing the extensive use of parliamentary resources to finance the administrative, staffing, advertising, and campaigning costs of the political parties. In other words, in the interests of fairness and transparency, a clear line needs to be drawn between a party's parliamentary and organisational functions. This study also recommends that the job of monitoring and administering MPs' allowances, including travel costs, should be the responsibility of a fully independent body, such as an appropriately resourced Remuneration Authority.

Evolving party system

New Zealand's transition from a two-party to a multiparty system has followed a familiar path. In his study of the party systems of Western Europe, Gordon Smith identifies three main causes of change: first, the *electorate*; second, the *parties* themselves; and third, the *political institutions*, especially the electoral system (1989). According to Smith, what goes on in the electorate has the greatest influence on the process of party system change. The loyalty of voters towards particular parties is said to partially reflect 'the social structure and the cleavage patterns within it' (1989, p. 354). But change is unlikely to be sparked by the electorate alone. Rather, it results from a complex interaction between all three causal factors (see figure 12.1). For instance, while an increase in the number of social cleavages, such as ethnicity, religion and socio-economic class, may provide fresh opportunities for new parties to be formed, their future growth is likely to be dependent on other variables as well. These may include the decline of a major party or the adoption of proportional representation. As Smith found, however, long-established major parties have an ability to resist the electoral challenge presented by the advent of new parties. His three-pronged account of party system change can be applied to recent developments in New Zealand.

The electorate

Although socio-economic class has traditionally been New Zealand's only significant cleavage, largely defining the social bases of support for National and Labour, by the early 1970s there were signs that voter attachments were becoming more tenuous. The formation of the world's first environmental party, Values, brought the 'new politics' of postmaterialism to the attention of voters for the first time. In 1980, a former cabinet minister, Matiu Rata, formed a Maori party, which he named Mana Motuhake. Although it failed to win any seats,[3] the new movement became a catalyst for change, providing Maori with an independent political voice and an alternative to voting Labour. At about the same time, the Social Credit Political League experienced a revival of support among small farmers and business owners,

Figure 12.1 Smith's model of party system change

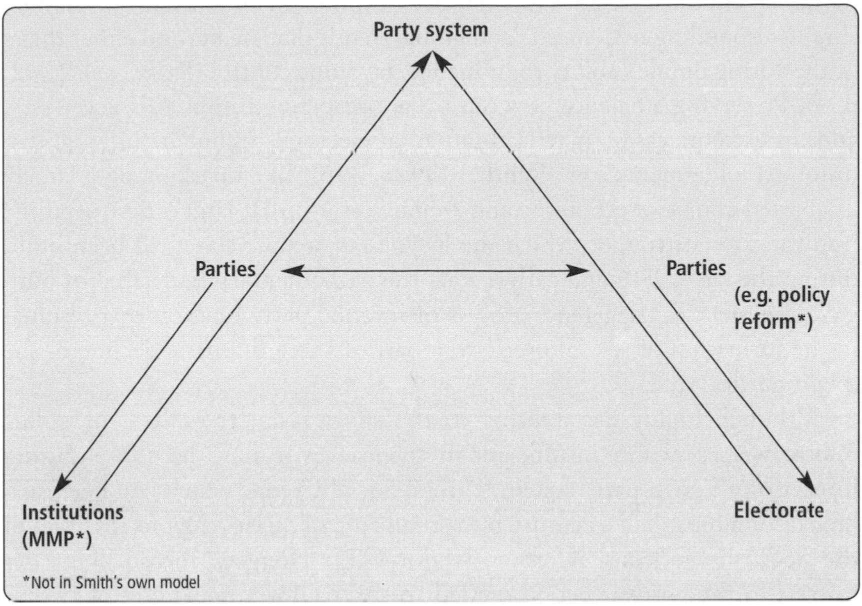

mostly on modest incomes. At its prime in 1981, Social Credit attracted over 20 per cent support. Two years later the New Zealand party was created in opposition to the interventionist economic policies and autocratic leadership of prime minister Robert Muldoon. It appealed to many young National voters, especially white-collar workers and professionals in the wealthy city suburbs. While National managed to retain its core support in the farming and business sectors, as did Labour among trade unionists and those on low incomes, by the 1980s and 1990s there were signs that those longstanding links had begun to weaken. The main beneficiaries of this gradual process of voter dealignment were the minor parties, initially NewLabour and the Greens, and later New Zealand First, ACT, and the Alliance. As we have seen, the fluctuating electoral fortunes of the various parties continued throughout the decade and into the new century (for discussions on this topic, see Vowles and Aimer 1993, Vowles et al. 1995; Vowles et al. 1998; Vowles et al. 2002; and Vowles et al. 2004). By 2004, while the Alliance had all but disappeared, a new political movement, the Maori party, had begun to chip away at yet another cornerstone of Labour's social base of electoral support.

The parties

The catalyst for this gradual loosening of attachment to the two major parties was the policy transformation that took place within the parties themselves. While political leaders have an ability to adapt to the wishes of their voters, equally they are independent agents who may impose their will in particular circumstances. In an increasing number of circumstances, they are simply responding to domestic and global trends that are beyond either theirs or the voting public's ability to influence, let alone control (Parry et al. 1992, p. 4). Preserving a balance between these competing impulses is never easy, and, in extreme cases, 'may lead either to electoral decline or internal disunity, even fragmentation' (Smith 1989, p. 356). In embarking on a largely uncharted course of economic and welfare reform that largely destroyed the postwar consensus upon which the Keynesian welfare state had been built, during the late 1980s and early 1990s the parliamentary leadership of both governing parties triggered a process of internal party division that resulted in the formation of several breakaway parties and a dramatic decline in the major parties' vote.

Although highly destabilising in the short term, the effects of policy reform were probably insufficient in themselves to have had an enduring impact on the two-party system. Unlike Social Credit, which had been sustained for almost half a century by a small core of quasi-religious disciples of the Scottish monetary reformer, Major C.H. Douglas, the small parties formed in the postwar period tended to survive for a maximum of two or three elections before being dissolved (Values) or collapsing back into the parent party (New Zealand party). So daunting had the task of electing even one minor party MP under the first-past-the-post (FPP) electoral system become, that most parties either collapsed under a mountain of campaign debt or succumbed to ideological disputation and division.

The political institutions

Whereas the radical policy agendas of the two major parties provided the 'trigger for change', the advent of proportional representation gave it legitimacy and electoral viability. Without MMP, there is little reason to believe that the status of the minor parties would have been any more secure than it was in the 1970s and 1980s. While NewLabour was the driving force behind the Alliance, its goal of replacing Labour was based on the mistaken assumption that the latter's enthusiasm for free market reform precluded any future return to its social democratic roots. Under FPP, a Labour party repositioned on the centre-left not only would have thwarted the Alliance from achieving its ultimate goal, but also endangered its status as a separate electoral organisation. New Zealand First is likely to have faced an even more uncertain future under FPP, its survival being largely dependent on the ability of Winston Peters to retain the marginal seat of Tauranga against inevitably strong challenges from National and Labour.

Paradoxically, while the advent of MMP provided the minor parties with fresh opportunities for political representation and influence, it failed to challenge the electoral dominance of the major parties, especially Labour. After an initial flurry of support for the Alliance at the 1993 election and New Zealand First three years later, the two-party vote began to consolidate around its substantial core. Towards the end of Clark's first term as prime minister and into her second, support for Labour reached the previously unimaginable height of over 50 per cent (neither major party has achieved more than 50 per cent of the vote since 1951). As Smith (1989) found in his study of party system change in Denmark, the Netherlands, Belgium, and the United Kingdom, long-established parties have demonstrated an ability to withstand most of the challenges posed by new parties. Among the resources they have been able to deploy to their advantage are proven organisational strength, an ability to retain a foothold in the electoral middle ground, and extensive experience in parliament and government.

By dominating its more radical Alliance (1999–2002) and Progressive (2002–05) partners, Labour was able to provide generally stable and moderate government to a public made weary by constant change. While Clark was criticised for a lack of strategic planning, or ability to see the big picture, she proved to be without peer as a short-term tactical thinker. Her practical political skills were vital to the government's success and included the brokering of legislative agreements with National (on free trade with Singapore) and all but one of the minor parliamentary parties. Her decisive responses to overseas crises, such as the invasions of Afghanistan and Iraq, and sensitivity to the frequent shifts of opinion among 'middle' New Zealand, reinforce the overall impression of a highly pragmatic politician. Of course, such a characterisation hardly fits that of a radical socialist, the evidence for which tends to be drawn from her early career as a political activist and backbench opponent of American foreign policy. Clark is arguably the most non-ideological and flexible prime minister of modern times. Indeed, it was only when she came up against the more morally and ideologically motivated race-based policies of National's new leader, Don Brash, that she appeared to lose touch with mainstream opinion.

Although its major party status has never been in doubt, National's transition to MMP proved to be more difficult than that of Labour. The party's early mistakes were largely tactical—for example, had National gone into opposition in 1996 rather than agreeing to the demanding coalition terms set by New Zealand First, it may well have been strongly placed to win the following two elections. Instead, the party's reputation was tarnished by a series of events, including growing disillusionment with coalition government among its grassroots party members and the wider public, a successful coup on the leadership of Jim Bolger, and the subsequent collapse of the coalition. The new prime minister, Jenny Shipley, remained in power with the unlikely support of some opportunistic defectors from New Zealand First and the Alliance, although it became increasingly obvious that there was no real prospect of a fourth successive term in office. However, apart from Bill English's brief tenure as leader, support for National remained firm, partly as a result of its organisational strength and residual core of voter support, but also because it was the only other party capable of heading a coalition government.

Guide to the sustainability of the minor parties

While the minor parties provide voters with a range of vote-splitting and coalition-building options during the course of an election campaign, popular support has been difficult to sustain, especially in government. Had the number of social cleavages increased or the debate over the neoliberal reforms retained its intensity, there may have been less reason to doubt the long-term sustainability of several of the minor parties as electoral organisations. Among the key challenges to their future success, four stand out:

1. Preserving the distinctiveness of their core values

The clustering of voters in the moderate centre of the left–right dimension (centripetal voting) poses a significant dilemma for minor parties, regardless of where they are positioned in relation to their competitors. If they decide to outflank their rivals, thereby creating a sense of ideological space, they will be competing for relatively few votes. This outlier approach, which has been adopted by both ACT and the Alliance, tends to produce internal conflict between a party's ideological purists and its pragmatists, with the latter urging the dilution of any policies that stand in the way of electoral success. An alternative approach is to explicitly brand the minor party as a 'centre' party capable of appealing to mainstream opinion. While allowing the small party to fish in a much larger electoral pool, such an approach risks the loss of any distinctiveness of value and belief.

Even in the event that it adopts an outlier position, there is no guarantee that a minor party will be able to protect its policies from being adopted by its competitors. In New Zealand, as in many other party systems, emerging parties are often regarded as laboratories for new ideas. The expressed commitment of the established parties to the environment in the mid-1970s, for example, was largely due to the popularity of the Values party among young voters (Miller 1987). Similarly, the electoral traction gained by New Zealand First on race relations, especially on affirmative action and Treaty matters, gave Brash the confidence to adopt it as the issue upon which to launch National's recovery in the polls. While the tendency to adopt the ideas of others is nothing new, it can strip a party of its reason for existence, a problem that ACT and United Future are likely to encounter in the event that the National leader takes his party any further to the right on policies relating to the economy and traditional values.

2. Building a robust organisation capable of surviving the inevitable departure from politics of the founding leader

Because most of the small parliamentary parties have limited access to their own finance, professional expertise and personnel, they are becoming increasingly dependent on the resources of the state. In extreme cases, the extra-parliamentary administration is little more than a post office box number or is nominally attached to the electorate office of an MP. This development has a number of important implications, not least in transferring any remaining powers from party activists and officials to the party's parliamentary elite, especially the party leader. It also leaves the organisation largely impotent in the event that the party loses its seats in parliament.

Those most at risk from this trend are the three parties with electorate bases, specifically New Zealand First, United Future, and the Progressives. Each is reliant on its founding leader for the electorate seat that guarantees representation in the event that the party fails to meet the 5 per cent threshold. As the party's insurance against an election rout, the leader is likely to be largely immune from internal scrutiny or review. More than that, however, in each case the leader has become the personification of the party to a point where no important organisational, candidate-selection, or policy decisions can be made without his direct intervention. As the recipient of the lion's share of the party's parliamentary resources, including the hiring of campaign and advisory staff, it is fair to conclude that the leader of the personality-based party enjoys a greater degree of overall independence than would ever be countenanced in the other parties.

Because of the extent to which personality-based parties rely on their leader, questions must be asked about their sustainability in the inevitable event that the leader either loses his electorate seat or is removed or retires as leader. Of the three parties already mentioned, the Progressive party is in the most vulnerable position, partly as a result of its consistently low level of public support, but also because advancing age is likely to force Anderton's retirement at or before the 2008 election. United Future and New Zealand First are in a somewhat less parlous state, their leaders being a few years younger, although it is hard to come up with a realistic scenario in which either has a long-term future in parliament.

3. Achieving credibility as a partner in government

Consistent with the experience of coalition government in several other countries, junior coalition partners are apt to be punished by their voters, even in the face of evidence that they have made a positive contribution to stable and effective government. The reasons for this are complex and, in the case of New Zealand, may reflect the public's unfamiliarity with the trade-offs that are an integral feature of coalition formation and government. Small parties that make demands of their senior coalition partner are often accused of unreasonableness (images of the 'tail wagging the dog' spring to mind). Equally, those that are perceived to be too cooperative may be charged with ineffectualness, even impotence. While it may be in the short-term interests of the senior coalition partner to take credit for the government's successes and deflect blame for its failings, it has made the minor parties increasingly wary of the electoral costs of coalition. A safer option, and one clearly preferred by United Future and many Green party activists in 2002, is to remain apart from the government while guaranteeing either confidence and supply or qualified legislative support.

As discussed in chapter 11, small parties can learn much from the coalition experiences of New Zealand First, the Alliance, and the Progressives. A 'Survival Kit' for intending junior coalition partners may well include the need to have a coalition strategy in place well before the election; enter negotiations with a short but substantive shopping list of policies, preferably with one defining policy upon which the junior coalition partner can stake its reputation; all else being equal, always choose the major party whose electoral support is most divergent from their own; and, in the interests of internal party unity, insist on some flexibility with respect to whipping, thereby allowing the junior partner to preserve its integrity where there is fundamental disagreement with proposed government action.

4. Finding ways to reach or circumvent the 5 per cent threshold

For those parties that lack an electorate seat, the 5 per cent threshold has proved to be a significant barrier to their future as electoral organisations. The Greens and ACT have been the parties most directly affected, although the threshold would have as much importance for New Zealand First and United Future in the event that either Peters or Dunne lost their seats of Tauranga and Ohariu-Belmont in a three-way contest involving a resurgent National party. But the party most at risk during the period of 2002 to 2005 was ACT, which lost its only electorate seat (Wellington Central) in 1999. As an artefact of the neo-liberal experiment of the 1980s and 1990s, it was a victim of the dramatic rise of National under the leadership of Brash, a politician whose core economic and social policy assumptions are almost identical to those of the small free market party.

Conclusion

As our discussion suggests, despite the vitality and adaptability of New Zealand's political parties, the future shape of the party system is as uncertain today as it was when MMP was first introduced. The long-term sustainability of each and every minor party is ultimately dependent upon an ability to nurture a distinct constituency capable of guaranteeing a continuing presence in the New Zealand parliament. On this basis, the Green and Maori parties may well be best placed to survive the vagaries of the rapidly evolving multiparty and electoral environments. This said, there are absolutely no grounds for disputing the primacy of parties within the New Zealand political system. Individual parties will come and go, but New Zealand will surely retain its strong tradition of representation and government by party.

Notes

1 The models discussed in this chapter contain features of the schema of party organisation presented by Whiteley and Seyd (2002). However, the four models of participation offered by these two scholars—extinction, leadership, plebiscitary, and participatory—don't entirely fit the New Zealand experience and give insufficient attention to the role of party delegates. Besides, as they themselves admit, the extinction model is now considered to be an unlikely outcome of party system decline.
2 *New Zealand Herald*, 9 June 2004, p. A6.
3 Mana Motuhake's Sandra Lee won the party's first seat, the general seat of Auckland Central, in 1993. By then, however, the Mana Motuhake was part of the Alliance.

Further reading

Katz, R.S. 2002, 'The Internal Life of Parties', in Luther, K.R. and F. Muller-Rommel (eds), *Political Parties in the New Europe: Political and Analytical Changes*, Oxford University Press, Oxford, pp. 87–118.
Scarrow, S.E. 2000, 'Parties without Members? Party Organization in a Changing Electoral Environment', in Dalton, R.J. and M.P. Wattenberg (eds), *Parties Without Partisans: Political Change in Advanced Industrial Democracies*, Oxford University Press, Oxford, pp. 79–101.
Seyd, P, and P. Whiteley 2004, 'British Party Members: An Overview', in *Party Politics*, 10/4, pp. 355–66.
Smith, G. 1989, 'A System Perspective on Party System Change', *Journal of Theoretical Politics*, 1/3, pp. 349–63.
Whiteley, P. and P. Seyd 2002, *High-Intensity Participation: The Dynamics of Party Activism in Britain*, The University of Michigan Press, Ann Arbor, Michigan.

Appendix: New Zealand General Election Results, 1935–2002

Election	Party	% vote	Seats	Government
1935	Labour	46.1	53	Labour
	United/Reform	32.9	19	
	Other	21.0	8	
	Total		80	
1938	Labour	55.8	53	Labour
	National	40.3	25	
	Other	3.9	2	
	Total		80	
1943	Labour	47.6	45	Labour
	National	42.8	34	
	Other	9.6	1	
	Total		81	
1946	Labour	51.3	42	Labour
	National	48.4	38	
	Other	0.3	0	
	Total		80	
1949	Labour	47.2	34	
	National	51.9	46	National
	Other	0.9	0	
	Total		80	
1951	Labour	45.8	30	
	National	54.0	50	National
	Other	0.2	0	
	Total		80	
1954	Labour	44.1	35	
	National	44.3	45	National
	Social Credit	11.3	0	
	Total		80	

Election	Party	% vote	Seats	Government
1957	Labour	48.3	41	Labour
	National	44.2	39	
	Social Credit	7.2	0	
	Total		80	
1960	Labour	43.4	34	
	National	47.6	46	National
	Social Credit	8.6	0	
	Total		80	
1963	Labour	43.7	35	
	National	47.1	45	National
	Social Credit	7.9	0	
	Total		80	
1966	Labour	41.4	35	
	National	43.6	44	National
	Social Credit	14.5	1	
	Total		80	
1969	Labour	44.2	39	
	National	45.2	45	National
	Social Credit	9.1	0	
	Total		84	
1972	Labour	48.4	55	Labour
	National	41.5	32	
	Social Credit	6.7	0	
	Values	2.0	0	
	Total		87	
1975	Labour	39.6	32	
	National	47.6	55	National
	Social Credit	7.4	0	
	Values	5.2	0	
	Total		87	
1978	Labour	40.4	40	
	National	39.8	51	National
	Social Credit	16.1	1	
	Values	2.4	0	
	Total		92	
1981	Labour	39.0	43	
	National	38.8	47	National
	Social Credit	20.7	2	
	Total		92	
1984	Labour	43.0	56	Labour
	National	35.9	37	
	Social Credit	7.6	2	
	New Zealand	12.2	0	
	Total		95	

Election	Party	% vote	Seats	Government
1987	Labour	48.0	57	Labour
	National	44.0	40	
	Democrat (Social Credit)	5.7	0	
	Total		97	
1990	Labour	35.1	29	
	National	47.8	67	National
	Green	6.8	0	
	New Labour	5.2	1	
	Total		97	
1993	Labour	34.7	45	
	National	35.1	50	National
	Alliance	18.2	2	
	New Zealand First	8.4	2	
	Total		99	
1996	Labour	28.2	37	
	National	33.8	44	National/NZ First
	Alliance	10.1	13	
	New Zealand First	13.4	17	
	ACT	6.1	8	
	United	0.9	1	
	Total		120	
1999	Labour	38.7	49	Labour/Alliance
	National	30.5	39	
	Alliance	7.7	10	
	New Zealand First	4.3	5	
	ACT	7.0	9	
	Green	5.2	7	
	United	0.5	1	
	Total		120	
2002	Labour	41.3	52	Labour/Progressive
	National	20.9	27	
	New Zealand First	10.4	13	
	ACT	7.1	9	
	Green	7.0	9	
	United Future	6.7	8	
	Progressive	1.7	2	
	Total		120	

Bibliography

Aimer, P. 1987, 'The New Zealand Party', in H. Gold (ed.), *New Zealand Politics in Perspective*, Longman Paul, Wellington, pp. 189–98.

Aimer, P. 1990, 'Good People and Big Movers: Aspects of Political Finance in New Zealand in 1990'. Unpublished paper presented to the Australasian Study of Parliament Group, Hobart, 21–22 September.

Aimer, P. 2003, 'United Future' in R. Miller (ed.), *New Zealand Government and Politics*, Oxford University Press, Melbourne, 3rd edition, pp. 293–304.

Anson, S. 1991, *Hawke: An Emotional Life*, Penguin, Ringwood.

Armstrong, J. 2004, 'Brash Ready to Come Out Swinging', *New Zealand Herald*, 17–18 January, p. A24.

Asher, H. 1995, *Polling and the Public: What Every Citizen Should Know*, Congressional Quarterly, Washington D.C., 3rd edition.

Atkinson, J. 2004, 'The Campaign on Television', in J. Vowles, P. Aimer, S. Banducci, J. Karp and R. Miller (eds), *Voters' Veto: The 2002 Election in New Zealand and the Consolidation of Minority Government*, Auckland University Press, Auckland, pp. 48–67.

Atkinson, J. 2004a, 'Television', in J. Hayward, J. and C. Rudd (eds), *Political Communications in New Zealand*, Pearson/Prentice Hall, Auckland, pp. 136–58.

Bale, T. 2003a, 'News, Newszak, New Zealand: The Role, Performance and Impact of Television in the General Election of 2002', in J. Boston, S. Church, S. Levine, E. McLeay and N.S. Roberts (eds), *New Zealand Votes: The General Election of 2002*, Victoria University Press, Wellington, pp. 217–34.

Bale, T. 2003b, 'The Greens', in R. Miller (ed.), *New Zealand Government and Politics*, Oxford University Press, Melbourne, 3rd edition, pp. 283–292.

Barber, J.D. 1972, *The Presidential Character: Predicting Performance in the White House*, Prentice-Hall, Englewood Cliffs.

Barker, F. 1998, 'Party Policy Positioning: The New Zealand Labour Party in Opposition 1990–1996', MA thesis, Victoria University, Wellington.

Bassett, M. 1976, *The Third Labour Government: A Personal History*, The Dunmore Press, Palmerston North.

Bassett, M. 1982, *Three Party Politics in New Zealand, 1911–1931*, Historical Publications, Auckland.

Bassett, M. 1993, *Sir Joseph Ward: A Political Biography*, Auckland University Press, Auckland.

Bassett, M. 1995, *Coates of Kaipara*, Auckland University Press, Auckland.

Bassett, M. 2000, *Tomorrow Comes the Song: A Life of Peter Fraser*, Penguin, Auckland.

Bell, D. 1983, *The End of Ideology: On the Exhaustion of Political Ideas in the Fifties*, Harvard University Press, Cambridge Mass., 2nd edition.

Bennie, L., J. Brand and J. Mitchell 1997, *How Scotland Votes: Scottish Parties and Elections*, Manchester University Press, Manchester.

Berry, R. 2004a, 'Attacks on Other Leaders Leave ACT Members Uneasy', *New Zealand Herald*, 10 March, p. A5.

Berry, R. 2004b, 'Clark to Take Another Look', *New Zealand Herald*, 24 February, p. A1.

Betz, H. and S. Immerfall 1998, *The New Politics of the Right: Neo-Populist Parties and Movements in Established Democracies*, St Martin's Press, New York.

Bickerton, J., A. Gagnon and P.J. Smith 1999, *Ties That Bind: Parties and Voters in Canada*, Oxford University Press, Don Mills Ont.

Blair, T. 1998, *The Third Way: New Politics for the New Century*, Fabian Society, London.

Blondel, J. 1968, 'Party Systems and Patterns of Government in Western Democracies', *Canadian Journal of Political Science*, 1/2, pp. 180–203.

Blondel, J. 1984, 'Political Leadership in the Commonwealth: The British Legacy', in H.D. Clarke and M.M. Czudnowski (eds), *Political Elites in Anglo-American Democracies: Changes in Stable Regimes*, Northern Illinois University Press, DeKalb Ill., pp. 309–35.

Blondel, J. 1987, *Political Leadership: Towards a General Analysis*, Sage, London.

Blondel, J. 2001, 'Keynote Address', European Consortium for Political Research Conference, University of Kent, Canterbury, 4 September.

Blondel, J. 2002, 'Party Government, Patronage, and Party Decline in Western Europe', in Gunther, R., J. R. Montero, and J. J. Linz (eds), *Political Parties: Old Concepts and New Challenges*, Oxford University Press, Oxford, pp. 233–56.

Blondel, J. and M. Cotta (eds) 2000, *The Nature of Party Government: A Comparative European Perspective,* Palgrave, Basingstoke.

Boston, J. 1997, 'Coalition Formation', in R. Miller (ed.), *New Zealand Politics in Transition*, Oxford University Press, Auckland, pp. 94–107.

Boston, J. 2001, 'Forming a Government' in R. Miller (ed.), *New Zealand Government and Politics*, Oxford University Press, Melbourne, 2nd edition, pp. 117–31.

Boston, J. 2003, 'Forming a Government' in R. Miller (ed.), *New Zealand Government and Politics*, Oxford University Press, Melbourne, 3rd edition, pp. 117–34.

Boston, J., S. Levine, E. McLeay and N.S. Roberts (eds) 1997, *From Campaign to Coalition: New Zealand's First General Election Under Proportional Representation*, The Dunmore Press, Palmerston North.

Boston, J., S. Church, S. Levine, E. McLeay and N.S. Roberts (eds) 2000, *Left Turn: The New Zealand General Election of 1999*, Victoria University Press, Wellington.

Boston, J., S. Church, S. Levine, E. McLeay and N.S. Roberts (eds) 2003, *New Zealand Votes: The General Election of 2002*, Victoria University Press, Wellington.

Bowler, S. and D.M. Farrell (eds) 1992, *Electoral Strategies and Political Marketing*, St Martin's Press, New York.

Bradbury, J. and J. Mitchell 2001, 'Devolution', *Parliamentary Affairs*, 54/2, pp. 257–75.

Brash, D. 2004, 'Nationhood', Orewa Rotary Club, 27 January, <www.national.org.nz>.

Broughton, D. and M. Donovan (eds) 1999, *Changing Party Systems in Western Europe*, Pinter, London.

Brown, B. 1962, *The Rise of New Zealand Labour: A History of the New Zealand Labour Party from 1916–1940*, Price Milburn, Wellington.

Budge, I. 1993, 'Direct Democracy: Setting Appropriate Terms of Debate', in D. Held (ed.), *Prospects for Democracy: North, South, East, West*, Polity Press, Cambridge, pp 136–55.

Budge, I. and H. Keman 1990, *Parties and Democracy: Coalition Formation and Government Functioning in Twenty States*, Oxford University Press, Oxford.

Burns, J.M. 1965, *Presidential Government: The Crucible of Leadership*, Avon Books, New York.

Bush, G. 2003, 'Local Government' in R. Miller (ed.), *New Zealand Government and Politics*, Oxford University Press, Melbourne, 3rd edition, pp. 161–70.

Butler, D. and D. Kavanagh 2002, *The British General Election of 2001*, Palgrave, Houndmills, Basingstoke.

Campbell, D. 1998, 'New Rules on Party Funding', *The (Glasgow) Herald*, 14 October.

Campbell, G. 2003, 'Creamed Corn', *New Zealand Listener*, 89/3299, August 2–8.

Carmines, E.G. 1991, 'The Logic of Party Alignments', *Journal of Theoretical Politics*, 3/1, pp. 65–80.

Carty, R.K., W. Cross and L. Young 2000, *Rebuilding Canadian Party Politics*, University of British Columbia Press, Vancouver.

Catt, H. 1997, 'Women, Maori and Minorities: Microrepresentation and MMP', in J. Boston, S. Levine, E. McLeay and N.S. Roberts (eds), *From Campaign to Coalition: New Zealand's First General Election Under Proportional Representation*, The Dunmore Press, Palmerston North, pp. 199–206.

Catt, H. 1997a, 'New Zealand', in P. Norris (ed.), *Passages to Power: Legislative Recruitment in Advanced Democracies*, Cambridge University Press, Cambridge, pp. 137–57.

Catt, H. 1999, *Democracy in Practice*, Routledge, London.

Chadwick, A. and R. Heffernan (eds) 2003, *The New Labour Reader*, Polity, Cambridge.

Chapman, R., 1963, 'The Response to Labour and the Question of Parallelism of Opinion, 1928–1960', in R. Chapman and K. Sinclair (eds), *Studies of a Small Democracy*, Pauls Books, Auckland, pp. 221–54.

Chapman, R. 1969, *The Political Scene 1919–1931*, Heinemann, Auckland.

Chapman, R. 1981, 'From Labour to National', in W.H. Oliver (ed.), *The Oxford History of New Zealand*, Oxford University Press, Wellington, pp. 333–68.

Chapman, R., W.K. Jackson and A.V. Mitchell 1962, *New Zealand Politics in Action: The 1960 General Election*, Oxford University Press, London.

Chisholm, D. 2002, 'The Aftermath of the Ambush', *Sunday Star Times*, 14 July, p. A11.

Church, S. 2004, 'Televised Leaders' Debates', in J. Hayward, J. and C. Rudd (eds), *Political Communications in New Zealand*, Pearson/Prentice Hall, Auckland, pp. 159–82.

Clark, H. 2003, 'Address to the New Zealand Labour Party Conference', Convention Centre, Christchurch, 8 November.

Clark, M. (ed.) 2001, *Three Labour Leaders: Nordmeyer, Kirk, Rowling*, The Dunmore Press, Pamerston North.

Clarke, P. 1991, *A Question of Leadership: Gladstone to Thatcher*, Hamish Hamilton, London.

Clarke, P. 1992, 'Margaret Thatcher's Leadership in Historical Perspective', in *Parliamentary Affairs*, 45/1, pp. 1–17.

Coe, R.D. and C.K. Wilber (eds) 1985, *Capitalism and Democracy: Schumpeter Revisited*, University of Notre Dame Press, Notre Dame, Indiana.

Coleman, J.J. 1996, *Party Decline in America: Policy, Politics and the Fiscal State*, Princeton University Press, Princeton.

Cross, W. and L. Young 2004, 'The Contours of Political Party Membership in Canada', in *Party Politics*, 10/4, pp. 427–45.

Daalder, H. 2002, 'Parties: Denied, Dismissed, or Redundant? A Critique', in Gunther, R., J. R. Montero, and J. J. Linz (eds), *Political Parties: Old Concepts and New Challenges*, Oxford University Press, Oxford, pp. 39–57.

Dalton, R.J. 2000, 'The Decline of Party Identifications', in Dalton, R.J. and M.P. Wattenberg (eds) 2000, *Parties Without Partisans: Political Change in Advanced Industrial Democracies*, Oxford University Press, Oxford, pp. 19–36.

Dalton, R.J. and M.P. Wattenberg (eds) 2000, *Parties Without Partisans: Political Change in Advanced Industrial Democracies*, Oxford University Press, Oxford.

Dalziel, R. 1981, 'The Politics of Settlement', in W.H. Oliver (ed.), *The Oxford History of New Zealand*, Oxford University Press, Oxford, pp. 87–111.

Dalziel, R. 1986, *Julius Vogel: Business Politician*, Auckland University Press/Oxford University Press, Auckland.

De Winter, L. 2002, 'Parties and Government Formation, Portfolio Allocation, and Policy Definition', in Luther, K.R. and F. Muller-Rommel (eds), *Political Parties in the New Europe: Political and Analytical Changes*, Oxford University Press, Oxford, pp. 171–206.

Debnam, G. 1994, 'Overcoming the Iron Law? The Role of the Policy Committees on the New Zealand Labour Party', in K. Lawson (ed.), *How Political Parties Work: Perspectives from Within,* Praeger, Westport, pp. 55–72.

Denver, D. 1988, 'Britain: Centralised Parties with Decentralised Selection', in M. Gallagher and M. Marsh (eds), *Candidate Selection in Comparative Perspective: The Secret Garden of Politics*, Sage, London, pp. 47–71.

Denver, D. and G. Hands 2002, 'Post-Fordism in the Constituencies? The Continuing Development of Constituency Campaigning in Britain', in D.M. Farrell and R. Schmitt-Beck (eds), *Do Political Campaigns Matter? Campaign Effects in Elections and Referendums*, Routledge, London, pp 108–126.

Douglas, R. 1993, *Unfinished Business*, Random House, Auckland.

Downs, A. 1957, *An Economic Theory of Democracy*, Harper and Row, New York.

Du Chateau, C. 2003, 'The Helen and Heather Show: Inside the PM's Inner Sanctum', *Canvas (Weekend Herald)*, 8–9 March 2003, pp 19–21.

Durie, M.H. 1997, 'Mana Maori Motuhake', in R. Miller (ed.), *New Zealand Politics in Transition*, Oxford University Press, Auckland, pp. 372–85.

Duverger, M. 1964, *Political Parties: Their Organisation and Activity in the Modern State*, Methuen, London.

Easton, B. (ed.) 1989, *The Making of Rogernomics*, Auckland University Press, Auckland.

Edwards, B. 2001, *Helen: Portrait of a Prime Minister*, Exisle Publishing, Auckland.

Eichbaum, C. 1999, 'The Politics and Economics of the Third Way', in S. Chatterjee, P. Conway, P. Dalziel, C. Eichbaum, P. Harris, B. Philpott and R. Shaw, *The New Politics: A Third Way for New Zealand*, Dunmore Press, Palmerston North, pp. 33–62.

Eldersveld, S.J. and H. Walton 2000, *Political Parties in American Society*, St Martin's, Boston, 2nd edition.

Electoral Commission 1996, *The NZ Electoral Compendium*, Electoral Commission, Wellington.

Electoral Commission 1999, *The NZ Electoral Compendium*, Electoral Commission, Wellington, 2nd edition.

Electoral Commission 2002, *The NZ Electoral Compendium*, Electoral Commission, Wellington, 3rd edition.

Epstein, L. 1967, *Political Parties in Western Democracies*, Frederick A. Praeger, New York.

Eunson, K. 2001, *Mirrors on the Hill: Reflections of New Zealand's Political Leaders*, Dunmore Press, Palmerston North.

Farrell, D.M. 2001, *Electoral Systems: A Comparative Introduction*, Palgrave, Basingstoke.

Farrell, D.M. 2002, 'Campaign Modernization and the West European Party', in Luther, K.R. and F. Muller-Rommel (eds), *Political Parties in the New Europe: Political and Analytical Changes*, Oxford University Press, Oxford, pp. 63–84.

Farrell, D.M. and R. Schmitt-Beck (eds) 2002, *Do Political Campaigns Matter? Campaign Effects in Elections and Referendums*, Routledge, London.

Farrell, D.M. and P. Webb 2000, 'Political Parties as Campaign Organizations', in Dalton, R.J. and M.P. Wattenberg (eds), *Parties Without Partisans: Political Change in Advanced Industrial Democracies*, Oxford University Press, Oxford, pp. 102–128.

Favretto, I. 2003, *The Long Search for a Third Way: The British Labour Party and the Italian Left Since 1945*, Palgrave MacMillan, Houndmills, Basingstoke, Hampshire.

Fielding, S. 2003, *The Labour Party: Continuity and Change in the Making of 'New' Labour*, Palgrave MacMillan, Houndmills, Basingstoke, Hampshire.

Finnie, R. and H. McLeish 1999, 'The Negotiation Diaries', *Scottish Affairs*, No. 28, pp. 51–61.

Flanagan, S.C. 1987, 'Response to R. Inglehart's "Value Change in Industrial Society"', *American Political Science Review*, 81/4.

Foley, M. 1993, *The Rise of the British Presidency*, Manchester University Press, Manchester.

Freud, S. and W.C. Bullitt 1967, *Thomas Woodrow Wilson: A Psychological Study*, Weidenfeld-Nicholson, London.

Gallagher, M. 2003, 'Stability and Turmoil: Analysis of the Results', in M. Gallagher, M. Marsh and P. Mitchell (eds) 2003, *How Ireland Voted 2002*, Palgrave Macmillan, Houndmills, Basingstoke, pp. 88–118.

Gallagher, M. and M. Marsh (eds) 1998, *Candidate Selection in Comparative Perspective: The Secret Garden of Politics*, Sage, London.

Gallagher, M. and M. Marsh 2004, 'Party Membership in Ireland: The Members of Fine Gael', in *Party Politics*, 10/4, pp. 407–26.

Gallagher, M., M. Marsh and P. Mitchell (eds) 2003, *How Ireland Voted 2002*, Palgrave Macmillan, Houndmills, Basingstoke.

Garner, R. and R. Kelly 1998, *British Political Parties Today*, Manchester University Press, Manchester, 2nd edition.

Garnier, T. 1978, 'The Parliamentary Press Gallery', in S. Levine (ed.), *Politics in New Zealand*, George Allen and Unwin, Sydney, pp. 149–59.

George, A.L. and J.L. George 1956, *Woodrow Wilson and Colonel House: A Personality Study*, John Day, New York.

Gibson, R. and S. Ward 2000, 'British Political Activity in Cyberspace: New Media, Same Impact?' in R. Gibson and S. Ward (eds), *Reinvigorating Democracy? British Politics and the Internet*, Ashgate, Aldershot, Hampshire, pp. 107–28.

Gibson, R.K., M. Margolis, D. Resnick and S.J. Ward 2003, 'Election Campaigning on the WWW in the USA and UK', in *Party Politics*, 9/1, pp. 47–75.

Giddens, A. 1998, *The Third Way: The Renewal of Social Democracy*, Polity Press, Cambridge.

Giddens, A. 1998, *The Third Way and its Critics*, Polity Press, Cambridge.

Godfrey, D.C. 2003, 'Princes Street Branch: Generational Change and Modernisation of the New Zealand Labour Party 1960–2000', MA Thesis, University of Auckland.

Graham, B.D. 1963, 'The Country Party Idea in New Zealand Politics, 1901–1935', in R. Chapman and K. Sinclair (eds), *Studies of a Small Democracy*, Pauls Books, Auckland, pp. 175–200.

Grofman, B. and A. Lijphart (eds) 1986, *Electoral Laws and Their Political Consequences*, Agathon Press, New York.

Gunther, R., J. R. Montero, and J. J. Linz (eds) 2002, *Political Parties: Old Concepts and New Challenges*, Oxford University Press, Oxford.

Gustafson, B. 1976, *From the Cradle to the Grave: A Biography of Michael Joseph Savage*, Reed Methuen, Auckland.

Gustafson, B. 1980, *Labour's Path to Political Independence: The Origins and Establishment of the New Zealand Labour Party, 1900–19*, Auckland University Press, Auckland.

Gustafson, B. 1986a, *From the Cradle to the Grave: A Biography of Michael Joseph Savage*, Reed Methuen, Auckland.

Gustafson, B. 1986b, *The First Fifty Years: A History of the New Zealand National Party*, Reed Methuen, Auckland.

Gustafson, B. 1989, 'The Labour Party', in H. Gold (ed.), *New Zealand Politics in Perspective*, Longman Paul, Auckland, 2nd edition, pp. 199–222.

Gustafson, B. 1997, 'The National Party', in R. Miller (ed.), *New Zealand Politics in Transition*. Oxford University Press, Auckland, pp. 137–46.

Gustafson, B. 2000, *His Way: A Biography of Robert Muldoon*, Auckland University Press, Auckland.

Gustafson, B. 1992, 'The Labour Party', in H. Gold (ed.), *New Zealand Politics in Perspective*, Longman Paul, Auckland, 3rd edition, pp. 263–88.

Hamer, D. 1988, *The New Zealand Liberals: The Years of Power, 1891–1912*, Auckland University Press, Auckland.

Harmel, R. 2002, 'Party Organizational Change: Competing Explanations?', in Luther, K.R. and F. Muller-Rommel (eds), *Political Parties in the New Europe: Political and Analytical Changes*, Oxford University Press, Oxford, pp. 119–142.

Harris, P. 1997, 'The Electoral Commission', in R. Miller (ed.), *New Zealand Politics in Transition,* Oxford University Press, Auckland, pp. 212–22.

Harris, R. 2004, 'Bewitched—10 Years of Blair', *New Zealand Herald*, 22 July, p. B4.

Hassan, G. and C. Warhurst (eds) 2000, *The New Scottish Politics: The First Year of the Scottish Parliament and Beyond*, The Stationery Office, Edinburgh.

Hayward, S. and A. Whitehorn 1991, 'Leadership Selection: Which Method?' Unpublished research paper presented to the Douglas Coldwell Foundation, Canada.

Hayward, J. and C. Rudd (eds) 2004, *Political Communications in New Zealand*, Pearson/Prentice Hall, Auckland.

Heidar, K. and J. Saglie 2001, 'A Decline of Party Activity? Intra-party Participation in Norway 1991–2000'. Unpublished paper presented to the European Consortium of Political Research General Conference, University of Kent, Canterbury.

Held, D. (ed.) 1993, *Prospects for Democracy: North, South, East, West*, Polity Press, Cambridge.

Henderson, J. 1980, 'Muldoon and Rowling: A Preliminary Analysis of Contrasting Personalities', in *Political Science*, 32/1, pp. 26–46.

Henderson, J. 1991, 'Labour's Modern Prime Ministers and the Party: A Study of Contrasting Political Styles'. Paper presented to Stout Research Centre, Victoria University of Wellington.

Henderson, J. 1992, 'Labour's Modern Prime Ministers and the Party: A Study of Contrasting Political Styles', in M. Clark (ed.), *The Labour Party After 75 Years*, Victoria University of Wellington, pp. 98–117.

Henderson, J. 2001, 'Prime Minister', in R. Miller (ed.), *New Zealand Government and Politics*, Oxford University Press, Melbourne, pp. 106–16.

Hug, S. 2001, *Altering Party Systems: Strategic Behaviour and the Emergence of New Political Parties in Western Democracies*, The University of Michigan Press, Ann Arbor.

Hunt, G. 2000, The Future for First-Past-the-Post Elections to the House of Commons: Pragmatism and Political Will in the Face of Constitutional Change, Green College, Oxford, Reuter Foundation Paper Number 132.

Hunt, G. 2003, 'Newcomer has Little Time to Succeed', *The National Business Review*, 31 October, p. 10.

Hunt, J. (Chair) 2001, *Report of the MMP Review Committee*, House of Representatives, Wellington.

Ignazi, P. 1996, 'The Crisis or Parties and the Rise of New Political Parties', *Party Politics*, 2/4, pp. 549–66.

Inglehart, R. 1977, *The Silent Revolution: Changing Values and Political Styles Among Western Publics*, Princeton University Press, Princeton N.J.

Jackson, K. 1987, *The Dilemma of Parliament*, Allen and Unwin, Wellington.

James, C. 1986, *The Quiet Revolution: Turbulence and Transition in Contemporary New Zealand*, Port Nicholson Press, Wellington.

James, C. 2004, 'Herculean Effort Needed by Hide to Overcome Hurdles', *New Zealand Herald*, 15 June, p. A11.

Jenkins, R. 1964, *Asquith*, Collins, London.

Jenkins, R. (Chair) 1998, *The Report of the Independent Commission on the Voting System*, Home Office, London.

Jenkins, R. 2001, *Churchill*, Macmillan, London.

Johansson, J. 2003, 'Leadership and the Campaign', in J. Boston, S. Church, S. Levine, E. McLeay and N.S. Roberts (eds) 2003, *New Zealand Votes: The General Election of 2002*, Victoria University Press, Wellington, pp. 59–74.

Judge, D. 1999, *Representation: Theory and Practice in Britain*, Routledge, London.

Karp, J. 2001, 'Members of Parliament and Representation', in J. Vowles, P. Aimer, J. Karp, S. Banducci, R. Miller and A. Sullivan, *Proportional Representation on Trial: The 1999 New Zealand General Election and the Fate of MMP*, Auckland University Press, Auckland, pp. 130–45.

Katz, R.S. 1997, *Democracy and Elections*, Oxford University Press, New York.

Katz, R.S. 2002, 'The Internal Life of Parties', in Luther, K.R. and F. Muller-Rommel (eds), *Political Parties in the New Europe: Political and Analytical Changes*, Oxford University Press, Oxford, pp. 87–118.

Katz, R.S. and P. Mair (eds) 1994, *How Parties Organise: Change and Adaptation in Party Organisations in Western Democracies*, Sage, London.

Katz, R.S. and P. Mair, 'Party Organisation, Party Democracy, and the Emergence of the Cartel Party', in P. Mair, *Party System Change: Approaches and Interpretations*, Oxford University Press, New York, pp. 93–119.

Katz, R.S. and P. Mair 2002, 'The Ascendancy of the Party in Public Office: Party Organizational Change in Twentieth-Century Democracies', in Gunther, R., J.R. Montero, and J.J. Linz (eds), *Political Parties: Old Concepts and New Challenges*, Oxford University Press, Oxford, pp. 113–35.

Kavanagh, D. 1987, 'Margaret Thatcher: The Mobilizing Style of Prime Minister', in H.D. Clarke and M.M. Czudnowski (eds), *Political Elites in Anglo-American Democracies: Changes in Stable Regimes*, Northern Illinois University Press, DeKalb Ill., pp. 177–208.

Key, V.O. 1961, *Public Opinion and American Democracy*, Alfred A. Knopf, New York.

Kirchheimer, O. 1966, 'The Transformation of the Western European Party Systems, in J. LaPalombara and M. Weiner (eds*)*, *Political Parties and Political Development*, Princeton University Press, Princeton, pp. 177–200.

Kirkpatrick, J. 1974, *Political Woman*, Basic Books, New York.

Laugeson, R. 1997, 'A Media Perspective on the 1996 Election Campaign', in Boston, J., S. Levine, E. McLeay and N.S. Roberts (eds) 1997, *From Campaign to Coalition: New Zealand's First General Election Under Proportional Representation*, The Dunmore Press, Palmerston North, pp. 67–74.

Laver, M. 1989, 'Party Competition and Party System Change: The Interaction of Coalition Bargaining and Electoral Competition', *Journal of Theoretical Politics*, 1/3, pp. 301–24.

Laver, M. 1999, 'The Irish Party System Approaching the Millennium', in M. Marsh and P. Mitchell (eds), *How Ireland Voted 1997*, Westview Press, Boulder Colorado, pp 264–76.

Laws, M. 1998, *The Demon Profession*, Harper Collins, Auckland.

Lawson, K. and P.H. Merkl (eds) 1988, *When Parties Fail: Emerging Alternative Organisations*, Princeton University Press, Princeton.

Laycock, D. 2002, *The New Right and Democracy in Canada: Understanding Reform and the Canadian Alliance*, Oxford University Press, Don Mills Ont.

Levine, S. 1979, *The New Zealand Political System: Politics in a Small Society*, George Allen and Unwin, Auckland.

Lijphart, A. 1984, *Democracies: Patterns of Majoritarian and Consensus Government in Twenty-One Countries*, Yale University Press, New Haven.

Lijphart, A. 1999, *Patterns of Democracy: Government Forms and Performance in Thirty-Six Countries*, Yale University Press, New Haven.

Lipset, S.M. 1960, *Political Man. The Social Bases of Politics*, Doubleday, Garden City.

Lipset, S.M. and S. Rokkan (eds) 1967, *Party Systems and Voter Alignments: Cross-National Perspectives*, The Free Press, New York.

Luther, K.R. and F. Muller-Rommel (eds) 2002, *Political Parties in the New Europe: Political and Analytical Changes*, Oxford University Press, Oxford.

MacLeod, C. 1999, 'Coalition Feels the Strain', *The (Glasgow) Herald*, 1999, p. 11.

Mair, P. 1996, 'Party Organizations: From Civil Society to the State', in R.S. Katz and P. Mair (eds), *How Parties Organize: Change and Adaptation in Party Organizations in Western Democracies*, Sage, London, pp. 1–22.

Mair, P. 1997, *Party System Change: Approaches and Interpretations*, Oxford University Press, New York.

Mair, P. 1999, 'Party Competition and the Changing Party System', in J. Coakley and M. Gallagher (eds), *Politics in the Republic of Ireland*, Routledge, London, 3rd edition, pp 127–51.

Maloney, W. 1998, 'Contracting Out the Participation Function: Social Capital and Chequebook Participation', in J. Van Deth, M. Maraffi, K. Newton and P. Whiteley (eds), *Social Capital and European Democracy*, Routledge, London.

Maor, M. 1997, *Political Parties and Party Systems: Comparative Approaches and the British Experience*, Routledge, London.

Maor, M. 1998, *Parties, Conflicts and Coalitions in Western Europe: Organisational Determinants of Coalition Bargaining*, Routledge, London.

Marsh, I. 1995, *Beyond the Two Party System: Political Representation, Economic Competitiveness and Australian Politics*, Cambridge University Press, Cambridge.

Martin, J.E. 2004, *The House: New Zealand's House of Representatives 1854–2004*, Dunmore Press, Palmerston North.

May, J.D. 1973, 'Opinion Structure of Political Parties: The Special Law of Curvilinear Disparity', *Political Studies*, 21, pp. 135–51.

Mazlish, B. 1972, *In Search of Nixon: A Psychohistorical Inquiry*, Basic Books, New York.

McAllister, I. 2002, 'Calculating or Capricious? The New Politics of Late Deciding Voters', in Farrell, D.M. and R. Schmitt-Beck (eds), *Do Political Campaigns Matter? Campaign Effects in Elections and Referendums*, Routledge, London, pp. 22–40.

McAllister, I. 1997, 'Australia', in Norris, P. (ed.), *Passages to Power: Legislative Recruitment in Advanced Democracies*, Cambridge University Press, Cambridge, pp. 15–32.

McKenzie, B. 2002, 'Left Without a Choice? Labour, Social Democracy and the Third Way in New Zealand and Britain', MA thesis, Department of Political Studies, University of Auckland.

McLeay, E. 2000, 'The New Parliament', in J. Boston, S. Church, S. Levine, E. McLeay and N.S. Roberts (eds), *Left Turn: The New Zealand General Election of 1999*, Victoria University Press, Wellington, pp. 203–16.

McLeay, E. 2003, 'Representation, Selection, Election: The 2002 Parliament', in J. Boston, S. Church, S. Levine, E. McLeay and N.S. Roberts (eds), *New Zealand Votes: The General Election of 2002*, Victoria University Press, Wellington, pp. 283–308.

McLeay, E. 2000, 'The New Parliament', in J. Boston, S. Church, S. Levine, E. McLeay and N.S. Roberts (eds), *Left Turn: The New Zealand General Election of 1999*, Victoria University Press, Wellington, pp. 203–16.

McMillan, N. 1993, *Top of the Greasy Pole: New Zealand Prime Ministers of Recent Times*, John McIndoe Publishers, Dunedin.

Mershon, C. 2002, *The Costs of Coalition*, Stanford University Press, Stanford Calif.

Miller, R. 1985, 'Social Credit/The Democratic Party', in H. Gold (ed.), *New Zealand Politics in Perspective*, Longman Paul, Auckland, pp. 204–15.

Miller, R. 1987, 'Social Credit: An Analysis of New Zealand's Perennial Third Party'. PhD thesis, University of Auckland.

Miller, R. 1991, 'NewLabour: A Chip off the Old Block?' Paper presented to the New Zealand Political Studies Association Conference, University of Waikato, Hamilton.

Miller, R. 1991, 'Postmaterialism and Green Party Activism in New Zealand', *Political Science*, 43/2, pp. 43–66.

Miller, R. 1995, 'Is There a Blue-Green Constituency in New Zealand?' Paper presented to the N.Z. Political Studies Association Conference, Victoria University of Wellington, 1 September.

Miller, R. 1997, 'New Zealand First', in R. Miller (ed.), *New Zealand Politics in Transition*, Oxford University Press, Auckland, pp. 165–76.

Miller, R. 1998, 'New Zealand First', in H. G. Betz and S. Immerfall (eds), *The New Politics of the Right: Neo-Populist Parties and Movements in Established Democracies*. St Martin's Press, New York, pp. 203–10.

Miller, R. 1998a, 'Coalition Government: The People's Choice?', in J. Vowles, P. Aimer, S. Banducci and J. Karp (eds), *Voter's Victory? New Zealand's First Election Under Proportional Representation*, Auckland University Press, Auckland, pp. 120–34.

Miller, R. 2002, 'Coalition Government: The Labour-Alliance Pact', in J. Vowles, P. Aimer, J. Karp, S. Banducci, R. Miller, and A. Sullivan, *Proportional Representation on Trial: The 1999 New Zealand General Election and the Fate of MMP*, Auckland University Press, Auckland, pp. 114–29.

Miller, R. 2003, 'Labour', in R. Miller (ed.), *New Zealand Government and Politics*, Oxford University Press, Melbourne, 3rd edition, pp. 226–41.

Miller, R. 2004, 'Who Stood for Office and Why?' in J. Vowles, P. Aimer, S. Banducci, J. Karp and R. Miller (eds), *Voters' Veto: The 2002 Election in New Zealand and the Consolidation of Minority Government*, Auckland University Press, Auckland, pp. 85–103.

Miller, R. 2004, 'Parties and Electioneering', in J. Hayward and C. Rudd (eds), *Political Communications in New Zealand*, Prentice Hall, Auckland.

Miller, R. and H. Catt 1993, *Season of Discontent: By-elections and the Bolger Government*, The Dunmore Press, Palmerston North.

Miller, R. and J. Karp 2004, 'A Vote for Coalition Government', in J. Vowles, P. Aimer, S. Banducci, J. Karp and R. Miller (eds), *Voters' Veto: The 2002 Election in New Zealand and the Consolidation of Minority Government*, Auckland University Press, Auckland, pp. 134–49.

Miller, R. and J. Vowles 1989, 'Delegates Revisited: A Sociology of New Zealand's National and Labour Parties in 1988'. Paper presented to the Australasian Political Studies Association Conference, University of New South Wales, Sydney.

Milne, R.S. 1966, *Political Parties in New Zealand*, Clarendon Press, Oxford.

Ministry of Social Development (New Zealand) 2005, 'The Social Report, 2004', 8 December, <http.//socialreport.msd.govt.nz>.

Mitchell. A. 1966, *Government by Party: Parliament and Politics in New Zealand*, Whitcombe and Tombs, Auckland.

Mitchell, P. 1999, 'Government Formation: A Tale of Two Coalitions', in M. Marsh and P. Mitchell (eds), *How Ireland Voted 1997*, Westview Press, Boulder Colorado, pp. 243–63.

Mitchell, P. 2003, 'Government Formation in 2002: "You can have any kind of government as long as it's Fianna Fail"', in M. Gallagher, M. Marsh and P. Mitchell (eds), *How Ireland Voted 2002*, Palgrave MacMillan, Houndmills, Basingstoke, Hampshire, pp. 214–29.

Mulgan, R. 1989, *Democracy and Power in New Zealand*, Oxford University Press, Auckland.

Mulgan, R. 1997, *Politics in New Zealand*, Auckland University Press, Auckland, 2nd edition.

Muller, W.C. and K. Strom 1999, *Policy, Office, or Votes? How Political Parties in Western Europe Make Hard Decisions*, Cambridge University Press, Cambridge.

Muller-Rommell, F. and G. Pridham (eds) 1991, *Small Parties in Western Europe: Comparative and National Perspectives*, Sage, London.

Murphy, B.D. 1975, 'Political Opinion Polling in New Zealand', in S. Levine (ed.), *New Zealand Politics: A Reader*, Cheshire, Melbourne, pp. 163–70.

Nagel, J. 1994, 'How Many Parties will New Zealand Have Under MMP?' in *Political Science*, 26/2, pp. 139–60.

Neill, Lord 1998, *Standards in Public Life: The Funding of Political Parties in the United Kingdom*, Stationery Office, London.

Nixon, P. and H. Johansson 1999, 'Transparency Through Technology: The Internet and Political Parties', in B.N. Hague and B.D. Loader (eds), *Digital Democracy: Discourse and Decision-making in the Digital Age*, Routledge, London, pp. 135–53.

Norris, P. (ed.) 1997, *Passages to Power: Legislative Recruitment in Advanced Democracies*, Cambridge University Press, Cambridge.

Norris, P. 2000, *A Virtuous Circle: Political Communications in Postindustrial Societies*, Cambridge University Press, Cambridge.

Norris, P. 2002a, *Democratic Phoenix: Reinventing Political Activism*, Cambridge University Press, Cambridge.

Norris, P. 2002b, 'Do Campaign Communications Matter for Civic Engagement? American Elections from Eisenhower to George W. Bush', in D.M. Farrell and R. Schmitt-Beck (eds), *Do Political Campaigns Matter? Campaign Effects in Elections and Referendums*, Routledge, London, pp 127–44.

Norris, P. 2003, 'Preaching to the Converted? Pluralism, Participation and Party Websites', in *Party Politics*, 9/1, pp. 21–45.

Oliver, W.H. 1989, 'The Labour Caucus and Economic Policy Formation, 1981–1984', in B. Easton (ed.), *The Making of Rogernomics*, Auckland University Press, Auckland, pp. 11–52.

Olssen, E. 1981, 'Towards a New Society', in W.H. Oliver (ed.), *The Oxford History of New Zealand*, Oxford University Press, Wellington, pp. 250–78.

Orsman, B. 2002, 'The Man For Whom the Worm Turned Up Trumps', *New Zealand Herald*, 17 July, p. A5.

O'Sullivan, F. 2002, 'Empress is Losing Her Clothes', *New Zealand Herald*, 15 July, p. D2.

O'Sullivan, F. 2003, 'Seeking Ideas from Like Minds', *New Zealand Herald*, 10 July, p. A18.

O'Sullivan, F. and V. Small 2002, 'The Cost of Democracy', *New Zealand Herald*, 29–30 June.

Palmer, G. and M. Palmer 1997, *Bridled Power: New Zealand Government Under MMP*, Auckland, Oxford University Press.

Panebianco, A. 1988, *Political Parties: Organization and Power*, Cambridge University Press, Cambridge.

Parry, G., G. Moyser and N. Day 1992, *Political Participation and Democracy in Britain*, Cambridge University Press, Cambridge.

Pedersen, K., L. Bille, R. Buch, J. Elklit, B. Hansen and H.J. Nielsen 2004, 'Sleeping or Active Partners? Danish Party Members at the Turn of the Millenium', in *Party Politics*, 10/4, pp. 367–84.

Poguntke, T. 2002, 'Party Organizational Linkage: Parties Without Firm Social Roots?', in Luther, K.R. and F. Muller-Rommel (eds), *Political Parties in the New Europe: Political and Analytical Changes*, Oxford University Press, Oxford, pp. 43–62.

Puhle, H. 2002, 'Still the Age of Catch-allism? *Volksparteien* and *Parteienstaat* in Crisis and Re-equilibration', in Gunther, R., J.R. Montero, and J.J. Linz (eds), *Political Parties: Old Concepts and New Challenges*, Oxford University Press, Oxford.

Putnam, R.D. (ed.) 2002, *Democracies in Flux: The Evolution of Social Capital in Contemporary Society*, Oxford University Press, New York.

Putnam, R.D. 2000, *Bowling Alone: The Collapse and Revival of American Community*, Simon and Schuster, New York.

Putnam, R.D. 1997, 'Democracy in America at Century's End', in A. Hadenius (ed.), *Democracy's Victory and Crisis*, Cambridge University Press, New York, pp 27–70.

Rae, D.W. 1967, *The Political Consequences of Electoral Laws*, Yale University Press, New Haven, pp. 87–103 (especially pp. 98–9).

Rae, D.W. and M. Taylor 1970, *The Analysis of Political Cleavages*, Yale University Press, New Haven.

Rainbow, S. 1993, *Green Politics*, Oxford University Press, Auckland.

Ranney, A. 1981, 'Candidate Selection', in D. Butler et al (eds), *Democracy at the Polls: A Comparative Study of Competitive National Elections*, American Enterprise Institute, Washington D.C., pp. 75–106.

Reid, N. 1999, 'Acting on a Vision: An Analysis of the Ideological and Policy Developments of Act New Zealand'. MA thesis, Department of Political Studies, University of Auckland.

Rentoul, J. 2003, *Tony Blair: Prime Minister*, Time Warner Books, London.

Richardson, A. 1983, *Participation*, Routledge and Kegan Paul, London.

Richardson, L. 1981, 'Parties and Political Change', in W.H. Oliver (ed.), *The Oxford History of New Zealand*, Oxford University Press, Wellington, pp. 197–225.

Riker, W.H. 1986, 'Duverger's Law Revisited', in B. Grofman and A. Lijphart (eds), *Electoral Laws and Their Political Consequences*, Agathon, New York, pp. 19–42.

Roberts, N.S. 1987, 'Nats, Fat Cats and Democrats: The Opposition Parties', in J. Boston and M. Holland (eds), *The Fourth Labour Government: Radical Politics in New Zealand*, Oxford University Press, Auckland, pp. 36–53.

Roberts, N.S. 1975, 'The New Zealand General Election of 1972', in S. Levine (ed.), *New Zealand Politics: A Reader*, Cheshire, Melbourne, pp 99–114.

Robinson, A. 1967, 'Class Voting in New Zealand: A Comment on Alford's Comparison of Class Voting in the Anglo-American Political Systems', in Lipset, S.M. and S. Rokkan (eds), *Party Systems and Voter Alignments: Cross-National Perspectives*, The Free Press, New York, pp. 95–114.

Saglie, J. and K. Heidar 2004, 'Democracy Within Norwegian Political Parties: Complacency or Pressure for Change?', in *Party Politics*, 10/4, pp. 385–406.

Salmond, R. 2003, 'Choosing Candidates: Labour and National in 2002', in J. Boston, S. Church, S. Levine, E. McLeay and N.S. Roberts (eds), *New Zealand Votes: The General Election of 2002*, Victoria University Press, Wellington, pp. 192–208.

Sartori, G. 1987, *The Theory of Democracy Revisited*, Chatham House Publishers, Chatham, New Jersey.

Sartori, G. 1986, 'The Influence of Electoral Systems: Faulty Laws or Faulty Method?' in B. Grofman and A. Lijphart (eds), *Electoral Laws and Their Political Consequences*, Agathon, New York, pp. 43–68.

Sartori, G. 1976, *Parties and Party Systems: A Framework for Analysis*, Cambridge University Press, Cambridge.

Scammell, M. 1995, *Designer Politics: How Elections are Won*, St Martins Press, New York.

Scarrow, S.E. 1996, *Parties and their Members: Organising for Victory in Britain and Germany*, Oxford University Press, New York.

Scarrow, S.E. 2000, 'Parties without Members? Party Organization in a Changing Electoral Environment', in Dalton, R.J. and M.P. Wattenberg (eds), *Parties Without Partisans: Political Change in Advanced Industrial Democracies*, Oxford University Press, Oxford, pp. 79–101.

Schedler, A. 1996, 'Anti-Political-Establishment Parties', in *Party Politics*, 2/3, pp. 291–312.

Schlesinger, A.M. 1978, *Robert Kennedy and His Times*, Andre Deutsch, London.

Schumpeter, J.A. 1976, *Capitalism, Socialism and Democracy*, George Allen and Unwin, London.

Seyd, P. and P. Whiteley 2002, *New Labour's Grassroots: The Transformation of the Labour Party Membership*, Palgrave/MacMillan, Basingstoke, Hampshire.

Seyd, P, and P. Whiteley 2004, 'British Party Members: An Overview', in *Party Politics*, 10/4, pp. 355–66.

Shea, D.M. and J.C. Green (eds) 1994, *The State of the Parties: The Changing Role of Contemporary American Parties,* Rowman and Littlefield, Lanham Md.

Shorter, C.B. 1974, 'Political Thought in New Zealand: The Ideologies, the Values and Beliefs of the New Zealand National and Labour Parliamentary Parties', MA Thesis, University of Auckland.

Sinclair, K. 1969, *William Pember-Reeves*, Reed, Wellington.

Sinclair, K. 1976, *Walter Nash*, Auckland University Press, Auckland.

Smith, G. 1989, 'A System Perspective on Party System Change', *Journal of Theoretical Politics*, 1/3, pp. 349–63.

Smith, J. and H. Bakvis 2002, 'Canadian General Elections and the Money Question', in W. Cross (ed.), *Political Parties, Representation and Electoral Democracy*, Oxford University Press, Don Mills Ont., pp. 132–44.

Sorrenson, K. 1986, 'A History of Maori Representation in Parliament', in J. Wallace (Chair), *Towards a Better Democracy, Report of the Royal Commission on the Electoral System*, Government Printer, Wellington, Appendix B.

Stanbury, W.T. 2001, 'Regulating Federal Party and Candidate Finances in a Dynamic Environment', in H.G. Thorburn and A. Whitehorn (eds), *Party Politics in Canada*, Prentice Hall, Toronto, 8th edition, pp. 179–205.

Stern, G. 1993, *Leaders and Leadership*, London School of Economics Publication, London.

Stone, W.J., R.B. Rapoport, and M.B. Schneider 2004, 'Party Members in a Three-Party Election: Major-Party and Reform Activism in the 1996 American Presidential Election', in *Party Politics*, 10/4, pp. 445–68.

Strachan, D. 1985, 'A Party Transformed: Organizational Change in the New Zealand Labour Party 1974–82', in H. Gold (ed.), *New Zealand Politics in Perspective*, Longman Paul, Auckland, pp. 159–71.

Street, M. 1997, 'The Labour Party', in R. Miller (ed.), *New Zealand Politics in Transition*, Oxford University Press, Auckland, pp. 147–55.

Sullivan, A. and D. Margaritis, 'Maori Voting Patterns in 1999', in J. Boston, S. Church, S. Levine, E. McLeay and N.S. Roberts (eds), *Left Turn: The New Zealand General Election of 1999*, Victoria University Press, Wellington, pp. 175–83.

Sundquist, J.L. 1983, *Dynamics of the Party System: Alignment and Realignment of Political Parties in the United States*, Brookings Institution, Washington D.C.

Taagepera, R. and B. Grofman 1985, 'Rethinking Duverger's Law: Predicting the Effective Number of Parties in Plurality and PR Systems', *European Journal of Political Research*, 13, pp. 341–52.

Taylor, K. 2004, 'Single Body for Elections Suggested', *New Zealand Herald*, 15 January.

Thomas, G.P. 2000, 'Should political parties be funded by the state?', in L. Robins and B. Jones (eds), *Debates in British Politics Today*, Manchester University Press, Manchester, pp. 158–72.

Trent, J.S. and R.V. Friedenberg (eds) 1991, *Political Campaign Communication: Principles and Practices*, Praeger, New York, 2nd edition.

Trotter, C. 2001, 'Alliance', in R. Miller (ed.), *New Zealand Government and Politics*, Oxford University Press, Melbourne, pp. 252–61.

Tunnah, H. 2004, 'Wanted—New Brash-pack MPs', *New Zealand Herald*, 9 July, p. A6.

Vaughan, G. 2003, 'What Sort of Business?', *The Independent: New Zealand's Business Weekly*, 20 August, p. 6.

Volkens, A. and H. Klingemann 2002, 'Parties, Ideologies and Issues. Stability and Change in Fifteen European Party Systems 1945–1998', in Luther, K.R. and F. Muller-Rommel (eds), *Political Parties in the New Europe: Political and Analytical Changes*, Oxford University Press, Oxford, pp. 143–68.

Von Beyme, K. 1985, *Political Parties in Western Democracies*, Gower, Aldershot.

Vowles, J. 2003, 'Voting Behaviour', in R. Miller (ed.), *New Zealand Government and Politics*, Oxford University Press, Melbourne, 3rd edition, pp. 188–200.

Vowles, J. and P. Aimer 1993, *Voters' Vengeance: The 1990 Election in New Zealand and the fate of the Fourth Labour Government*, Auckland University Press, Auckland.

Vowles, J., P. Aimer, H. Catt, J. Lamare and R. Miller 1995, *Towards Consensus? The 1993 General Election in New Zealand and the Transition to Proportional Representation*, Auckland University Press, Auckland.

Vowles, J., P. Aimer, S. Banducci and J. Karp (eds) 1998, *Voters' Victory. New Zealand's First Election Under Proportional Representation,* Auckland University Press, Auckland.

Vowles, J., P. Aimer, J. Karp, S. Banducci, R. Miller and A. Sullivan 2002, *Proportional Representation on Trial: The 1999 New Zealand General Election and the Fate of MMP*, Auckland University Press, Auckland.

Vowles, J., P. Aimer, S. Banducci, J. Karp and R. Miller (eds) 2004, *Voters' Veto: The 2002 Election in New Zealand and the Consolidation of Minority Government*, Auckland University Press, Auckland.

Wallace, J. (Chair) 1986, *Towards a Better Democracy: Report of the [New Zealand] Royal Commission on the Electoral System*, Government Printer, Wellington.

Ware, A. 1987, *Citizens, Parties and the State: A Reappraisal*, Polity Press, Cambridge.

Ware, A. 1996, *Political Parties and Party Systems*, Oxford University Press, Oxford.

Watkin, T. 2002, 'In the Spin Cycle', *Weekend Herald*, 20–21 July, p. G1.

Watt, E. 2004, 'Email MPs Fail to Click On', *Sunday Star Times*, 11 July, p. A7.

Webb, P. 2000, *The Modern British Party System*, Sage, London.

Webb, P. 2002, 'Parties and Party Systems: More Continuity than Change', in *Parliamentary Affairs*, 55/2, pp. 363–76.

Weber, M. 1958, *The Protestant Ethic and the Spirit of Capitalism*, Charles Scribner's Sons, New York (A translation by Talcott Parsons).

Wheen, F. 2000, 'The Nutty Professor: Stating the Obvious and Anthony Giddens', *The Guardian*, 1 March.

White, J.K. and P.J. Davies 1998, *Political Parties and the Collapse of the Old Orders*, State University of New York Press, Albany N.Y.

Whiteley, P. and P. Seyd 2002, *High-Intensity Participation: The Dynamics of Party Activism in Britain*, The University of Michigan Press, Ann Arbor.

Wilkes, C. 1978, 'The Great New Zealand Melodrama: Television and the 1975 General Election', in S. Levine (ed.), *Politics in New Zealand: A Reader*, George Allen and Unwin, Sydney, 2nd edition, pp 207–21.

Wilson, M. 1989, *Labour in Government: 1984–87*, Allen and Unwin, Wellington.

Winetrobe, B. 2001, *Realising the Vision: A Parliament with a Purpose: An Audit of the First Year of the Scottish Parliament*, The Constitution Unit, University of London.

Winter, L. and P. Dumont 1999, 'Belgium: Party System(s) on the Eve of Disintegration?' in D. Broughton and M. Donovan (eds), *Changing Party Systems in Western Europe*, Pinter, London, pp. 183–206.

Wolinetz, S.B. 1979, 'The Transformation of Western European Party Systems Revisited', *West European Politics*, 2, pp. 4–28.

Wolinetz, S.B. (ed.) 1988, *Parties and Party Systems in Liberal Democracies*, Routledge, London.

Wolinetz, S.B. 2002, 'Beyond the Catch-All Party: Approaches to the Study of Parties and Party Organization in Contemporary Democracies', in Gunther, R., J.R. Montero, and J.J. Linz (eds), *Political Parties: Old Concepts and New Challenges*, Oxford University Press, Oxford, pp. 136–65.

Wood, A. 2001, 'National', in R. Miller (ed.), *New Zealand Government and Politics*, Oxford University Press, Melbourne, 2nd edition, pp. 242–51.

Wood, A. 2003, 'National', in R. Miller (ed.), *New Zealand Government and Politics*, Oxford University Press, Melbourne, 3rd edition, pp. 251–60.

Young, A. 2002, 'Into the Valley of Electoral Death', *Weekend Herald*, 3-4 August, p. B3.

Young, A. 2003, 'Brash's Inner Circle', *Weekend Herald*, 1–2 November, p. A6.

Index